AMERICA
OUR NEXT CHAPTER

AMERICA
OUR NEXT CHAPTER

TOUGH QUESTIONS, STRAIGHT ANSWERS

SENATOR
CHUCK HAGEL

WITH PETER KAMINSKY

ecco
An Imprint of HarperCollins*Publishers*

HarperCollins books may be purchased for educational, business, or sales promotional use. For information, please write: Special Markets Department, HarperCollins Publishers, 10 East 53rd Street, New York, NY 10022.

FIRST EDITION

Designed by Daniel Lagin

Library of Congress Cataloging-in-Publication Data is available upon request.

ISBN: 978-0-06-143696-3

08 09 10 11 12   QWF   10 9 8 7 6 5 4 3 2 1

For Allyn and Ziller—who will write America's next chapter.

The dogmas of the quiet past are inadequate to the stormy present. The occasion is piled high with difficulty, and we must rise with the occasion. As our case is new, so we must think anew and act anew. We must disenthrall ourselves, and then we shall save our country.

—ABRAHAM LINCOLN

CONTENTS

PROLOGUE: WHERE I COME FROM   I

PART I: REINTRODUCING AMERICA TO THE WORLD

CHAPTER 1
LIT BY LIGHTNING   19

CHAPTER 2
IRAQ I: REALITY, ILLUSION, AND POLITICS   37

CHAPTER 3
IRAQ II: WHERE WAS CONGRESS?   53

CHAPTER 4
FIRE IN THE HOLY LAND: ISRAEL AND THE ARABS   67

CHAPTER 5
AYATOLLAHS, BLUE JEANS, AND NUKES: THE QUESTION OF IRAN   83

CONTENTS

CHAPTER 6
CHINA: A SEAT AT THE TABLE
101

CHAPTER 7
OPTICS: SEEING THE WORLD THROUGH A WIDER LENS
117

CHAPTER 8
TERRORISM VERSUS TOLERANCE
137

CHAPTER 9
WHO SPEAKS UP FOR THE RIFLEMAN?
149

CHAPTER 10
OUR SWORD AND SHIELD
159

PART II: CITIZENSHIP, SERVICE, DEMOCRACY

CHAPTER 11
"ALWAYS SHOULDER THE WHEEL"
175

CHAPTER 12
CRABS OR PRAIRIE DOGS: POLITICS AND PARALYSIS
191

CHAPTER 13
BEYOND GRIDLOCK: A NEW ELECTORAL SCENARIO?
205

PART III: SENSE AND DOLLARS

CHAPTER 14
COMPETITIVENESS: STAYING IN THE GAME
215

CHAPTER 15
ENTITLED?
241

CONTENTS

PART IV: LEADERSHIP

CHAPTER 16
MY MOUNT RUSHMORE   261

ACKNOWLEDGMENTS   283

INDEX   287

AMERICA

OUR NEXT CHAPTER

PROLOGUE

WHERE I COME FROM

Above all, I think of myself as an American. If you had asked my dad, he would have said the same thing. That's how we thought out in the Sand Hills of Nebraska, in Ainsworth where I grew up in the 1950s. It was like a hundred other small towns in the western part of the state: a couple of churches, a hardware store, a movie theater that always had a double feature, two gas stations, and an American Legion post. It was the kind of town where if you rolled down your car windows and turned the radio up loud, the whole town could hear Buddy Holly singing "Peggy Sue" from one end of Main Street to the other. Just down the road in Rushville, my great-grandfather and great-grandmother, Herman and Bertha Hagel, lived in an apartment above the bakery and across the street from Wefso's drugstore. Herman and Bertha shared their small apartment with two grown sons, wounded vets from World War I who got by on small disability pensions.

From the vantage point of sixty years, I suppose you could say life was tough back then, but I was a kid and kids pretty much accept life the way it comes and think that's the way things are supposed to be. Whatever was true in Ainsworth, I thought, was probably true everywhere. Maybe it had something to do with the wide-open environment and the big skies that seemed to take in all of creation. Those immense skies define the prairie states as much as the rolling sameness of the landscape. When you grow up like that, there's an openness that you feel and a sense of belonging to something larger than yourself. You don't dwell on it. You just know it's there and it's part of you that you carry all through your life.

I've learned a lot that has broadened my perspective since then. But many of the things I held to be true as a boy have stayed with me. Perhaps the most fundamental is the idea of service. It was never a question with me or any of my people. Service was simply what people did. It's the way neighbors helped each other and looked out for one another. It's what the French historian Alexis de Tocqueville found so remarkable about our democracy and its people in the nineteenth century. When a barn needed to be built, he marveled, the neighbors came together and pitched in to build it. There's a common purpose here in doing something important and good for your neighbor, and an understanding that maybe tomorrow your neighbor can do something important and good for you, too. Service to others. Service to your country.

Service meant that when your country called, you answered the call. It would never have occurred to anyone to question it. If the president said he needed you, that was enough. It was enough for me at the age of twenty-one, which is how I eventually found myself pinned down by Viet Cong rifle fire, badly burned, with my wounded brother in my arms.

I got my belief in service from my dad and mom, and people like them, "the greatest generation." As I often do, I thought about those World War II vets recently as I was preparing to get on a plane and fly to western Nebraska from Omaha. Before I left, my staff brought me a photo album that they had found as they were reorganizing our office. There was a photo of my father when he was the commander of American Legion Post #79 in Ainsworth back in the early 1950s. My father was a three-time commander of the American Legion Post and my mother was a three-time president of the Legion Auxiliary.

I thumbed through the album, reliving the Legion events that stretched all through my childhood: I remembered my father preparing for Legion meetings, the Fourth of July, Veterans Day, Memorial Day, parades, and of course, the somber cemetery visits, the gravestones with their small flags flapping in the wind that always blows across the plains. "Taps" seems to echo longer on the prairie. I stopped at one photo of my dad in his Legion uniform. I remembered that when he was first elected commander he did not own a full Legion uniform. Those blue uniforms cost money, and like a lot of young vets after World War II, my folks had more immediate needs—such as feeding and clothing four young boys. This was a cause of great concern to him. It was like a soldier not having a proper uniform. And I remember my mother promising him, "Charlie, we'll get that uniform. We're going to be able to do that." And they did.

My mother made sure of that. My brothers and I inherited our father's Legion uniform and it has fallen to me to preserve this family treasure. I keep it cleaned and pressed, the same way my mother did until she passed away.

I still believe, as my father did, in serving our country. But history has taught me that we must require better answers than we have been given before we ask our young men and women to sacrifice their lives for a greater cause. And when lives and families are put at risk, those questions should be probing, serious, and unrelenting. I would go so far as to say that it is unpatriotic not to ask them.

I do not believe the people's representatives pressed these questions strongly enough in the run-up to the Iraq War. It was our responsibility to do so, to demand a clearer purpose and more defined objectives. Instead, both the House and the Senate were an amen corner for every administration claim, laying aside our responsibility to be ever-vigilant in safeguarding the people's interests. I believe the national news media were complicit in this as well. They too were slow to ask the tough and probing questions. The results have been one of the greatest foreign policy fiascos in the history of our republic, the hemorrhaging of our national treasure and the sacrifice of thousands of young lives in the meat grinder of a Mideast conflict. Those who died gave their lives for the noble purpose of defending America. It was their leaders who failed them by committing them to a strategy that was flawed in its premises and botched in its execution. For the men and women on the ground, though, it was enough that their country asked. Their sacrifice is no less than the price paid by those who perished in the waters of Pearl Harbor or in the blasted ruins of the Alamo.

Like their fathers before them, the men and women who have slogged through the alleys of Fallujah and the caves of Kandahar set the bar for the rest of us. It is our duty to live up to their expectations and to put the needs of their brothers- and sisters-in-arms first.

It is the blunders of that war, the paralysis of a political system that did not question it, and the dangers as well as the opportunities of a rapidly changing world that have moved me to write this book. From where we stand now, how do we begin to write the next chapters of America's story?

I believe we do so by looking—without preconceptions or illusions—at where we are today, considering our strengths and our weaknesses, and only then mapping out a path to the future. That is not to say that this is a book that seeks to predict the future course of events; human affairs are too complex and quick-changing to undertake that kind of political and historical soothsaying. But we can clearly discern trends, both the alarming ones that beset us and the positive ones that have made America great.

In Part I, I will look at our evolving role in the world community, both as a superpower and as one member of the community of nations. I will take up our recent blunders and the reasons for them, most notably the misadventure in Iraq, and will also examine the root causes of extremism and how our nation should confront it. And in a brief survey, I'll examine other pressing challenges and exhilarating opportunities that face all of us across the globe, specifically in the Middle East, Russia, China, and India.

Part II takes up the current state of the American body politic, in particular the two cornerstones of our democracy: the rights and obligations of citizens, and the alchemy that transforms the concept of service into the life-blood of citizenship (and how we can and must strengthen the idea of service). I will also address the pitfalls and paralysis that have taken control of our political culture, as well as the search for new ideas that can redefine and revitalize our political system.

Part III deals with America's future role in a competitive world marketplace and the practicalities of economics in a broad context. I'll address the transformational potential of the global free market and the costs of such global challenges as climate change, the failing report card for our educational system in science and math, the urgent needs of our national infrastructure, and the largely bogus challenge of outsourcing (with its twin, the emotionally overwrought immigration question). I will also examine the often-overlooked opportunities of a world in need of the tremendous productive capacity of America, as all nations seek everything from new energy sources to medicines that will sustain a graying world population. Affecting every discussion of American economics are the heavy burdens placed upon our system by unsustainable entitlement programs, rising health-care costs, and the servicing of our national debt that eats up a larger and larger percentage of our federal budget.

Finally, in Part IV I offer some thoughts on the vital question of leadership. With great leaders, America has never faltered, even in the most trying times. Our present era is such a time. Once again we need great leaders. But in a system where reelection is everything, we have lost the ability to look beyond immediate self-interest to take stock of the long-term interests of our nation and of the peoples of the world. If we built Mount Rushmore today, who would belong on it? I will offer my own personal answer in hopes that all Americans will give some thought to who belongs on their individual Mount Rushmore—and why.

These next years can be inspiring, positive, constructive chapters for America, or they could turn out differently and quite dangerously. I take the view that they will be great chapters. We can succeed and we can lead, if we're wise enough to understand what we must do and not foolish enough to believe that somehow America's greatness is preordained. Our success will be the result of hard work, smart and informed policy, and strong and enlightened leadership.

Although the press of current events gives us a telescoped perspective in which recent history occupies the largest part of the frame, it is important that we look at things with a wider perspective than that of the startling events of 9/11 and their aftermath in Afghanistan and Iraq. Stepping back for the long view, America finds itself in a unique position today. Unique in history. In the early twenty-first century, we stand alone as the world's only superpower. No matter how much we have squandered in treasure and good will in recent years, we still lead the world by all measurements—politically, militarily, economically, technologically. Never before has one nation exerted so much influence throughout the globe.

How will history assess our stewardship as the leading power of our time? For the most part, I think it will do so positively. In the aftermath of World War II, America found itself locked in a conflict with totalitarianism. Eventually we triumphed in the most glorious of ways—without a shot being fired. Communism imploded. A system supposedly founded on the science of economics was defeated by the inexorable power of the free marketplace. This took place in the context of a world where America stood at the center of an international system made up of coalitions of common interest. Whether through the United Nations or NATO (the North Atlantic Treaty Organization), through the World Bank and International Monetary Fund, through fellowships, scholarships, conferences, and cultural exchanges, America reached across its borders and engaged the world and was, in turn, enriched by its contacts with other nations, other cultures.

After the unspeakable horrors of the first half of the twentieth century, in the second half peace prevailed (for the most part), science advanced, and prosperity uplifted billions of people. To be sure, for those who lived through conflicts in Africa, the Balkans, and Southeast Asia, the horror of war darkened those decades too, but for most of humanity, the tale of the half-century of America's preeminence is largely one of progress.

Nowhere did the change inherent in this flooding tide of history appear more clearly to me than when my brother Tom and I returned to Vietnam in 1999 to hoist the flag over the new American consulate in Ho Chi Minh City. The bustling street was different from the shabby war-torn thoroughfare in the city we had known as Saigon thirty-one years before. I was struck by a jarring incongruity of images before me. On one side of the street, a supersized statue of Ho Chi Minh (the Communist leader of Vietnam from 1946 to 1969) dominated the peaceful green landscape of a city park. Across the street, a Ford showroom featured a gleaming display of new cars: Broncos with all the options, pick-up trucks, and a flashy Mustang with the top down. The contrast could not have been more stark: in the park, the omnipresent Marxist leader stared vacantly at a scene of commerce far different from any he could have imagined—a glittering beacon of the capitalist system that has propelled Vietnam to the first rank of the world's fastest-growing economies. Nothing could more clearly capture the new realities of the twenty-first century.

Alongside the great upswelling of progress and prosperity represented by a surging Vietnam, or the reborn bustle of the Czech Republic, or the thrilling ascent of Ireland, or the success of the enormous skilled professional class that is transforming India, there has been a powerful and much less hopeful counterforce: the despair that stalks two and a half billion people who live in poverty and squalor. We find them in the slums of Caracas and Lagos; and among the vast legions of unemployed young men across the Islamic world, who are easy prey for extremist preachers who promise regeneration through violence; we see them in the countless millions who have no awareness of the transforming power of the Internet; in the drought-stricken swath of the sub-Sahara among those with no crops to raise and no water with which to raise them. Until the progress that lifted so many in the twentieth century is extended to those who were left behind, stability will be at best short-lived and at worst a prelude to even greater chaos in the twenty-first century.

Like the challenges that the world faced in 1945, when much of it lay in ruins, its economies shattered, and its peoples dispirited, once again we face a world beset by conflict and in need of leadership. We found a way forward then and I believe we will again. Perhaps the great issue of our times is how to complete the progress of the twentieth century by extending it to these two and a half billion people for whom nothing else matters beyond finding their next meal and a safe place to sleep through the night. This will require solutions that are a product of the twenty-first century. It calls for a new frame of reference, one that embraces the reality of a multipolar world. Economic power has become more diffuse around the globe: The information that empowers that diffusion spreads instantaneously through the same Internet that carries jihadist calls to arms and twenty-four-hour news cycles that can enflame as easily as they can inform. With more weapons of great destructive power in the hands of more and more nations, the margins for error are much slimmer than ever before. Add to that the ticking time bombs of environmental and social issues, and this new century presents the people of our great green planet with a demanding and critical agenda.

America can lead, but it cannot go it alone. We have seen the pitfalls of that kind of cocksure policy in the bitter experience of Iraq. It is imperative that we enlist the aid of friends and, just as important, that we engage our adversaries on whatever areas of common interest we can find. If we do not, you can be sure that the Chinese or the Indians or the European Community or some combination of third parties will see to it that world order is maintained according to their interests, which are not always the same as America's. Our ability to play a leading role rests, as it always has, on the wisdom of our leaders—but just as much it relies on the strength of our republic and our people.

Maintaining America's leadership position will largely depend on how well we maintain our competitive position in the global economy. And for that, the truth is that we have too long neglected the great first-order challenges that confront us: trade, energy, deficit spending, entitlement programs, a decaying infrastructure, education, and immigration reform, to name the chief issues that I will explore later in the book.

We need to fundamentally rethink the U.S. financial system. Up until the staggering inflationary pressures of the 1970s, the financial system of the United States and the world was based on the principle that long-term capital would fund short-term debt. Today that system has become a financial market based on short-term credit used to finance long-term debt. So when we have a crisis like the subprime mortgage implosion, there is no "shock absorber" in the markets to handle the jolt because the markets are overly dependent on short-term credit. There is no reservoir of capital to back up the large short-term debt; everything is based on credit. We're living on borrowed money and borrowed time. In a global financial market, the kind of subprime mortgage shock that we saw in 2007 ripples out across the world causing banks to close and "runs" on bank deposits in Europe and elsewhere. Just this one crisis will affect the world's financial markets well into 2008. In the fall of 2007, the Treasury Department pushed leading U.S. banks to create a fund to purchase assets in the most traumatized segment of the credit market. The fund was intended to be a safety net of $80 billion or more to help stabilize the dangerously troubled housing market. This action was an unusual intervention by the government into the workings of financial markets. It was unprecedented and was further evidence of the seriousness and consequences of the subprime mortgage crisis. This is a clear example of the new reality of the interconnected global economy that we live in today.

Consider these facts, if you doubt that we face great financial challenges:

- Over the next seventy-five years, our nation faces $47 trillion in unfunded liabilities on our entitlement programs.
- Today's individual savings rate in America is at an all-time low and our personal debt is at an all-time high.
- $2.2 trillion (45 percent) of U.S. debt held by the public (of a total of $5 trillion) is held by foreign investors.
- In 2000, the United States had 50 percent of the total valuation of all global initial public offerings (IPOs), while in 2005, the United States had only 5 percent.
- Finally, according to the American Society of Civil Engineers, the current condition of our nation's major infrastructure systems earns a grade of D.

Only a strong America that systematically and honestly addresses these challenges can help to welcome the rising new powers of the world to history's table, and only a strong America— not just militarily strong but economically and morally fit as well—can hope to lead in this reordered world. I am not talking about a belligerently powerful or arrogant superpower. Instead I am proposing a return to an honest and invigorated nation, one based on neighborly goodwill and common sense—much like the America that men such as Harry Truman, Gen. George Marshall, and Dwight D. Eisenhower helped to create in the post–World War II era. Through their strong and imaginative leadership, coherent policies, and responsible way of managing both politics and government, they sustained our great nation and the world.

On the question of politics, those presidents, as well as legislators such as Bob Dole and Pat Moynihan, knew and showed by example that politics and effective leadership is not a zero-sum game, where success only counts if it brings a corresponding defeat across the aisle. That's not politics: It's electoral Russian roulette. Politics, at its best, is about bringing people together for the common good. It should be uplifting and help educate and inform citizens with responsible debate about the issues of the day. We don't have the luxury of waiting out the gridlock that comes from the exhausting partisan battles that have divided this nation in recent years. The urgency of our unsettled times demands that America acts wisely, with resolve and a common purpose. We expect our leaders not to bicker, but to govern. How any body politic responds to political paralysis will always determine the fate of nations. History is quite clear on this point.

For Americans to believe once again in our political system—and by believe in, I mean participate in it with their votes and their active involvement—they have to believe their elected leaders. Too often, the only thing you can say for certain about so many of our elected representatives is that they want to be reelected and they never act without first considering how any decision will affect them in the focus groups, the polls, the fundraising sweepstakes, and ultimately the ballot box. Every action, decision, and vote is politically calibrated. That is a prescription for precisely the kind of dead end toward which the two parties have marched us—preaching to their respective choirs, and covering their respective butts with safe votes. That's not leadership, that's marketing—and people know it. That's why the American people are so turned off: why more of them vote for *American Idol* than an American president.

There was another time that America faced this kind of stale, impotent party politics. It was the 1850s. The answer, of course, was a new party, the Republican Party, my party. I wonder, if Abe Lincoln were alive today, if he would throw his hands up at the whole mess and decide it was time for another party, beholden to no one. I'm not sure that we're quite at that point—but, on the other hand, I'm not so sure we are not. At the very least we need more independent leadership, with an independent platform not captive to the restraints of party politics.

The bond between a people and their party or their government is based on the same currency that matters most in life: trust. If you debase that currency and people don't trust or believe what you've said, then you can't govern. America learned that the hard way during the Vietnam War. If you listen to the tapes released by the Johnson Library, on which President Lyndon B. Johnson and Senator Richard Russell discuss Vietnam in the mid-1960s, you will hear President Johnson confess that we couldn't win in Vietnam, but we couldn't pull out because he didn't want to be the first president to lose a war. Senator Russell said (and I'm paraphrasing): "Get out. It's unfair to project this country into a situation where on the outside you're saying 'Stay steady, stay the course, there's lights at the end of the tunnel, we can win' when privately you are saying we can't win. That's wrong."

I wish someone had told me when I was sitting on a burning tank in a Vietnamese rice paddy that I was fighting for a lost cause just to save a president's legacy. I volunteered to go to Vietnam to defend our nation, not to save LBJ's place in history.

The cold political calculation I heard on those tapes made me vow that I would never—ever—remain silent when that kind of thinking put more American lives at risk in any conflict. That's how an administration gets to a point where the American people and the Congress can no longer believe in it. When people stopped believing that the war was winnable, they stopped believing Johnson, and his days as a leader were numbered. In the heady times of the Great Society and the Voting Rights Act, he had been a true leader. He faced up to the power structure and said, "This is where I stand!" People trusted him as a man of principle. When he debased his currency, he lost his connection to the people—and a leader is nothing without it.

At the end of the day, I don't think any leader gets into trouble for saying exactly what he or she thinks, provided you are informed and educated on the issues. People can tell if you are speaking from the heart and the gut. You rarely fool them, and if you do, it's only temporary, so there's no percentage in being too cute or too cautious. You just deal with the issue, straight up and straight out.

More important than your string of statements on any issue is making sure that people understand that you believe what you're saying. We are so conditioned by the prepackaged product of political consultants that too many modern-day politicians ricochet all over the place. People know the difference between a genuine statement and the overly rehearsed sound bite. To be effective, leaders must be directed and motivated and anchored in something far greater than the next set of polls, political calculations, or even the next election. And if you're not willing to do that, or lack the courage, you cannot lead. It was courageous and farsighted leadership more than 200 years ago that created a remarkable and precious form of government with honest, competent, and accountable leadership. That kind of leadership is what America needs now as we begin to write our next chapter.

PART I

REINTRODUCING AMERICA
TO THE WORLD

CHAPTER 1

LIT BY LIGHTNING

What has not America lost by her want of character with foreign nations and how many errors and follies would she not have avoided, if the justice and propriety of her measures had, in every instance, been previously tried by the light in which they would probably appear to the unbiased part of mankind?

—FEDERALIST PAPER #63

Politicians are fond of saying that we live in unprecedented times—as if the challenges of today are somehow greater and more important than those of the past. By definition, today's challenges have great consequence for tomorrow, but that has been true of every "today" going back to the beginning of time. What is different about our modern world is that the combination of weapons of incalculable destructive power and an interdependent global society mean that history will not be as forgiving of mistakes and foreign policy blunders as it has been in the past. There is little margin for error in a point-and-click world.

The stakes are higher—but what it takes to play and win remains the same: leadership, strength, and the willingness of our nation to work together with others for our common interests. Those interests, shared by all mankind, have not changed in ten thousand years. All people want peace, security, food on the table, a future for their children. Even though the twenty-first century's problems may look bigger or more challenging, I think we can take heart from our track record as a country. So far we have survived and, by and large, we have prospered. True, we never seem to solve one problem without creating another, but the point is we do solve them. Sometimes it is not without great pain and sacrifice, but we should never forget that no matter how difficult our current challenges may look, America has always risen above the greatest dangers and, in so doing, we have helped to build a better world.

Throughout history there have been nations that have been leaders. For the last one hundred years, America has filled that role. The strength of our economy, its tremendous productive capacity shaped by entrepreneurship, the openness of our political system, and the spirit of cooperation and citizenship among our people have brought us to a position of immense power and influence. Does this make us better than other countries? Probably not, but it does mean—given our overwhelming power—that today's challenges squarely confront this nation as they do no other.

I have always been fascinated with the historian Arnold Toynbee's theory of the rise and fall of civilizations. "Civilization is a movement and not a condition, a voyage and not a harbor," he wrote as he considered the fate of the world's great civilizations. In other words, a civilization is like a story, with a beginning, a middle, and an end. Every great civilization has succeeded because it has organized the energies of its people to meet a challenge. For the ancient Babylonians the challenge was harnessing the power of the Tigris and Euphrates Rivers. For the church of the Middle Ages it was offering order to communities terrorized by chaos and anarchy. For sixteenth-century Spain it was tapping the seemingly inexhaustible riches of the New World. For America it was "e pluribus unum," creating one nation out of a melting pot of peoples.

Earlier civilizations declined because there came a time when they became complacent about their power and could no longer meet the challenges of the day. For example, the mighty Roman Empire fell apart when the legions it depended on for public order were "outsourced" to barbarian mercenaries. The traditions of service and sacrifice that defined Roman citizenship and led it to greatness disappeared as the citizens grew fat and happy on the spoils of empire. Rome was just one more case of a universal principle according to Toynbee: "Civilizations die from suicide, not by murder."

Challenge and response, rise and fall, these have been the

unchanging laws of human history . . . *so far*. For if they were truly as constant and immutable as the speed of light or the pull of gravity, then I would not be talking from such a positive perspective about America's next chapter.

We Americans are not born better than those ancient empire builders. We probably have the same proportion of go-getters and, balancing the equation, the same proportion of laggards. What America has that is different is *an open political, educational, and economic system* that in the space of two centuries has time and again proved itself capable of generating ever-increasing amounts of wealth and ever greater opportunities for people to better their lives and those of their children.

The difference between America and the preeminent powers of the past is that our continued success is not at the expense of the rest of the world. The great scientific advances of the last sixty years have meant bigger markets, greater progress, and more prosperity and opportunities for more people everywhere. A wealthy and powerful China or India or Europe does not have to mean a corresponding decline in the quality of life for America. Instead, the advancement of other nations as they join the world's free-market community creates a rising tide that, for the most part, lifts us all. True, some jobs have moved overseas, but as I will argue in chapter fourteen those jobs, which were a heritage of an early industrial era, were always destined to leave. The challenge is to create new jobs to take their place.

Counterbalancing this story of progress are new, more global threats: Terror, religious extremism, nuclear proliferation, the scourge of new and virulent health pandemics, poverty and despair, and the specter of ecological collapse through climate change are not challenges that can be met and overcome through the imposition of one nation's will and unrivaled military power. What will be required are enhanced and strengthened multilateral relationships and institutions, expanded trade, and more cultural, educational, and scientific exchanges. In this way we can nurture those things that bring people together. This must be our twenty-first-century frame of reference: one that accepts, in fact demands, American leadership. But we can lead only to the extent that we are trusted and respected in the world—not feared. Our goal must be inspirational leadership, moral authority, and confidence that America's purpose is noble and that its interests are shared by the rest of humanity.

So where does this leave us? With the fall of our primary adversary of the last half of the twentieth century, the Soviet Union, the forces that govern international life are realigning. The end of the Cold War changed international relationships; it changed the focus and deployment of our armed forces and military resources; it altered the reach of our economy, global investment patterns, domestic budgets, and the balance of power. The nuclear standoff of the Cold War took place in a bipolar world, one that was less complex than the multipolar world of today.

For all of its anxiety, the era between the Berlin airlift and the fall of the Berlin wall took place in a world of minimal open conflict because the dominant powers, the Soviet bloc and the West, both worked to contain issues before the world descended into the chaos of conventional war—or worse, nuclear Armageddon. If a dictator or warlord started to make trouble, he was put back in his box by the great powers before he drew the rest of the world into the maelstrom of war. Yes, we had our Idi Amins and our Pol Pots, and they wreaked murderous havoc on their people, destroying millions of lives, but we avoided a world war whose casualties would have been numbered in tens—if not hundreds—of millions. So long as the most important decisions were made in Washington and Moscow, the armed truce held.

In contrast, the world we live in now is far more dangerous, far more combustible, far more hair-triggered than ever before, because it is far more interconnected. To understand it, to lead and live in it, will require a new frame of reference. We need a way of looking at the world that reverses the optics, so to speak. We Americans have always seen things through a lens that magnified our position and appeared to keep the world at a distance. But that is not the reality of the twenty-first century, and in the contest of history, reality always trumps ideology. This means, as John F. Kennedy said with great foresight in 1963, "The purpose of foreign policy is not to provide an outlet for our own sentiments of hope or indignation; it is to shape real events in a real world."

Any serious analysis of the international system in these opening years of a new millennium starts with the clear understanding of an America that stands alone as the world's only superpower. Though we have been challenged, and though we have no doubt made missteps, America nonetheless leads the world by all reasonable measurements—politically, militarily, economically, culturally, technologically. Never before has one nation exerted so much influence. Our opportunities are enormous and exhilarating. But they are not a blank check, nor do they come without significant risks.

We must ask ourselves what being a superpower means in a world of numerous emerging power bases, both economic and geopolitical. Our strength, built on the twin pillars of our open democracy and the dynamism of our economic system, may be unrivaled, but there is no question that the trend so far in the twenty-first century is toward the diffusion of power. More countries are projecting more issues out on to the world stage. The days of a very few nations making the rules and imposing their will on humanity are gone.

Paradoxically, things were simpler and therefore, for many of us, more comfortable and less anxiety-producing even with the nuclear sword of Damocles hanging over us during the Cold War. As long as we knew, or thought we knew, that our adversary was the monolith of Soviet Communism, it didn't take a lot of subtlety to figure out who was right and who was wrong on any international issue. If the Russians backed something, then we generally opposed it. Whether this was always wise or prudent didn't enter into the evaluation. There were good guys and bad guys. Simple.

I remember the first time that I had a real sense of the stakes in global power politics. I was in Mr. Sheridan's history class at St. Bonaventure High School, in Columbus, Nebraska. Every one of us, no doubt, remembers a teacher, coach, neighbor, or family member to whom we looked up and who, in turn, took an interest in us. Tom Sheridan did that for me. He led me to an understanding that today's events are no less a part of history than the building of the Suez Canal or the heroic last stand of the 300 Spartans at Thermopylae.

Mr. Sheridan made us read *Newsweek* and *Time*. Every week there was a big story that we studied: an earthquake in Turkey, a revolution in Venezuela, drought in the Midwest, reports of conflict in South Vietnam (a little-known nation in Asia that not many of us could quickly point to on the pull-down map in front of the blackboard). Mr. Sheridan would always look for a way to relate these stories to our lives, our community, our nation. We learned to see world events as something more than answers on a pop quiz. He made us understand that it was somebody's mom or dad, cousin or uncle, girlfriend or boyfriend, who faced the consequences of disasters and upheavals—both natural and man-made.

During the Cuban Missile Crisis in the fall of 1962, Mr. Sheridan's class learned that world events impacted us even in the wide-open and seemingly isolated spaces of Nebraska. Day by day, we watched the progress of the Russian ships carrying their deadly cargo within striking distance of every town in the United States—even Columbus, Nebraska! This was serious business. What was it that Slim Pickens said, playing the role of a gonzo B-52 pilot in *Dr. Strangelove*? "This here is nuclear combat toe-to-toe with the Russkies." It didn't seem so far-fetched that fateful autumn.

For the first time, the unthinkable seemed very possible. The world hung in the balance and we knew it. I was absolutely transfixed by this long-distance, slow-motion dance of warships and missiles on the high seas. The leading figures in the drama also commanded my attention: JFK, Dean Rusk, Robert McNamara, LBJ, Walt Rostow, Bobby Kennedy, and Ted Sorensen (a Nebraskan). At that point they became as fascinating to me as Elvis or Paul Hornung or James Dean. History was exciting and meaningful. Those who made it were stars. It was only later that I began to understand that the luminaries of Kennedy's Camelot were as human, as fallible, as the folks in my hometown, or yours. They were capable of great achievements but also of blunders with equally great consequences for the nation and, as it turned out in a few short years, for the Hagel family itself.

Had the intellectual giants of the Kennedy administration—in a mixture of hubris and folly—not upped the ante in Vietnam, there would probably have been no Tonkin Gulf resolution, no U.S. buildup, no political paralysis that kept LBJ and Nixon from extricating our country from what came to be a tragic mess. I think of the fifty-eight thousand students from classes like Mr. Sheridan's all over America who died in Vietnam and wonder what they'd be doing today. That's always one the great tragedies and consequences of war: the "what ifs".

JFK's predecessor Dwight D. Eisenhower was, in his day, often looked on as an uninvolved and not very forceful leader. But having studied his life and presidency, I have come to a different conclusion. He was a paragon as a soldier and a general, and as a leader, he understood—as did other leaders of the World War II

generation—that war, once it is unleashed, is always uncontrollable, unpredictable, and painful far beyond the predications of
those who beat the drum the loudest. To be sure, there is sometimes no other recourse than war, but it always must be the last
alternative.

Eisenhower emerged as a farsighted statesman in 1954 when
the French forces, which had sought to restore the colonial system in Indochina after World War II, were encircled at Dien
Bien Phu. Against all predictions, the ragtag army of Ho Chi
Minh had thrown a great European power back on its heels.
The situation was grim. The French leader, Charles de Gaulle,
pleaded with President Eisenhower to employ U.S. airpower
to rescue his forces. Eisenhower, who led the D-Day invasion
that liberated France, refused. He did not see how our interests
would be served by reinserting the United States in an Asian
conflict when we had just negotiated an armistice in Korea that
extricated us from another Asian war. Furthermore, Eisenhower
understood that "the winds of change" (as British prime minister
Harold Macmillan would later refer to the end of colonialism in
Africa) were blowing away old European-denominated political
systems everywhere in the world.

The way Ike saw it, the French were involved in a colonial
conflict in Vietnam, and America could not and would not be
a party to propping up a system that was rightfully in its death
throes. Furthermore, as an experienced military officer and
geopolitical strategist, he knew that even with the addition of
overwhelming U.S. airpower, Indochina was a lost cause for the
French. Our assistance at that moment would have only put off a

greater disaster for the French while ensuring a costly entanglement for America.

Eisenhower understood one of history's immutable principles: getting into war is much easier than getting out. I believe that it was this realization that moved another statesman-general, Colin Powell, to put forward his famous Pottery Barn caution during the run-up to Iraq ("you break it, you own it"). Listening closely to our career military leaders is a measure of responsible governance and wisdom. This is certainly one lesson that I had hoped we had learned from Vietnam before we embarked upon a path that brought us disaster in Iraq. Although as more and more of the behind-the-scenes stories of Iraq come to light, it seems that politics largely won out over the more sober and realistic advice of our military leaders.

Our military perspective was thrown off balance—as was everything else in American life—when al-Qaeda turned civilian airplanes into guided missiles. The jolting gong of September 11, 2001 demonstrated that the greatest threat to peace does not necessarily come from strong nations, but from weak ones. Terrorists find sanctuary in failed or failing states, in unresolved regional conflicts, and extremism preys on the misery born of endemic poverty and despair. No single state, including the United States, even with its vast military and economic power, can meet this challenge alone.

We should therefore welcome the inevitable emergence of robust new economies and regional powers, and encourage their pursuit of stability and progress. China will continue to become a bigger and bigger factor in world affairs, as will India, a united

Europe, Brazil, and Southeast Asia. Political and military power will become more diffuse as more nations follow our path to economic success. This does not mean a diminished, weakened, or less relevant America. It does mean that the reality of the rest of this century will be one of more leading players on the international stage.

For America to participate and lead in this reconfigured world, we need a clearheaded understanding of where we are. When the Berlin wall came down and the Soviet system melted away like a sand castle in the tide, the alignment of power in the world was transformed. We have not yet fully adjusted to this metamorphosis. When, after World War II, we found ourselves similarly on top of the international order, we approached world leadership as part of a community of nations, and the results were staggeringly successful. Europe and Asia were rebuilt, economies were transformed, and science and technology brought their benefits to most of the world's people. America was the head of this global march toward progress because of its leadership and vision, not because of its imposition of power.

This was an extraordinary turn in world affairs: leadership and international cooperation founded on coalitions of common interests. In the past, nations led because of overwhelming power, and they tended to dominate through intimidation and even brutality. Europe ruled the world in the nineteenth century by virtue of its gunboats and its occupying armies. These colonial powers drew much of their strength and their wealth from their imperial dominions. So-called lesser nations were not seen as partners in progress; instead they were viewed as properties. Nations—even whole continents—were absorbed by the European economies largely for the benefit of the colonial power. Within this context the great powers got along to the extent that they carved up the world and stayed out of each other's way. Conflict emerged when they contested control of the wealth produced by colonial possessions.

That world is gone. Instead of a giant pink swath on the map mostly controlled by Britain (and to a lesser extent, other European countries), Africa is now a continent of fifty-three sovereign states. Take this a step farther and look at the composition of the United Nations, which now numbers 192 nations, many of them former colonies.

This marks quite a change from the immediate post–World War II era when the United States led a war-wracked and prostrate community of nations in the United Nations' early years. Compared to those simpler times, creating coalitions of common interest among so many more nations today is a task akin to herding cats, except that some of today's cats have nuclear weapons. While all nations share a potential for growth, they also share the ability to descend into chaos and carry their neighbors down with them. Furthermore, in this increasingly interdependent world, we are all close neighbors in a smaller, more densely populated neighborhood.

The United Nations is one example of the kind of wide-angle thinking that can bring nations and peoples together. The good that it has done is a result of farsighted statesmen (and -women) having the vision to see that progress can only come through cooperation. No country can go it alone. History, geography, resources, and geopolitical strategic interests bind us together. We can move forward together: If we don't, we will fail together. That seems especially true today, but on reflection, it has been true throughout the modern era. After all, it was the assassination of an archduke in a place that few people could even pronounce (Bosnia and Herzegovina) that drew Europe and America into a world war that killed millions.

Whenever the bell tolls, it truly tolls for all of us. America has always known this although the Iraq War (and our overall policy in the Middle East) departed from this principle. I would go farther and say whenever we as Americans are unilateral in our actions or isolate ourselves in global decision making, the results are almost always costly for us as well as the world. Tariffs that seek to protect failing industries cut us off from the benefits of a more productive world and divert us from the task of re-training our workforce to make it more competitive. Failure to engage all nations in a concerted effort to address climate change and man-made greenhouse gas emissions brings us closer to the detonation of an ecological time bomb. At the same time, our immigration policy is undermining our own national interests by restricting the visas of the highly educated people from other countries who have the talents to augment homegrown scientists and engineers to sustain the twenty-first-century industries that must be embraced by our evolving economy.

An unwillingness to engage adversaries only isolates them more and strengthens the hand of extremists. Look at Iran: It is a proud nation with a three-thousand-year history and eighty million people, two-thirds of them under the age of thirty. Although we strongly disagree with their nuclear policy, we cannot refuse to speak to them as if we were angry parents sending a misbehaving kid to his room without dinner. Dialogue and engagement are the only way to strengthen the forces of moderation in a very complicated and dangerous world, the only way to convert mistrustful strangers into neighbors who—while they may not love each other—can at least coexist. Fortress America, isolated from the world, and going her own way without regard for the interests of others, is not viable—and never was.

At the same time, a strong America is vital to global stability. Great nations lead through the well-considered exercise of all the instruments of power—military, economic, and diplomatic. The greater the power, the greater the responsibility.

It may seem strange to say in this multipolar world, but the time has come for America to reintroduce herself to the global community. The facts of the matter are that the world is in the midst of an unprecedented generational shift. There have been four and a half billion people born since the end of the Vietnam War; that means that two-thirds of all the humans ever born are alive today. The America that rescued Europe and Asia from militarism and fascism is a distant and fading memory to most of the world's citizens. The heroism of prior generations connected us to freedom, fairness, justice, and prosperity. The current generation knows little or nothing of this. Among most of the world's 1.5 billion Muslims, we are viewed negatively. Even the citizens of our oldest and staunchest allies, including Great Britain and

NATO partners such as Turkey and Spain, have an unfavorable view of us.

Some of this is inevitable: great powers are always resented. But for the most part this dangerously negative view of America is a misperception that can be explained in large part by the current administration's unwillingness to act in concert with others. Too often, the world's perception—and many times the reality—of an arrogant America, dictating the terms of engagement, strong-arming allies, and imposing our will has alienated our allies and undermined our own interests.

America must make a focused and deliberate effort over the next few years to reintroduce herself to the world. Our foreign policy should concentrate on public diplomacy, strengthening and working closely with multilateral institutions. It must call for international engagement at every level in every field. Extending and adding free-trade agreements with the nations of the world, building on the successes of military-to-military programs of the past, expansion of our recent successes in constructing a seamless network of intelligence-gathering and -sharing with our allies, and visa and immigration reform are some of the areas that call for our attention over the next few years. And, perhaps above all, we must strive to include those nations that have not shared in the progress of recent decades.

Now, as it has been since our founding, the United States' purpose in foreign policy is to chart a new course in a world that is, as Ronald Reagan said in his second inaugural address, "lit by lightning." So much is changing and will change, but so much of what America is and always has been endures. We will continue to succeed to the extent that our foreign policy transcends the hubris that comes with great power and the mistaken belief that our resources are without end. Nowhere has this tension been more apparent than our disastrous misadventure in Iraq.

CHAPTER 2

IRAQ I

REALITY, ILLUSION, AND POLITICS

There was little good that came out of the Vietnam War and its aftermath, a conflict that cost fifty-eight thousand American lives and millions more among the people of Vietnam, Cambodia, and Laos. Still, all historical events, even great tragedies, offer lessons for future generations, if we are willing to listen and learn. The past can inform the present and the future. Thirty years later—while the question of Iraq was being debated—I was initially confident that the lessons of Vietnam, bought at such a high price in American blood and treasure, would provide our political and military leaders with some hard won perspective before sending American troops to the Middle East.

What were the lessons of Vietnam?

I believe they were very clear and straightforward, and can only be ignored at our peril. As I said on the Senate floor in 1998 when Iraq was first being discussed, "If our nation decides to risk the lives of young American men and women we must do so for a clear purpose, with a clear understanding of the possible intended and unintended consequences . . . and a reasonable assurance of success." No war policy will be successful unless it is supported by the American people, and furthermore, that support needs to be sustainable over the long run. All other alternatives should always be exhausted before committing a nation to war, and if war is the decision, then we must go to war with overpowering force and have an exit strategy. As I mentioned earlier, I have long held the belief, and shared it with my colleagues, particularly in the fever-pitched debate leading up to the invasion of Iraq: *It's easy to get into war, but not easy to get out of war.*

To the astonishment of those of us who lived through the agony of Vietnam, these lessons were ignored in the run-up to the Iraq War. The administration cherry-picked intelligence to fit its policy, used fear and the threat of terrorism to intensify its war sloganeering (particularly in speeches by the vice president), and dampened the possibility of dissent by denying that it had decided to go to war even though it had already made that decision before the debate even began.

It is shocking how little Congress or the media challenged the Bush administration. This is not too far-removed from the way the tragedy in Vietnam unfolded forty years earlier. Unlike Vietnam, however—which did not represent vital strategic security interests for America—the war in Iraq and its consequences are playing out against a backdrop of the world's largest reserves of petroleum, and the contagion of a virulent strain of religious fanaticism that threatens to inflame the entire Middle East.

In the wake of the 9/11 attacks, the administration's intent and the nation's steady drift toward war were unmistakable and alarming. In an otherwise quiet summer in 2002, on July 31 and August 1 the Senate Foreign Relations Committee held "Hearings to Examine Threats, Responses, and Regional Considerations Surrounding Iraq." We called as witnesses some of the top experts on Iraq and the Middle East for two full days of probing testimony and questions.

My statement at those hearings reflected many of the questions that shaped my thinking during that time:

How do we accomplish regime change in Iraq given the complexities and challenges of the current regional environment? The deep Israeli-Palestinian conflict continues; our relations with Syria are proper though strained; we have no relationship with Iran; Egypt, Saudi Arabia, Turkey, and Jordan have warned us about dangerous unintended consequences if we take unilateral military action against Iraq; and Afghanistan remains a piece of very difficult unfinished business, an unpredictable but critical investment for the United States and our allies.

I can think of no historical case where the United States succeeded in an enterprise of such gravity and complexity as regime change in Iraq without the support of a regional and international coalition. We have a lot of work to do on the diplomatic track. Not just for military operations against Iraq, should that day come, but for the day after, when the interests and intrigues of outside powers could undermine the fragility of an Iraqi government in transition, whoever governs in Iraq after Saddam Hussein.

An American military operation in Iraq could require a commitment in Iraq that could last for years and extend well beyond the day of Saddam's departure. The American people need to understand the political, economic, and military magnitude and risks that would be inevitable if we invaded Iraq.

Given the gravity and uncertainty of the situation in the Middle East, Joe Biden and I decided to get our own close-up assessment of a region that seemed on the verge of war. Our itinerary for a seven-day trip to the Middle East in December 2002 included meetings with King Abdullah II in Jordan, Prime Minister Ariel Sharon in Israel, President Bashar al-Assad in Syria, newly elected Prime Minister Abdullah Gul in Turkey, General Tommy Franks at USCENTCOM (Central Command) headquarters in Qatar, and Prince Turki al-Faisal of Saudi Arabia. Not one Arab leader expressed support for possible American military action in Iraq. To the contrary, they all shared deep concern about this possibility and its consequences as well as the lack of progress on the Palestinian issue. On that same trip, although Israel's top security officials pledged their support for whatever we planned to do in Iraq, they also said to us, in effect, "Do you really understand what you are getting yourselves into?"

Meeting privately as we did with leaders and experts produced candid, unvarnished information. That alone made it a valuable trip at a critical time, but the most memorable part of our Mideast fact-finding mission was the side trip that Biden and I made into Kurdistan. The Kurds were one of the few success stories in the Middle East. In the ten years that America had enforced no-fly zones in the northern and southern parts of Iraq, this long-oppressed people had tasted freedom and prosperity.

Their fellow Kurds in Turkey and Iran were still denied many basic human rights. But with Saddam effectively contained after the 1991 Gulf War, the Iraqi Kurds achieved a degree of autonomy and prosperity they had never known, though not without a measure of conflict and instability at first. From 1994 to 1998, the Kurdistan Democratic Party of Masoud Barzani and the Patriotic Union of Kurdistan of Jalal Talabani fought a bloody civil war. After the parties settled their differences in 1998—thanks to U.S. mediation—the shackles came off in northern Iraq. With a few billion dollars a year in UN-sanctioned oil contracts (as well as black market deals), and a nascent business and economic relationship with Turkey, the Kurdistan region of Iraq entered what seemed like a golden age.

As Biden and I were making our way toward the Turkish-Iraqi border with a military escort, we were given VIP treatment as the first two U.S. senators to visit the region. We were driven to the front of the long line, past the miles of patiently waiting trucks with radio speakers blaring everything from traditional prayer summons to Johnny Cash. At the border, our Turkish escort handed us over to a detachment of the Kurdish *peshmerga*, a term that literally means "those who face death." These were the legendary Kurdish guerilla fighters who, though outgunned and outnumbered, had fought so valiantly against Saddam Hussein.

During the five-hour ride, I called my mother in Lincoln, Nebraska on a satellite phone. Typical of Mother's conversations—

"You shouldn't be there, take care of yourself, and are you getting enough to eat?" But what wasn't typical was that she was dying of lung cancer and would be gone in a month. She was so happy to hear from me. Joe asked to talk to her and that brightened her day since she knew how much I liked and respected Joe Biden.

After hours of a pitch-black, nerve-wracking, high-speed night ride through winding mountain roads to Erbil, the capital of Kurdistan, we were greeted at the guesthouse by a large and enthusiastic group of well-wishers, and were treated to a spectacular feast, despite the late hour. We were far from home, but it felt like home. I liked these people, and they were genuinely happy to receive two elected representatives of America.

Visiting a refugee camp the next day, however, was a swift reminder of the troubles these people had been facing, and surviving. The refugee camp in Erbil was reserved for internally displaced persons from Kirkuk, a land that remained under Saddam's control at that time. Kirkuk is a significant oil-producing region, the largest in the north of Iraq. Its oil resources make it a strategic prize, and an intensely symbolic one for the Kurds, many of whom think of Kirkuk as the "Kurdish Jerusalem." For several years, Saddam had been seeking to alter its demographic character by expelling Kurdish families and replacing them with Arab families from farther south.

Conditions were wretched—but that's part of the definition of refugee camps everywhere, from Gaza to Cambodia to Darfur. They're all miserable; it's simply a matter of degree. No running water, no electricity, sewage and trash everywhere, mud, grime, noise. Festering in such conditions, these people were not disposed to live peacefully with the Iraqi Arabs who had forcibly taken their homes.

But the camp was just the beginning of our descent—however brief—into the hell that all Kurds had lived through under Saddam before the Gulf War. We were given an unforgettable look into the soul of their suffering when, after our speech to the Kurdistan National Assembly, we were taken to a large receiving hall. Hundreds of women waited for us there, all dressed in the black chador, traditional Islamic dress. Most of these women were the wives and daughters of Kurdish families from the Barzan region, where in the 1980s an estimated eight thousand men were killed or "disappeared," according to human rights groups, as Saddam's retribution against Kurdish freedom fighters. Also present were survivors of Saddam's chemical weapons attack on the Kurdish town of Halabja, which occurred during the Iraqi *Anfal* (military campaign) against the Kurds in 1988.

As these women told us their stories of unspeakable horror, an unsettling sound, a pulsing wailing, began to sweep the room. It was the Islamic woman's ancient anthem of suffering, loss, and mourning. The dictionary word for this sound of bereavement is "ululating," but really it is a sound beyond words. It is pure anguish. The noise grew like a wave until the whole crowd took it up, pouring all their anger and horror into this communal cry. It was a moment that told the tale of Saddam's reign of terror in the most visceral and emotional way. It dispelled any doubts about the reports of his grisly brutality, and the cruelty that had led him to use chemical weapons against his own people.

Our trip to Kurdistan gave us an on-the-ground perspective

on how Saddam was being contained. The Butcher of Baghdad was hemmed in by the no-fly zones enforced by the United States, Britain, and France. Economically he was equally hampered by international trade embargoes that were taking a serious toll on the economy. This did not mean he was no longer a threat; he had shown in the past that he was very resilient, dangerously unpredictable, and very willing to use his military against neighbors and even his own people: whatever it took to survive.

Still, at the time of our visit with the Kurds, Saddam controlled only 40 percent of the country. For ten years our F-16s—operating out of Saudi Arabia and Turkey—provided a protective umbrella for the Kurdish north (30 percent of the country) and, to a lesser degree, the Shia south (another 30 percent). The Kurds prospered more in those ten years than at any time in their history.

As for the issue of weapons of mass destruction, our trip turned up no evidence or even strong suspicions of evidence of Saddam's possessing them. In spite of this, the war crowd in the administration grasped for every shred of intelligence no matter how far-fetched, and, in the most chilling and colorful turns of phrase, ominously warned that Iraq was getting close to a nuclear break-out. No solid intelligence ever supported the Bush administration's most exaggerated contention that Saddam Hussein possessed weapons of mass destruction, might be in the process of reconstituting his weapons program, or transferring such technology to terrorist groups. Yet President

Bush implied as much when he portentously said on October 7, 2002: "Facing clear evidence of peril, we cannot wait for the final proof—the smoking gun—that could come in the form of a mushroom cloud."

"What clear proof?" I wanted to know. I was not aware of any such evidence.

A few months earlier, the late Lebanese prime minister Rafik Hariri had invited former Senate Majority Leader George Mitchell and me to a small private dinner at the Four Seasons Hotel in Washington. At that dinner the prime minister told us that Saddam had no weapons of mass destruction. Hariri said that Saddam was playing games with the United States. He asked, why did we think Saddam possessed these weapons? The prime minister said that Saddam had gotten rid of his WMD stockpile and capability to produce them after the 1991 Gulf War. George and I looked at each other; neither of us immediately responded to the prime minister's question. After a moment, I said, "Because the president of the United States and our government are telling us that Saddam Hussein has weapons of mass destruction."

Hariri's argument was backed up by the man who knew the most about Iraq's nuclear weapons programs, Mohamed ElBaradei, director general of the International Atomic Energy Agency. ElBaradei reported that there was no compelling evidence of a reconstituted Iraqi nuclear program. But his assessment, informed by on-the-ground inspections, was disparaged by an administration that would not let facts stand in the way of the roll-out of "Shock and Awe," the embarrassing and ridiculous name given to our initial military attack on Baghdad.

ElBaradei's counterpart was Hans Blix, the chief UN weapons inspector responsible for Iraq's chemical, biological, and missile programs. Blix's inspectors indicated that Iraq's reporting on these programs was wanting—there was much unaccounted for. But Blix did not believe that, absent any real evidence, it merited a case for war. If anything, it argued for more aggressive and intrusive UN weapons inspections. But he, too, had his analysis and integrity challenged by those itching to remake the Middle East. I had met with ElBaradei and Blix on different occasions in 2002 and believed they had the best and most timely information and analysis on whether Saddam possessed weapons of mass destruction or could and would reconstitute WMD programs.

Another worrying sign of the administration's rush to war was the role and influence of Iraqi exile Ahmad Chalabi. Chalabi had inserted himself into United States–Iraq policy during the Clinton administration. The CIA, which provided Chalabi with tens of millions of dollars in the years following the 1991 Gulf War, finally gave up on Chalabi's failed schemes and cut off his funding in 1996. During the remainder of the Clinton administration, Chalabi's base of support came almost exclusively from outside the executive branch—some influential members of Congress, and staff and neoconservatives at the American Enterprise Institute. An effective Washington operator even after his funding was removed, he was tireless in urging Congress to pass the Iraq Liberation Act of 1998, a significant legislative marker offering "regime change" as a new direction for U.S. policy toward Iraq. The State Department continued to engage Chalabi and other Iraqi opposition figures, but with modest expectations about either his potential for leadership among Iraqi exiles or his purported influence inside Iraq.

In 2002, the disagreements over Chalabi in the Bush administration soon mirrored the infighting over the war itself. Chalabi counted top officials in the office of the vice president and the Pentagon as his strongest advocates and allies: I. Lewis "Scooter" Libby and John Hannah in Vice President Cheney's office, and Deputy Secretary of Defense Paul Wolfowitz, Undersecretary of Defense for Policy J. Douglas Feith, and Defense Policy Board Chairman Richard Perle at the Pentagon, as well as some members of Congress. The State Department and the CIA were skeptical of Chalabi and, at a minimum, did not consider a post-Saddam Iraq as a likely precursor to a Chalabi coronation, as many of the neoconservatives had believed.

Chalabi's disproportionate influence struck me as both odd and ominous. I was never personally exposed to Chalabi's widely reported and alleged charm, but his record gave me pause— convicted in absentia of bank fraud in Jordan—and there were many unanswered questions about the use or misuse of CIA and State Department funding by his Iraq National Congress. I realized, of course, that there are few angels when dealing with Iraq and Iraqi exile politics. But the absolute confidence placed in Chalabi by some at the top of the administration seemed to me misguided at best, irresponsible at worst.

Senator Patrick Leahy shared my reservations about Chalabi and together we placed a hold on funding for the INC's Information Collection Program in 2002. I also pressed the administration on the role of Chalabi and the Iraq National Congress in the lead-up to the war. Secretary of State Powell and Deputy Secretary Richard Armitage were skeptical of Chalabi's sources and influence and did not believe that he was the only horse we should ride into Baghdad. The State Department's Future of Iraq Project had cast a wider net among Iraqi opposition figures. But its detailed findings were ignored by the Department of Defense (DoD). Chalabi's direct lines to the office of the vice president and to the Pentagon and funding from DoD continued unchecked.

Soon after Saddam was deposed by U.S. forces, my misgivings about Chalabi proved well founded. The Iraqi defectors served up by the Iraq National Congress prior to the war, including the notorious "Curveball," were shown to be the source of some of the most egregious faulty intelligence on Iraq's WMD programs. Placed in charge of Iraqi de-Baathification in 2003, Chalabi undertook a purge of such excess that it is considered one of the earliest and costliest mistakes of the Bush administration's handling of postwar Iraq. Chalabi maintained close ties with Iran and even entered into a tactical political alliance at one point with the anti-American Iraqi Shiite leader Muqtada al-Sadr. In an interview in February 2004, Chalabi arrogantly said this about his deceitful efforts to involve the United States in Iraq:

> As far as we're concerned we've been entirely successful. That tyrant Saddam is gone and the Americans are in Baghdad. What was said before is not important. The Bush

administration is looking for a scapegoat. We're ready to fall on our swords if he wants.

At the end of the day, the story of Chalabi is less an indictment of Chalabi himself than it is of those who promoted and defended him. It strikes me as unseemly that many neoconservatives would rather blame American public servants at the CIA or the State Department than blame Chalabi—someone who knowingly delivered false intelligence information and probably passed sensitive information to Iran. The defense of Chalabi is but one example and clear testimony of the duplicity the Bush administration used in its hyped marketing for going to war in Iraq, and an insult to those who have died, and continue to die, suffer, and sacrifice in Iraq.

The reality of Iraq, as we have come to know, was not as depicted by the administration. Saddam was growing weaker and more isolated under international sanctions. Time was not our enemy; it was our friend. The administration should have cultivated and supported Blix and used his assessments as the basis for a UN coalition effort to disarm Iraq. Like ElBaradei, however, Blix was dismissed as a peacenik who was actively undermining U.S. national interest. By early 2003, the headlong, foolhardy rush to war was charging full steam ahead. No time for diplomacy or to build a coalition—that would be selling out our national interest to the weak-kneed United Nations! It was a foregone conclusion that war was inevitable; all we needed to do was topple

Saddam and get our troops home before the heat of an Iraqi summer set in.

So why did we invade Iraq? I believe it was the triumph of the so-called neoconservative ideology, as well as Bush administration arrogance and incompetence that took America into this war of choice. This ideology presented a myopic vision of a democratic Middle East that would inject a large permanent American force presence in the region to act as the guarantor of a regional realignment. They believed that by taking the relatively easy step of toppling Saddam, they could begin to realize this vision through the use of America's unequaled military power, thereby establishing America's preeminence in the Middle East and bolstering the defense of Israel. They obviously made a convincing case to a president with very limited national security and foreign policy experience, who keenly felt the burden of leading the nation in the wake of the deadliest terrorist attack ever on American soil.

There was never any reliable evidence or intelligence linking Saddam Hussein and al-Qaeda or any terrorist group. But the Bush administration continued to propound this fabrication. They knew that America, thrown tragically off balance by the terrorist attack of 9/11, was susceptible to incessant administration warnings that more terrorist attacks were coming unless we acted against Saddam Hussein—one of the triumvirate of Bush's "axis of evil."

We would mount preemptive strikes against our enemy. No one disagreed with that. But the enemy was stateless terrorists, difficult to identify and find, and harder to seek out and kill. We took the strategically correct and responsible action in Afghanistan by going after clearly identifiable targets: terrorists, their infrastructure, their training camps, and their supporters. We should have stopped there and focused our resources, efforts, strategies, and energies on terrorist targets and terrorist organizations, and on rebuilding and strengthening our alliances for the next generation of global challenges and threats including terrorism. But the administration was dead set on invading Iraq.

Although the administration put forward geopolitical reasons for going into Iraq, their march to war succeeded not because of cool-headed rationalizations of global policy, but as a result of a sudden national tide of strong, visceral emotion. The rush to war was accelerated by—in fact could not have happened without—the emotional fallout from 9/11. The administration played this card with consummate skill. Some of its chief proponents were intoxicated with their own fantastic ambition: that by militarily deposing Saddam Hussein, they would somehow bring about democratic change in the Middle East. There was even talk that such action could bring about a more moderate form of global Islamic politics. The hubris of such assumptions—to bring democratic change and affect the course of religious history at the point of a gun in Iraq—is breathtaking. It's okay for a classroom exercise, but not for our elected leaders whose responsibility is the security and future of the United States.

Democracy, like faith, cannot be imposed. It must come from within. But the planners of our Iraq invasion believed in a democratic domino effect: We erect a democracy in Iraq and the rest of the nations of the Middle East would soon follow with their own democracies. It doesn't work that way; it never has and we have paid a very high price to relearn an old lesson, one that Michael Korda cites in *Ike: An American Hero*, his biography of Eisenhower. Korda writes that Eisenhower warned that "the United States has no business transforming itself into 'an occupying power in a seething Arab world' . . . and that if we should ever do so, 'I'm sure we would regret it.'" I wonder what Ike would think of our current predicament in the Middle East.

Misguided and dangerous ideology, not military necessity, landed us in Iraq. Taken in sum, this administration's hell-bent determination to go to war in Iraq was an historic blunder borne of an astounding amount of arrogance, ignorance, and incompetence. In my opinion, this misstep will play out to be the most dangerous and costly foreign policy debacle in our nation's history.

If the acclaimed author and historian Barbara Tuchman were alive today, she might be tempted to add a fifth chapter to her magnificent book, *The March of Folly*. Her book is about four monumental historical blunders: the Trojan War; the Renaissance popes who provoked the Protestant Secession; the British loss of the American colonies; and the Vietnam War. In fact, I feel certain she would add a fifth blunder: America's invasion and occupation of Iraq.

CHAPTER 3

IRAQ II

WHERE WAS CONGRESS?

O ne of the questions that future historians will consider is: "What was and what should have been the role of Congress in the lead up to and entry into war with Iraq?"

Congress held hearings, members met privately with the president and his National Security Council, and Congress debated and ultimately voted on an Iraqi War resolution. I knew (as did some of my colleagues) that there was a showdown coming between the administration and Congress when Alberto Gonzalez, who was White House counsel at the time, wrote a memo to the president that effectively said, "Mr. President, you don't really need a congressional resolution to go to war in Iraq because you have all the powers that you need as commander-in-chief to take whatever course of action you deem fit to protect this country."

This seemed preposterous to me and certainly not within the spirit or the letter of the Constitution. I called Andy Card, who was the president's chief of staff and told him, "I don't think you have a strong case, constitutionally. But more to the point, why would any president seriously consider taking a nation to war without Congress being with him?" I think the White House heard this same message from others like Joe Biden and Dick Lugar.

So a begrudging White House sent a war resolution to Congress for approval. It assured a very broad sweep of discretionary power. It not only authorized the use of force in Iraq—it implied the president could commit our forces anywhere in the Middle East, wherever the White House deemed it necessary, including Iran. *No* boundaries, *no* restrictions.

Early on in the process of negotiations between the White House and the Congress over the text of the resolution, Senate Majority Leader Tom Daschle reached out to me very quietly through our staffs. Many of my Republican colleagues vilified Daschle because of his role as the leading Democrat in the Senate. He was the very sharp point of the spear for many partisan battles. But I also knew Daschle as a fellow midwesterner and a person of instinctively moderate politics who tried to do the right thing, while seeking to give his party the edge in the Senate. He was also a fellow veteran. He told President Bush at a White House breakfast meeting during the second week in September that he opposed the draft resolution. But among the congressional leadership he was on his own. House Speaker Denny Hastert and Senate Republican Leader Trent Lott were ready to do the president's bidding regarding a resolution. House Minority Leader Dick Gephart, who was planning a run for president, decided he would support the president. I offered Daschle my counsel as he fought a lonely battle with both the congressional leadership and the administration to resist the Gonzalez draft in favor of a more reasonable alternative.

I also consulted with Joe Biden and encouraged him in his role as chairman of the Senate Foreign Relations Committee to take a stand and offer an alternative to the president's resolution. He and Lugar began drafting a resolution that granted much less expansive authority to the president. I immediately signed on. Biden-Lugar-Hagel advocated that the United States first seek a UN Security Council resolution calling for aggressive UN weapons inspections in Iraq, backed by force if necessary. If that resolution could not make it through the United Nations, Biden-Lugar-Hagel would have required the president to certify to Congress that the danger posed by Iraq's WMD programs could only be addressed through military action.

Although our efforts were not wholly successful, the eventual resolution was a substantial improvement over the initial draft. The interventions of Daschle, Biden, Lugar, and myself helped in that regard. Perhaps the most important thing that we thought we had achieved, in principle, was an understanding that the president would exhaust all diplomatic avenues before committing troops and beginning combat. This was an assurance that I was given personally by the president. Furthermore, he promised that he would seek a broad-based coalition before taking military action. I remember saying to him, quite specifically, "This has to be like your father did it in 1991. We had every Mideast nation except one siding with us. Also, the United Nations was firmly with us."

And he said, "That's what we're going to do."

I had also received similar assurance when I asked Secretary of Defense Donald Rumsfeld and Deputy Secretary Wolfowitz: How are you going to govern in Iraq after Saddam is gone? Who is going to govern? Where is the money coming from? What are you going to do with their army? How will you stabilize Iraq? Do we have enough troops? How will you secure their borders?

They reassured me on every count, "Senator, don't worry, we've got task forces on that, they've been working on it, they're coordinated, we know what we're doing."

Congress and the American public were hearing the steady beat of war drums from the Bush administration: We could not afford to give Iraq any more time, they said. Much of this argument was built around the urgency of taking military action against Iraq before the beginning of severe sand storms and heavy rain in April and May.

The administration's efforts had their desired effect. The resolution that enabled the president to go into Iraq passed the Senate 77–23 on October 10, 2002, and I voted for it.

Here is what I said, with a sense of deep foreboding, in a speech on the Senate floor, one day before the Senate passed the war resolution:

> We must look at the issue of a post-Saddam Iraq and the future of democracy and stability in the Middle East with more caution, realism, and humility. While the people of the Arab world need no education from America about

Saddam's record of deceit, aggression, and brutality, and while many Arabs may respect and desire the freedoms that the American model offers, imposing democracy through force in Iraq is a roll of the dice. A democratic effort cannot be maintained without building durable Iraqi political institutions and developing a regional and international commitment to Iraq's reconstruction. No small task. To succeed, our commitment must extend beyond the day after the fall of Baghdad, to the months and years after Saddam has gone. The American people must be told of the long-term commitment, risk, and cost of this undertaking.

I voted for the resolution based on the president's assurances that he would do everything possible to find a diplomatic solution before going to war. I continually received assurances from Secretary of State Powell and other senior administration officials that the president had not made a final decision to go to war. They argued that by voting for the Iraq War resolution, the Congress was strengthening the president's hand before the United Nations. I also believed it was important to give the president the strongest hand possible in order to maximize American influence, leverage, diplomacy, and power.

From the passage of the resolution to the overthrow of Saddam to the failed attempts at reconstruction of Iraq, there have been so many missteps, that the question of how we got into this mess has been obscured by finger pointing and blame shifting. The administration adopted a unilateralist policy, pushed it through a politically cautious Congress, and sold it through the lens of fear to the American people, who were inclined to trust their elected leaders in the aftermath of 9/11.

It all comes down to the fact that we were asked to vote on a resolution based on half truths, untruths, and wishful thinking. I voted for this resolution that gave the president the authority to go to war in Iraq *if all diplomatic efforts were exhausted and failed.* Unfortunately, it was not his intention to exhaust all diplomatic efforts. And, to answer a question that I believe you cannot duck, yes, I regret my vote that gave the president war-making authority. I believed him and his advisors. Like each member of Congress who cast a vote on this issue, I have to take responsibility for that decision.

Like most of the nation, Washington was caught up in pervasive sloganeering. Congress was told to support our commander-in-chief. Don't ask questions; line up behind the president. Some of us in Congress who dared to question the president's policies were vilified as unpatriotic, as traitors, and of course as disloyal Republicans. My mail attested to all of the above and worse.

I've always wondered whether my Republican colleagues would have been so unquestioning and supportive of going to war in Iraq had Bill Clinton been president. Both political parties failed to do their job in Congress. Congress abdicated its oversight responsibilities and fell silent and timid.

Too few of the uniformed leaders of the American military spoke out against what many believed was a terribly flawed plan to go to war in Iraq. There were courageous exceptions. General Eric Shinseki, chief-of-staff of the Army, testified to Congress that the military would need far greater manpower than we had planned for in order to achieve our objectives in Iraq. He was publicly humiliated by Rumsfeld and Wolfowitz, and left dangling and neutered over the last twelve months of his tenure. Marine Lt. General Greg Newbold, director of operations for the Joint Chiefs of Staff, resigned and walked away from a brilliant future and a fourth star in late 2002 because of his opposition to the administration's war plans.

Now that this war has dragged on longer than any conflict in our history (except for Vietnam), it is high time that we address the issue of how we can end America's involvement in Iraq honorably and responsibly.

The way forward must start with a basic understanding that has eluded this administration. Namely, America cannot simply impose its values and its will on other countries. The future of Iraq was always going to be determined by the Iraqis, not the Americans. There is no military solution for Iraq. Only the Iraqis can achieve the kind of political accommodation among themselves that leads to national political reconciliation. And it may well take many years before there is a cohesive political center in Iraq.

No matter how much we may want to help the people of Iraq, America's options have always been limited. For five years, we have tried to bring stability and security to Iraq, at a tremendous cost in American blood and treasure. But our policies sadly show that we misunderstood, misread, misplanned, and mismanaged our honorable intentions.

In September 2004, well before the administration acknowledged the downward spiral that was engulfing Iraq, I wrote letters to then National Security Advisor Condoleezza Rice and Secretary of State Powell stating my opinion, that U.S. strategy in Iraq was unsustainable. I said that Iraqi political reconciliation must be our core strategic objective.

But since Iraq first took center stage on our foreign policy agenda, we have failed to embrace a regional and international diplomatic commitment comparable in its significance, capacity, and vitality to our vast military occupation of Iraq.

I, along with a number of witnesses who appeared before the Foreign Relations Committee during hearings leading up to the Iraq invasion, distinguished military men like former USCENT-COM Commanders Generals Tony Zinni and Joseph Hoar and former National Security Advisor Dr. Zbigniew Brzezinski, warned the administration that American military might alone could not achieve our long-term objectives in Iraq.

As I wrote Rice and Powell in 2004, said again in my speech to the Council on Foreign Relations in 2005, and wrote in a 2007 op-ed in the *Financial Times*, we need to "internationalize" our efforts to help the Iraqis achieve a core of political stability. This means helping to establish a constructive regional security and political framework supported by the international community.

Iraqi political accommodation can be achieved only within a formalized standing regional structure that involves all of Iraq's Mideast neighbors, as well as the international community and leading international institutions such as the United Nations, the European Union (EU), NATO, the World Bank, and the International Monetary Fund. This requires direct U.S. engagement with Iran and Syria, another point I have raised continuously. This effort at diplomatic engagement must be disciplined and sustained. One-off, catch-as-catch-can meetings often produce little more than photo-ops and are no substitute for grounded, credible structures that can work through the problems and challenges and produce options that lead to actions. The 2006 Baker-Hamilton report of the Iraq Study Group offered similar conclusions. As I said at the time, the Bush administration could have embraced the seventy-nine recommendations of this report and used them as the foundation to build a new bipartisan consensus in Congress on how we could go forward in Iraq. The president chose not to do that, and he squandered a critical moment and opportunity.

It has always been clear that America alone cannot shoulder the burden of bringing stability and security in Iraq. Beginning in 2003 and continuing through 2007 and today, I have continuously argued for a U.S. strategy on Iraq that centered on international and regional diplomacy so that the power, resources, and influence of the entire world could be applied to rebuilding a post-Saddam Iraq.

I called for an international mediator under the auspices of the UN Security Council. That mediator would have the authority of the international community, and call on its expertise and resources. The mediator's mandate would be to engage Iraq's political, religious, ethnic, and tribal leaders in an inclusive political process *as well as* help shape and formalize a regional and international political and security framework for Iraq.

This approach would begin to take the American face off Iraq's political process, diminish the huge American military footprint, and further invest the region and the rest of the world in helping stabilize Iraq. Reversing Iraq's continued slide into chaos is a goal shared by nations around the world, especially in the Middle East. It is not in the interests of any of these nations to have Iraq in chaos. That is dangerous for everyone. Creating an international mediator and focusing on a constructive regional and international framework would build on this common interest.

In May 2007, I wrote President Bush, UN Secretary-General Ban Ki-moon, and Secretary of State Rice, urging them to consider my proposal for an international mediator, as well as other specific suggestions for an American policy shift in Iraq. Despite my status as the second-ranking Republican member of the Senate Foreign Relations Committee and third-ranking Republican on the Senate Intelligence Committee, my suggestions were summarily ignored. The White House never responded to my letter to the president; I received a very perfunctory cookie-cutter response from the assistant secretary of state for congressional affairs. And we wonder why we're in so much trouble in Iraq and the world!

In June, I pressed this proposal further when I met Secretary Rice in her office and when National Security Advisor Steven Hadley saw me privately in my office. Later that month, the U.S. Ambassador to the United Nations, Zalmay Khalilzad, told me that he personally supported my proposal. I later met privately with Ban Ki-moon, and urged him to consider it.

I urged this measure against the background of my deeply held belief that, yes, America has vital geopolitical, energy, and economic interests in Iraq and the Middle East, but in order to sustain an enduring presence, we require a new policy that the broad bipartisan majority of the American people can support. We should have begun a phased withdrawal and redeployment of U.S. troops from Iraq months ago. That is why when I wrote Rice and Powell in September 2004, it was with the strong belief that counterterrorism, border security, and training Iraqi forces needed to be our top priorities—not more troops. Nothing in the intervening years has changed that assessment.

Many of us have recognized our presence in Iraq for what it is—an occupation. As I said in my November 2005 speech to the Council on Foreign Relations, we must encourage and demand more responsibility from the Iraqis. U.S. military power is not, and cannot be, a surrogate or a crutch upon which Iraq can indefinitely depend. For five years, the U.S. military has been deployed as an occupying force in Iraq. That must change. It is wrong, and futile, for us to have put men and women in uniform in the middle of Iraq's civil war.

By the fall of 2006, it had become clear to me that the time had come for the United States to prepare to withdraw and redeploy from Iraq. On November 26, 2006, I published an op-ed in *The Washington Post* titled "Leaving Iraq, Honorably." In it, I called for the United States to begin planning for a phased troop withdrawal from Iraq. The facts on the ground no longer justified one-hundred-thirty thousand U.S. marines and soldiers deployed in Iraq and, with that deployment, the unending string of deaths and casualties that we continued to suffer.

For the same reasons, I opposed the president's decision in

January 2007 to escalate our military presence in Iraq (the so-called surge). That month, Joe Biden and I sponsored a Senate resolution that opposed the president's escalation, stating that our primary objective must be Iraqi political reconciliation and that we must establish a clear transition to a limited U.S. military mission in Iraq. Concretely we would help to ensure the territorial integrity of Iraq, conducting counterterrorism operations, border security, and accelerating the training of Iraqi Security Forces. We were joined in this effort by Senators Carl Levin and Olympia Snowe. We all felt very strongly that the time had come for the U.S. Congress to act and change the administration's flawed and failing strategy. As I said at the time, the president's decision was dangerously wrong-headed and drove America deeper into a dangerous swamp at a great cost.

The limited U.S. military mission in Iraq that we proposed would still have our forces protecting our national interests in the Middle East and around the world. This depended on a phased and significant withdrawal from the middle of Iraq's civil war. History, I believe, will show that the January 2007 Hagel-Biden resolution largely framed the core issues on Iraq taken up in subsequent debates. The damage this war has done to our country will play out for years to come. It has eroded our position and influence in the world, severely degraded our military force structure, further destabilized the Middle East, and seriously undermined Americans' trust in their leaders.

I have confidence in the wisdom of our people. The great challenge for America will be to avoid another march into an ill-conceived conflict. As I look at the dual experiences of Vietnam and Iraq there are, to be sure, substantial differences, but there is at least one common factor: Congress didn't do its job. It ceded its constitutionally mandated war-making powers to an ideologically driven executive branch.

This was a shameful dereliction of duty. The Constitution clearly establishes Congress's authority and responsibility regarding decisions to go to war. The course of events in Iraq has laid bare our failure to prepare for, plan for, and understand the broad consequences and implications of the Executive's unilateral decision to make war.

As Leslie Gelb, president emeritus of the Council on Foreign Relations, and Anne-Marie Slaughter, dean of the Woodrow Wilson School at Princeton University, wrote in an op-ed for *The Washington Post*:

> Our Founding Fathers wanted the declaration of war to concentrate the minds. Returning to the Constitution's text and making it work through legislation requiring joint deliberate action may be the only way to give the decision to make war the care it deserves.

Before committing troops, the American people should demand that the president request a declaration of war as required by the Constitution, and that Congress formally declare war, if and when the president believes that using our armed forces is in the vital national security interests of this country. This would make both the president and Congress more accountable for their actions—just as the Founders of our country intended.

"Original Intent"—what the Founders had in mind when they drafted the Constitution—is a notion that is most often applied to contentious social issues such as school busing or gay marriage. However, if anything rises to the level of original intent, I can conceive of nothing having weighed more heavily on the minds of Jefferson and Madison, Franklin and Washington than the decision to send our sons and daughters into battle and the face of death.

One of the clearest lessons of Iraq is that when the people's representatives fail to weigh in on the fateful decision to go to war, both the people and the system that represents them are grievously harmed.

In the years ahead, when another president and another Congress struggle with the question of another war in another dangerous corner of the world, will the lessons that Vietnam should have taught us and the lessons that Iraq has underscored guide our policy and decisions? I hope so—I pray so for our children who will be fighting the next war. Will we ever learn from the pages of blood and suffering that fill our history books?

If there is one place in the world where that question is urged upon us every day, it is in the Holy Land where the Arabs and Israelis have been locked in a mutual death grip for sixty years. That enmity explains much of the background to the Iraq War, and, as we shall see, much of the potential for conflict from Jerusalem, to Jalalabad, to Jakarta.

CHAPTER 4

FIRE IN THE HOLY LAND

ISRAEL AND THE ARABS

n June 1967, I was finishing army basic training at Fort Bliss, Texas. There was a war in Vietnam and we were going to take part in it. That's probably the only reason most of us knew where Vietnam was. The knowledge that you will be going into battle somewhere tends to focus your attention. But not many of us knew where the Gaza Strip was when, seemingly out of nowhere, the Six-Day War commenced. The first I heard of this far-off conflict was when our drill sergeant suggested that half of us would be going to Vietnam and the other half to the Gaza Strip, the Golan Heights, or the West Bank.

Golan Heights? Where was that?

"What do you like, Hagel, dry heat or hot and humid?" I remember being asked by Sergeant First Class William Joyce, who was a twenty-two-year army veteran and a master in the art of deadpan gallows humor.

Quickly, my fellow trainees and I developed an interest in the Middle East and the battles taking place in locations which, if any of us had heard of them, it had probably been as part of Sunday morning Bible studies, or in my case, Catholic catechism and religion classes.

For the next few days we followed the news on the radio. On Sunday morning, at the base doughnut shop, some of us crowded around the small television to get the news. This probably was the first time so much attention had been given to Sunday television at Ft. Bliss on any subject other than sports. No one knew whether this was the beginning of another world conflict or just another regional exchange between old enemies.

And then, suddenly, the Six-Day War was over, or so we thought. But as the months and years rolled by, the Middle East never left my consciousness. It had arrived dead center in my field of vision by virtue of that war and it has stayed there ever since. The issues that produced this conflict still remain unresolved and dangerously close to breaking out into a regional war that would inevitably drag in the world powers—not unlike the major wars of the twentieth century.

The echoes of those wars still reverberate everywhere: in the armed peace between India and Pakistan; in the patchwork of peoples and faiths fitfully glued together to make the country of Iraq; in the failed postcolonial states of Africa; in the still raw wounds of the Balkans; in the divided Korean peninsula. But they echo nowhere more ominously than in the Middle East, where the Arab-Israeli standoff was first set in motion by the Balfour Declaration of 1919 promising the Jewish people a homeland and the Arabs their own independent states.

Religious and geopolitical unrest in the Middle East remains the great unresolved crisis of our time. It is an explosive convergence of religious conflict, economic disparity, postcolonial struggle over identity and borders, and the chokepoint for global energy dependence. Iraq represents one aspect of this crisis, Iran another, and Lebanon yet another. The contemporary Middle East has been described, colorfully and accurately, by *New York Times* op-ed columnist Tom Friedman as on the "hinge of history," a region of unfulfilled promise, tragedy, and contradiction.

The fault lines run deep. It is the geographic focus of three of the world's great religions—Christianity, Judaism, and Islam— and, paradoxically, the site of some of the most horrific violence done in God's name. The rich history of Arab and Islamic con- tributions to culture and knowledge contrasts starkly in our own times with the crushing statistics produced yearly in the UN Arab Human Development Reports. They depict a region with minimal political freedom, scant scientific and technological in- novation, failing education systems, and nearly zero economic development outside the oil sector. There may be "seven-star" hotels in Dubai and Doha, but they exist alongside the squalor of the Palestinian refugee camps in Gaza, Lebanon, and Jordan. Modern state institutions in Iraq, Lebanon, and the Palestinian territories have all but collapsed into warring ethnic and sectar- ian factions. It is a region where the most pro-American Arab governments produce some of the most virulent anti-American terrorist recruits.

At its core is the struggle between Israelis and Palestinians, which is in many ways among the most complex and intractable problems of our time. This is not to say that there are not many other interrelated challenges in the Middle East—the democracy gap, terrorism, energy security, etc. But the Israeli-Palestinian conflict is the strategic epicenter of conflict, rooted in the aspirations of two peoples for the same narrow strip of territory. There is on the one hand the realization of the dream of the Jewish people to return to and live in peace in a sovereign Jewish state and, on the other hand, the emergence in the late twentieth century of Palestinian nationalism and the movement for their right to self-determination. The now solid consensus among the vast majority of Israelis and Palestinians for a "two-state solution" has raised the feasibility of a negotiated end to the conflict. But peace has been elusive. The Israeli-Palestinian standoff keeps the region on a treadmill of violence and despair.

A recent visit to an old Palestinian village on the West Bank reminded me again of the human perspective of this great tragedy. It is a point of view that falls under the radar of high-level shuttle diplomacy and of world leaders drawing lines on maps. The Arab-Israeli impasse is the sum of many smaller but serious frustrations and injustices in people's daily lives.

In 2007, our congressional delegation visited Aboud, a small Palestinian village on the West Bank. The people had always had one product that sustained them: olives that they grew on a hill overlooking the valley. For hundreds of years their olive groves have been blessed with a bountiful and peaceful stream flowing through them. If you had been looking for a place to deliver a Sermon on the Mount, Aboud would have been suitable.

At the small Catholic church, we met local dignitaries including an old man who had been the mayor, as his father had been.

We drank sweet tea and ate assorted cookies that the women in the village baked especially for us. The old man had a story to tell, not a happy one, about a wall that the Israelis were constructing through the heart of their olive groves. He told us the history of his people, generation upon generation, century upon century. His point was that Aboud was the sum of its people, its history, and through it all, its olive groves. Their year was lived according to the life cycle of the olives. Tending olives was more than just a job. It was who these people were.

One day the Israeli military arrived with bulldozers and ripped up acres of olives. "Why are you doing this?" the old man asked them. The answer was that they were making way for a security wall. Not only did it go through the heart of the olive groves, but it walled off the stream, without which the olive trees would not survive. Without its precious crop, it was only a matter of time until that village would go the way of its olive trees.

As the old man told the story, the villagers who were drinking tea with us looked on, occasionally nodding or joining in with a word or two. Clearly they still had a sense of dignity and self-respect, but also, the look of weary resignation and defeat.

"Where are your young people?" I asked.

They answered, "Why would our young people stay? What would they do?" Many had left to fight against the Israelis.

I understand their bitter resentment, but I also understand Israel's need to protect itself from terrorists sneaking across the border and blowing up their citizens in suicide attacks. What would we do, I wondered, if confronted with a similar danger? In considering the Middle East, at such times you stand back and say, with sorrow, will this ever end? Is there no way to stop this? Both sides are perpetuating the hatred and violence.

The Middle East need not be a region forever defined by endemic conflict or historical hatreds. Neither the Bible nor the Q'uran calls for enmity between these two peoples, but there will be no peace between Israel and her Arab neighbors without America's seizing the opportunity to lead in the pursuit of a resolution. Given the reality of the world's power politics, there is probably no other way. America cannot fix every problem in the world— nor should we try—but we must get the big issues and important relationships right and concentrate on those. The United States must focus its leadership and resources on ending the madness in the Middle East. The Israeli-Palestinian issue should be treated with the urgency it demands—by the United States, the United Nations, NATO, Israel, and the Arab countries. Beyond contributing to the destabilization of the Middle East, this issue has an enormous effect on global energy security.

Every day that passes without active and effective American mediation contributes to the further radicalization of Palestinian and Arab politics, and to the likelihood of greater terrorism being visited on the Israelis, which in turn will lead them to retaliate against Palestinians. Terrorist organizations such as al-Qaeda and Hezbollah have appropriated the Palestinian struggle for self-determination as a rationale for violence against Americans and Israelis. Failure to address this root cause will enable Hezbollah, Hamas—and terrorist groups even more troublesome— to gather the support of disaffected Muslims everywhere. This dynamic continues to undermine America's standing in the region and threatens the governments of Egypt, Jordan, and Saudi Arabia at a time when their support is critical for any Mideast resolution.

During the last twelve years, I made a point to develop a deeper understanding of the Middle East through frequent and, whenever possible, private and candid conversations with all of the regional leaders, including former Prime Ministers Ariel Sharon, Ehud Barak, and Shimon Peres of Israel, King Abdullah II of Jordan, President Hosni Mubarak of Egypt, Palestinian President Mahmoud Abbas, and many others.

These visits have only strengthened my belief that pursuing peace in the Middle East has been a high-risk endeavor for Israeli and Arab leaders. Prime Minister Yitzhak Rabin of Israel and President Anwar Sadat of Egypt were killed because they made peace. In his ground-breaking speech to the Israeli Knesset in November 1977, President Sadat said: "Peace is not a mere endorsement of written lines. Rather it is a rewriting of history." He was right. Those who have a stake in violence and conflict never want that history of bloodshed to be rewritten.

In the United States, president after president has brought Arab and Israeli leaders together over the years. Each time we have seen progress or its promise as a result of these efforts. And each time the region has slid back into violence. The Clinton years were the heyday of the "peace process."

While much maligned by Republicans and other critics, the Clinton administration efforts, when seen in retrospect, are notable for what they accomplished and for what they *nearly* accomplished. They brought Israeli and Arab officials together in regional economic conferences. They established the Oslo Process that achieved a peace treaty between Israel and Jordan and that brought us to the brink of peace between Israel and Syria. In a great missed opportunity (due to Palestinian intransigence), in July 2000, at Camp David, we came the closest yet to a negotiated end to the Israeli-Palestinian conflict.

The so-called Clinton parameters, the result of the intensive and often forgotten United States–brokered Israeli-Palestinian diplomacy that followed Camp David, represent the most comprehensive, detailed, and practical plan to date for an Israeli-Palestinian settlement and a two-state solution. Tragically, Palestinian leader Yasser Arafat wouldn't sign an accord that he believed he could not sell to his people and that would make him the target of a rejectionist fringe. He had 95 percent of what he asked for and then turned it down.

That was very puzzling to me and to many other observers. How do you get what appears to be such a good deal and then walk away from it? As it turned out, my travel schedule in December 2000 took me behind the scenes of this seeming paradox. I was in the Middle East and had gone to Damascus for a meeting with the late Hafez al-Assad, president of Syria. Assad was a shrewd man. I knew from my previous meetings with him that meetings with Assad were very long. He would spend the first part saying very little. The visitor did most of the talking and he used that time to size you up. Then he would speak, usually at great length. He could hold the floor for hours and would pride himself on never having to rest or excuse himself. "You would be well advised to skip your morning coffee and juice" was very practical advice from former Secretary of State James Baker.

We talked about Israel and the Golan Heights, and, not surprisingly, Assad said he was for peace, but Israel would, of course, have to give up the Golan Heights and East Jerusalem. I asked him his views on the Clinton-Barak-Arafat talks. What about Arafat's position on the deal that had been negotiated?

"He does not have the sole authority to make a deal," Assad said, simply and directly. What was left between the lines was his clear implication that not all Arab leaders would accept the deal and Arafat was overreaching his authority and position to imply he could speak for other Arabs.

My next stop was Israel for meetings with Prime Minister Barak and other Israeli leaders. While leaving my hotel room at the Sheraton in Damascus I received a call from my office in Washington to tell me that the Supreme Court had just ruled on the contested presidential election and that Governor Bush was now president-elect Bush.

My old friend Colin Powell, who was to be Bush's Secretary of State, located me and asked if I could make an assessment of the Clinton peace efforts in Israel. The incoming Bush administration did not want to obstruct any possibilities for progress. I said I would see what I could learn, and held a series of meetings with American Ambassador Martin Indyk, Barak, and others, after which I reported back to Powell. Barak was a direct man, but unlike Assad, he possessed a sense of humor and as we Nebraskans would say, "a good-natured outlook." He had risked everything politically to forge an historic Arab-Israeli compromise. The late Egyptian president Anwar Sadat and the late Israeli prime minister Menachem Begin were his role models. As for the Palestinians, he agreed with Assad's take: Arafat was good at meetings and press conferences, but, in the end, Arab politics would overtake him. He couldn't deliver.

Although the Clinton years did not end with an Arab-Israeli peace agreement, they remind us of how close we once were, and how far we are today from that elusive goal. The Clinton initiative would not have been possible without the prior leadership, vision, and intense efforts of President George H. W. Bush and Secretary of State Baker. They deserve great credit for teeing up the Clinton initiative. They demonstrated that true peace in the Middle East, and stability and security for Israel, could only result from a process aimed at a regionally oriented political settlement. Former American Middle East envoy Dennis Ross, who served under presidents George H. W. Bush and Clinton, once observed that a peace process is necessary because process absorbs events. Without a process, events become crises. He was right. Crisis diplomacy is no substitute for sustained, day-to-day engagement. Our inattention to this inescapable truth has crippled many of our efforts in the Middle East since 9/11.

Early in his administration, President George W. Bush made a dramatic bid to address the Israeli-Palestinian issue as a diplomatic complement to the U.S. strategy in the global "war on terrorism." On November 10, 2001, in a speech before the UN General Assembly, President Bush went further than any of his predecessors when he said:

We are working toward a day when two states, Israel and Palestine, live peacefully together within secure and recognized borders as called for by the Security Council resolutions.

But Bush's historic declaration, like so many in the sad record of this unending conflict, died on the vine. The wars in Iraq and Afghanistan soon consumed all of our energy and focus. True, there was an agreement on a "road map" for Israeli-Palestinian peace endorsed by the United States, Russia, the United Nations, and the European Union, but it was soon shunted to the back burner of U.S. foreign policy. From time to time, as events demanded, there was crisis diplomacy, several special envoys, the occasional "consultation" involving the secretary of state, and of course the press conferences and photo-ops. But despite a steady deterioration in the situation in the Middle East, there was never a sustained U.S. diplomatic process with the support and direct involvement of the president.

For the most part, ideology hijacked diplomacy during the Bush administration and statecraft gave way to a misinformed "democracy" agenda in the region. Of course democracy is important. But it can't take root in a region of explosive conflict and collapsing states, or in the absence of a diplomatic resolution of the political issues that are at the source of the conflict. In the end, we got Hamas in Palestine, Ahmadinejad in Iran, and failing states in Lebanon and Iraq. Not all of this should be blamed on the United States. But the sad reality is that we advanced neither democracy nor peace, and thereby lost our credibility in the process.

It is in Israel's interest, as much as in our own, that the United States is seen to be trustworthy by all the states in the Middle East. Our capacity to influence all parties in the Mideast conflict can only be effective if we are considered an honest broker of peace. That is the only way that our advice will be accepted. In situations where the question of war or peace is at issue, trust is the most valuable currency. Sadly, however, our currency has been seriously devalued. A poll conducted last year by Zogby International among our Arab allies (Egypt, Jordan, Lebanon, Morocco, Saudi Arabia, and the United Arab Emirates) found that only 12 percent of those polled expressed favorable attitudes toward the United States. As the perceptive *Washington Post* writer David Ignatius observed, "It isn't a tiny handful of people in the Arab world who oppose what America is doing. It's nearly everyone."

Being evenhanded does not mean that we cannot condemn the actions of Hezbollah and Hamas terrorists in their attacks or Israel's overreaction in 2006, when it engaged in relentless aerial bombardment of Lebanon for twenty-six straight days. Israel, like all sovereign nations, has the undeniable right to defend itself against terrorism and aggression. However, military retaliation—rightful or not—is not a political strategy that can end the threat posed by terrorist groups.

Extended military action has nearly destroyed Lebanon, killing innocent civilians, gutting its economy and infrastructure, and creating a humanitarian disaster within refugee camps whose only governance is chaos and violence. The result was a grave wounding of Lebanon's fragile democratic government and deepening hatred of Israel across the Middle East. In this conflict, the pursuit of tactical military victories at the expense of the core strategic objective of Arab-Israeli peace can only produce a hollow victory. The war against terrorists will not, ultimately, be won on the battlefield.

Too often in recent years, the need for a clear consistent Mideast policy has been obscured by the Iraq War—a conflict that has inadvertently, but undeniably, led to the recruitment of new terrorists who have, in turn, spawned new terror cells all over the world. America's policy must be grounded in an understanding of the complex history, competing interests, and varying perspectives of all parties. The alternative, an unending cycle of war, will continually drain Israel of its human capital, resources, and energy as it fights for its survival. The United States and Israel must understand that it does not serve us well to drift into an "us against the world" framing of the issue. That would marginalize America's global leadership and further isolate Israel.

One wonders what would have happened if Arafat could have or would have pushed through the deal worked out in the waning days of the Clinton administration. Without question the Palestinians are in a far worse position, drastically worse, than they were in January 2001. The radical Palestinian group Hamas now has total control of the Gaza Strip and Fatah is struggling to govern the Palestinian territory on the West Bank. The Palestinians are more fractured today than ever before. In addition, public services are basically nonexistent, unemployment is at a record high, health-care facilities are stretched beyond their limits. Every step toward peace and eventual statehood is countered by a step and a half backward. The electoral triumph of Hamas and the ill-conceived and disproportionate response of Israel against Lebanon after the kidnapping of three soldiers in July 2006 are but two of dozens of actions that have hardened hearts and produced a very difficult environment for Israeli and Palestinian leaders to reach any accord.

We are past the point of paying occasional attention to the Israeli-Palestinian issue and hoping that the parties will act reasonably and rationally to begin sorting out the differences between them. Given our position in the world, America has a responsibility to help shepherd the peace process to a successful conclusion. This requires our president to engage actively in the dangerous and politically risky business of peacemaking.

This is not to say that a positive outcome can be predetermined by American will and leadership. But we know that a peace settlement will not happen if the parties are left to their own devices. The challenge is immense and there is one important given that is not negotiable: A comprehensive solution should not include any compromise regarding Israel's Jewish identity, which must be assured. The Israeli people must be free to live in peace and security. Similarly, the Palestinian people must also have the same right to live in peace in Palestine with East Jerusalem as its capital, and with the same hope for a prosperous future.

A peace agreement can only work if it is supported by a massive economic development and assistance program for the Palestinians. If Palestinian leaders are willing to take risks for peace, they must have the possibility of economic benefits or the process is doomed to collapse. The lack of such aid and investment was the reason that Prime Minister Sharon's "Gaza First" plan to unilaterally withdraw Israeli settlers and military presence from Gaza turned from opportunity to tragedy with Hamas's takeover of Gaza in 2007. A broad regional economic strategy —including Israel, the Palestinians, and all the Arab states—is required to provide trade-based, sustainable growth, and to integrate the Middle East into the global economy. Such economic integration would bind Israel and the Arab states together in the joint venture of building a better future for their peoples.

The situation will ultimately require a regional security initiative that brings Israel and the Arab states together to implement a peace agreement. Region-wide confidence-building measures are required to avoid war, fight terrorism, and prevent the spread of weapons of mass destruction. So is the participation of the United Nations and perhaps NATO. Their roles could include a peacekeeping force once an agreement is reached. Recommending NATO's and Europe's close involvement in an already complex situation may sound surprising to some, but it shouldn't. The Greater Middle East is vital to the interests of all members of the Atlantic alliance—especially in our efforts to combat terrorism and the drive toward global energy security.

America's approach to the Middle East must be consistent and sustained. At its core, there will always be a special and historic bond with Israel exemplified by our continued commitment to Israel's defense. But this commitment cannot be at the expense of our Arab and Muslim relationships, which are in crisis. All of our interests will suffer if we are perceived as being implacably and irreversibly at odds with the Arab and Muslim world. Achieving a lasting resolution to the Arab-Israeli conflict is the best means of pushing political and religious extremists to the margins.

The Arab-Israeli conflict, like all great geopolitical questions, cannot be looked at in isolation. Like a stone dropped into a placid lake, its ripples extend out farther and farther. Egypt, Syria, Jordan, and Lebanon feel the effects most noticeably. Farther still, Afghanistan and Pakistan; and anything that impacts their political stability also affects the two emerging economic superpowers, India and China. On the immediate horizon, calling for a coherent policy, we find the conundrum that is Iran.

CHAPTER 5

AYATOLLAHS, BLUE JEANS, AND NUKES

THE QUESTION OF IRAN

The next president of the United States will face one of the most difficult national security decisions of modern times: what to do about an Iran that may be at the threshold of acquiring nuclear weapons. Some point to hopeful signs from our experience in North Korea as an indication that we can manage a nuclear Iran. Perhaps, but that is not a desirable outcome, and we should do all we can to avoid reaching that stage. The comparison with North Korea does not really hold. Kim Jong Il's government is a genuinely rogue regime whose nuclear ambitions and capacity for mischief have been more or less contained, though imperfectly, through the United Nations and a mature diplomatic structure that includes the United States, Russia, China, Japan, and South Korea. Patience and diplomacy, not saber rattling, has—for now—pulled North Korea back from the brink of a nuclear arms race.

No comparable regional diplomatic structure exists in the Middle East. An Iranian nuclear breakout would have dangerous consequences in a region characterized by unresolved and long-standing conflicts, including the overriding Arab-Israeli issue, a centuries-old sectarian divide in Islam, and the absence of mechanisms and institutions to promote diplomacy and conflict resolution. This is a potential nuclear match that could ignite a Middle East bonfire. Israel would not accept the possibility of an Iranian nuclear bomb and would react militarily. Because of the ancient fratricidal split between the two main branches of Islam, a Shiite (that is, Iranian) nuclear weapon could also spark a tit-for-tat escalation in proliferation among Arab Sunni nations such as Saudi Arabia, Egypt, and Syria, in addition to Turkey. Such proliferation would have grave implications for the people of the region and for global energy security. In this context we would do well to remind ourselves that while it is easy for nations to blunder into war, they never blunder into peace. It takes much more skill to cool passions than it does to inflame them.

America is the Great Power—not Iran. Because of the awesome responsibility that comes with such power, it falls to us to advance the proposition that the United States and Iran can overcome decades of mutual mistrust, suspicion, and hostility. The prospect of a nuclear-armed Iran calls for urgent and creative diplomacy by the United States, including direct bilateral talks. There can be no more excuses for not doing all we can to resolve one of the great strategic challenges of our time. Military strikes against Iran's nuclear facilities would signal a severe diplomatic failure and would have their own serious negative consequences for the United States and for our allies. Iran has the ability to retaliate in Iraq against our forces, in Lebanon against our Lebanese partners, against Israel, and potentially against us in Europe as well as here in America. The absence of a concentrated diplomatic effort to confront this issue is an abdication of our responsibility for our nation's security and for world leadership.

In dealing with Iran, we must not forget that every country is unique with its own particular history, culture, problems, strengths, and weaknesses. We cannot expect to approve of or agree with all the actions of the governments of every one of the world's countries. Nor can we simply ignore those with whom we disagree. Isolating nations is risky. It turns them inward, and makes their citizens susceptible to the most demagogic fear mongering. Unfortunately, that is what America's strategy has been over the last several years in dealing with Iran. We rebuffed an opportunity for direct dialogue in 2003 following our toppling of the Taliban regime in Afghanistan. And we never fully explored the possibility of greater bilateral dialogue during the time when the reformist Iranian president Ayatollah Mohammad Khatami was in office, from 1997 through 2002.

One of the world's oldest civilizations, Iran is a proud nation with a long, rich history. It is also, at the same time, a nation that is a state sponsor of terrorism. We must understand "both" Irans and factor both into our policies and strategic interests. Iran is not going away and whether we like it or not, there will be no peace or stability in the Middle East without Iran's participation. Iran has been a central power in the Middle East for centuries and will remain so. The historian Will Durant wrote, "Most of us spend too much time on the last twenty-four hours and too little on the last six thousand years." We must take the time to understand the country in this historical context, rather than reacting to every provocative statement its leaders serve up to pander to the most radical elements of public opinion.

Because of its strategic geopolitical position in the region, Iran holds important keys to Mideast stability and the world energy economy. Simply not engaging Iran is a dangerously simplistic approach to a complicated challenge. International problems don't go away. Unless they are dealt with they get worse—not better. The most irresponsible and dangerous course is to defer them. As John McLaughlin, the former deputy director of the Central Intelligence Agency wrote, "Even superpowers have to talk to bad guys."

Diplomacy that excludes adversaries is a contradiction in terms. Still, such diplomacy is often disparaged by critics as the first step on the road to appeasement when in fact, robust diplomatic effort is an essential component of any national security strategy that seeks to influence other nations and advance U.S. national interests without the use of force. It may involve compromise—most negotiations do—but the resulting compromise may be in the best interests of all parties. Finding areas of potential compromise and mutual interest is almost impossible in the absence of diplomacy.

For example, Iran cooperated with the United States on intelligence sharing and gathering after we invaded Afghanistan and drove out the Taliban. Why? Because replacing the Taliban, securing Iran's borders, and stopping great quantities of heroin from pouring into their country was clearly in Iran's self-interest.

The current lack of a diplomatic relationship with Iran leaves America with fewer options and less leverage to influence Iran's actions in the Middle East. Distasteful as we may find that country's rulers, the absence of any formal governmental relations with Iran ensures that we will continue to conduct this delicate international relationship through the press and speeches, as well as through surrogates and third parties, on issues of vital strategic importance to our national interests. Such a course can only result in diplomatic blind spots that will lead to misunderstandings, miscalculation, and, ultimately, conflict. Issues that should be minor disputes become tests of will. Our refusal to recognize Iran's influence does not decrease its influence, but rather increases it. This situation has created a disaster for United States–Iran relations for the better part of three decades, beginning with the overthrow of the shah and the hostage crisis.

In order to prevent this problem from escalating, the United States will need to engage Iran across a full range of issues including Iran's nuclear program, Iran's support for terrorism, Israel, Iraq, U.S. sanctions, and security assurances. Acknowledging this necessity should in no way confuse our position vis-à-vis Iran's dangerous, destabilizing, and threatening behavior. Iran provides material support to Hezbollah and Hamas, among others. It publicly threatens Israel, and is developing an increasingly advanced nuclear capability. It has contributed to instability in Iraq and Lebanon and it is no doubt responsible for some of the weapons and explosives used against U.S. and Iraqi military forces.

All those realities notwithstanding, just labeling Iran as part of the "axis of evil," and leaving it at that is dangerously short-sighted. As Tom Friedman has pointed out, Iran is a country that "regularly holds sort-of-free elections," where "women vote, hold office, are the majority of its university students, and are fully integrated in the workforce," and whose residents "were among the very few in the Muslim world to hold spontaneous pro–United States demonstrations" on September 11, 2001.

Even more promisingly, two-thirds of Iran's almost eighty million people are under the age of thirty—the vanguard of a generational shift that will shape its outlook toward the United States for decades to come. Large numbers of Iranian young people use the Internet, wear American jeans, listen to American music, and feel positive about America and the West. Many bristle under the ayatollahs' reactionary limitations on personal freedom. Therefore, we must not let rigidity or oversimplification of our attitudes toward Iran contribute to the alienation of a potentially pro-American generation by turning young Iranians away from us. They are our best hope for a peaceful Iran and, because of that, the hope of the Greater Middle East.

This is not to suggest that Iran is not ruled by fanatics who oppose us, but we must remember it is not a nation of robots all programmed by an evil genius. This is one of the most complicated and sophisticated political cultures in the world. It is both theocratic and democratic. Its democratic institutions are more developed than those in almost all other countries in the Middle

East or Central Asia, except for Israel. It is as inaccurate to think of all Iranians as anti-American fanatics as it is for them to think of us as a nation of anti-Islamic militarists.

Iran's governmental system is awash in intricacies and contradictions. At the top of the hierarchy is Ayatollah Ali Khamenei, the "Supreme Leader," and inheritor of the mantle of the Iranian revolution from Ayatollah Ruhollah Khomeini, who led the Iranian revolution that toppled the shah's regime. His is the most powerful position in Iran, and his predisposition is as anti-American and anti-Israeli as that of any world leader. But then it gets more complicated. The elections of Iran's past two presidents—the reformer Mohammad Khatami and the radical Mahmoud Ahmadinejad in 2006—were upsets: Both beat heavily favored candidates. The two men could not be more different politically. Think about this for a minute: upset presidential elections—in the supposedly hopelessly corrupt and authoritarian Middle East! That is part of the paradox of Iran.

Iran also has an elected parliament (the *Majles*) composed of both conservative and radical Islamists and more reform-oriented political parties. The Majles passes laws and at times challenges the perceived excesses of executive power. The result is far from perfect by American or European standards of democratic governance, where pluralism and open debate are accepted and even encouraged. But by regional standards, the complexity and sophistication of Iran's government are undeniable.

Iran is a patchwork of competing factions. America can either use this to our benefit, or, through intransigence, we can end up uniting all the factions against a commonly perceived threat—ourselves. As in America or any large complex society, power and influence in Iran evolve and shift. Reacting to it in a way that most benefits America requires strategic thinking, sound judgment, and wise policy rather than uninformed, broad-brush ideological reactions.

Of course we would like to see Iran free of nuclear weapons. The world would be far more secure if no one had nuclear weapons, or, at the very least, no new nations joined the nuclear club. We must work closely with our allies and world institutions to make every effort to ensure that this club does not grow. We know that any time a new nuclear weapon is developed, we move that much closer to accidental Armageddon. But the genie of nuclear armaments is already out of the bottle, no matter what Iran does. In this imperfect world, sovereign nation-states possessing nuclear weapons capability (as opposed to stateless terrorist groups) will often respond with some degree of responsible, or at least sane, behavior. These governments, however hostile they may be toward us, have some appreciation of the horrific results of a nuclear war and the consequences they would suffer in the form of retaliation meted out by larger nuclear powers like the United States or Russia or China. But we cannot count on rationality and logic should these weapons ever fall in the hands of terrorists for whom death is merely one step on the road to martyrdom. That's why it is so critically important that the United States lead a new effort to frame, structure, and build a twenty-first-century nuclear arms–control regime.

———————

The nations of the world must renew their commitment to stop the proliferation of weapons of mass destruction, because this threat is a menace to us all. The United States possesses the largest stockpile of nuclear weapons, and our actions must match our admonitions to other countries regarding these destructive devices. Iran will not be deterred from developing nuclear arms only because the United States and the EU say they must—especially if they feel threatened and if the United States, Great Britain, France, and Israel, among others, all retain their nuclear weapons. A perception exists in Muslim nations that we are saying it's okay for Christian and Jewish nations to have nuclear weapons and play by their own rules, but Muslim nations cannot (despite the reality that Pakistan and India are hardly Christian or Jewish nations). I have heard this charge from Muslim leaders. One can dismiss this point or trivialize it, but nevertheless, this perception exists and we must deal with it.

In a 1953 speech, President Eisenhower proposed a global nuclear framework to respond to the dangerous reality of nuclear weapons. Eisenhower's vision helped produce an international nuclear regime based on a simple premise: States that did not possess nuclear weapons would agree not to seek them but would be given access to nuclear technology, and states that did have nuclear weapons agreed to eventual nuclear disarmament. This was one of the Cold War's obvious but overlooked successes—no nuclear war.

But today, this framework is slowly failing. India, Pakistan, and North Korea have become "unofficial" nuclear weapons states; others, including Iran, may be seeking the same; disarmament by the nuclear weapons states has bogged down, leading non–nuclear weapons states to cry foul; sensitive information on uranium enrichment and plutonium reprocessing is spreading; the Comprehensive Test Ban Treaty that would ban nuclear tests remains in limbo; and negotiations to halt production of nuclear weapons material have stalled.

The world needs to establish a new global consensus on nuclear disarmament and nonproliferation—one that is relevant to the realities and challenges of the twenty-first century rather than to the Cold War confrontation between the United States and the Soviet Union. As the world's largest nuclear power, the United States has a responsibility to lead in this effort. There is no other way. In particular, we must once again convince the world that America has the clear intention of fulfilling the nuclear disarmament commitments that we have made. Building a new global nuclear consensus is the only way to achieve lasting solutions to challenges such as Iran's nuclear ambition.

Last summer, Senator Barack Obama and I introduced comprehensive nuclear nonproliferation legislation. Among other things, our bill would provide funding for an international fuel bank that would be administered by the International Atomic Energy Agency. This fuel bank has the potential to be a critical mechanism to help reduce the demand for sensitive nuclear technologies that could be used to produce nuclear weapons-grade uranium and plutonium. Our bill would also provide funding to enable the United States to work with other countries to develop the technology to identify sources of nuclear material. If Iran's nuclear intentions prove to be peaceful, as its leaders claim, this bill can put that to the test.

America's refusal to recognize Iran's status as a legitimate power does not decrease Iran's influence, but rather increases it. Engagement creates dialogue and opportunities to identify common interests, as well as to clarify disagreements. In a hazy, volatile environment, careless rhetoric and military movements that one side may believe are required to demonstrate resolve and strength can be misinterpreted as preparations for war. The risk of inadvertent conflict because of miscalculation is great. Because nations usually respond in their own self-interest, which most often leads to a consistent and predictable response, what is most dangerous is a nation whose behavior is inconsistent and unpredictable.

The United States must be cautious to avoid stepping down the same destructive path in Iran that led us into Iraq. We blundered into Iraq because of flawed intelligence, flawed assumptions, flawed judgments, and ideologically driven motives. We must not repeat these errors with Iran, and the best way to avoid them is to maintain an effective dialogue.

We still have the opportunity to open a new chapter by engaging Iran with a direct and strategic diplomatic initiative that will both seek to avoid a military confrontation. Let's put the burden on Iran and its rulers about the direction the ayatollahs choose for its young population—toward enduring conflict with the United States, or toward Iran's acceptance and integration into the world economy.

Iran has been much on my mind throughout my career in the Senate. I have gone back through my speeches, interviews, and policy studies, and from them put together what I believe to be a concise and straightforward way for the United States to deal with Iran. Some of the specifics may change by the time you read this but overall it is a course for a safer harbor than any we have found since the fall of the shah.

First, the United States should continue its efforts at the UN Security Council to keep international pressure on Iran regarding its nuclear program. Preventing an Iranian nuclear weapon is in the interests of both the United States and the world community—it is not just a United States–Iran issue. Iran's nuclear defiance must be perceived in Tehran as having consequences for its international standing.

Second, the United States should offer a wide-ranging diplomatic agenda for bilateral negotiations with Iran. Washington should make clear that everything is on the table with Tehran—an end to sanctions, diplomatic recognition, civil nuclear cooperation, investment in Iran's energy sector, World Bank loans, World Trade Organization (WTO) membership, Iraq, Afghanistan, regional security arrangements, etc.—if Iran abstains from a nuclear weapons program, ends support for terrorist groups, recognizes Israel, and engages in more constructive policies in Iraq.

Iran must change its behavior, not its regime, for an improved relationship with the United States—this should be made clear.

Regime change is desirable, but that should not be our objective. Bilateral talks with Iran would have no conditions and there would be no illusions that progress would be quick or easy, if progress is even possible. The UN secretary-general could host the first meeting, or some other agreeable venue could be arranged. It could be quiet or public. The point is that it needs to happen sooner rather than later, and it should be more than just the narrowly defined talks that took place in Geneva in 2003 or in Baghdad in 2007.

In making such an offer to Iran, America would be squarely placing the burden on Iran's rulers to respond to the opportunity for a new relationship with the United States. Let them think about the substantial carrots of improved relations, not just the sticks, and there may be a deal to be had.

This type of bold U.S. diplomacy would also create pressure from within Iranian society to begin direct talks with the United States. Most Iranians want the benefits of a good relationship with the United States and integration with the global economy. This initiative, I believe, would shake the regime to its core. But it falls to us to take the first step.

Third, the United States must find a new regional diplomatic strategy to deal with Iran, one that includes all of our regional allies. The agenda for this effort would include other issues such as Iraq and Afghanistan, nonproliferation, antiterrorism, and confidence-inspiring measures to avoid regional conflict. Refusing to engage Iran as a significant player in Persian Gulf security matters perpetuates dangerous geopolitical unpredictabilities.

In October of last year, I sent President Bush a letter urging him to consider just such a comprehensive strategy, emphasizing the critical importance of pursuing direct, unconditional, and comprehensive talks with the government of Iran. I told the president that I was increasingly concerned that our diplomatic strategy was stalling and that we were relying more and more on a single-track policy of pressure, sanctions, and escalating tensions. Unless there was a strategic shift in the coming months, the United States could find itself in a dangerous and increasingly isolated position regarding Iran. I also pointed out that Russia will be critically important to any U.S.-Iran regional peace plan or agreement.

I followed my letter to the president with a speech to the Center for Strategic and International Studies, where I warned that "loose talk of World War III, intimidation, threats, bellicose speeches only heighten the dangers we face in the world. Without offering solutions and building international alliances we only strengthen the hand of those who prey upon and play to a confused, frightened, and disorganized world. We must not play the Iranian president's game by allowing ourselves to recklessly ricochet into a conflict that could help unite Iran and the Muslim world behind the very extremists that we should be isolating. Our strategy must be smarter, and get beyond the Iranian president. We must demonstrate to the rest of Iran's leaders, the Iranian people, the Middle East, and the world that only an irresponsible Iranian president could take Iran into conflict, not the United States."

As I mentioned earlier, the fruits of positive engagement were very much in evidence when Iran cooperated with the United

States to break the power of the Taliban in Afghanistan, and even more when it invested heavily in the reconstruction of western Afghanistan in 2002–2003. This was not done out of a desire to assist American foreign policy goals. It was in the clear self-interest of Shiite Iran to disable the Sunni Taliban. The lesson learned is that both America and Iran found common interests and something productive came of it.

I know that Iranians of good will seek to further the relationship between our two nations. Over the years I have made a point to meet occasionally with Iran's permanent representatives to the United Nations—both Ambassador M. H. Nejad Hosseinian (who also has served as minister of heavy industries and deputy oil minister) and Javad Zarif (who has also served as deputy foreign minister). Both men are accomplished and clever diplomats who represented their country ably at the United Nations. While our conversations focused on those Iranian policies that harmed U.S. interests in the Middle East—such as support for terrorist groups opposed to Israel and providing arms for elements in Iraq who are killing Americans—we also discussed where diplomatic common ground might be found to end what is now almost thirty years of hostility between our two nations.

The United States must be prepared to act boldly and exploit opportunities to reframe our relationship with Iran. Engagement should not be limited to government-to-government contact. We must find new and imaginative ways to reach out to the Iranian people. Part of that initiative could be an offer to reopen a consulate in Tehran: not formal diplomatic relations, but a consulate to help encourage and facilitate people-to-people exchanges. All the nations of Europe and most of our allies in the Middle East and Asia already have diplomatic relations with Iran.

When America's Librarian of Congress James Billington returned from a visit to Iran in 2004, I called him to get his assessment. Dr. Billington was the first senior American official to visit Iran in many years. He told me he was struck by a normalcy among the Iranian people in their exchanges with him, their positive views toward the United States, their interests in the United States, and how open and engaged their young people were. These are very encouraging signs for the relationship between the United States and Iran, and we need to find ways to capitalize on this state of affairs within Iran. If we do not pursue a diplomatic option to end the animosity between our two nations, we can be assured that the region will grow progressively more dangerous and hostile toward the United States in the coming years.

While reaching out to Iran, we must always be clear-headed in grasping the reality of who is in charge there and what their objectives are—they may not be the same as ours. The ayatollahs may be vested in conflict with the United States, and if so, our strategy may need to be one of containment and confrontation. But we cannot know if that is the case unless we begin the diplomacy required to break out of the current cycle of hostility. Today's leaders will pass from the scene, so we must build bridges to the next generation of Iranians, many of whom are excited by the global economy and tired of heated rhetoric and reactionary politics. Thinking of the long term can offer hope and direction for what has become one of America's most intractable problems. There are much greater challenges and opportunities to which we must attend as a new superpower emerges three thousand miles to the east of Tehran: the People's Republic of China.

CHAPTER 6

CHINA

A SEAT AT THE TABLE

T here is something about the word "China" that evokes strong feelings among Americans. We respect the ancient culture and philosophy that underpins the Chinese civilization, and we respond positively to the Chinese people themselves on a personal level. We love Chinese food. Yet many Americans also instinctively fear and distrust this distant, different, and enormously populous nation that is once again rising to a prominent role in the world. By virtue of its size and economic strength it will be, alongside America, the major player on the world scene in this century.

There is no strategic relationship more important to the United States than China. At the same time there are few, if any, more open to contention and discord. From human rights and intellectual property rights to the balance of trade, we can expect continued strong differences with the Chinese. We must be realistic and clearheaded in our approach to these issues, and we must remain balanced and insightful. There are those who call for a new cold war with China based on a policy of economic, political, and military containment, but this kind of belligerence would be a disaster for our two nations and for the world.

First, such a policy would fail. China is and will remain a major factor in the world economy. Other nations would certainly refuse to join the United States in such a containment policy, and the result would contribute more toward our own isolation rather than China's. Second, such a policy today is simply wrong. History has shown that the way to encourage more open societies, human rights, and democratic development is through engagement, trade, communication, and direct contact among people. As Richard Nixon recommended nearly forty-one years ago in *Foreign Affairs* magazine: "For the long run, it means pulling China back into the world community—but as a great and progressing nation, not as the epicenter of world revolution." This has been the policy of every American president since Nixon. A constructive bilateral relationship with China is one of the most important steps America can take toward building a world more aligned with our interests and leadership.

We often think of America as a nation anchored by a strong middle class. If that is true, and I believe that it is, consider this fact: China currently has a middle class *as large as the population of the United States.* Three hundred million people investing in their country and the world.

We also need to recognize that there are still hundreds of millions of Chinese living in some degree of poverty. Still, China's direction is clearly toward further economic development and an ever-larger middle class. China's rate of growth has few historical parallels. A film of the Shanghai skyline over the last few years would more than anything show constant change like a time-lapse video of a plant going from seed to tree in a matter of minutes. Before the middle of this century, if it continues growing at its current rate, China's economy will be on the same order of magnitude as America's.

Over the last twenty-five years, China has "leapfrogged" many of the stages of economic development that America and Europe had gone through in the nineteenth and twentieth centuries. This is often the case with developing economies. Look at the resurgence of Japan after World War II. It had the benefit of America's (and Europe's) experience in the Industrial Revolution. New technologies have given China and other less-developed economies the opportunity to advance rapidly.

One of these new transforming technologies is cellular telephony, a business I was deeply involved in during the early 1980s. In much of the world, the expansion of telephonic communications through cell phones has moved ahead at a blistering pace because new markets don't have to lay expensive wires and invest tremendous sums of capital for a land-based telephone system the way America and other nations did a hundred years ago. Towers, antennas, and switches can quickly bring telephone service to millions of people. In the last twenty years, hundreds of millions of people have thus entered the world of instantaneous communications.

I was able to witness some of this transformation in China as my partners and I were building our businesses. In 1982, after resigning as deputy administrator of the Veterans Administration, I cashed in two insurance policies, sold my Buick, and went into partnership with three friends in a cellular telephone venture we called Collins, Hagel and Smith (later Collins, Hagel and Clark). This was before most people knew what cellular was and before you could even buy cell phones.

On January 1, 1984, I landed with a small group of business colleagues at the Beijing airport on a trip to market the new technology in China. To my surprise, the airport was nearly deserted. The sky was leaden gray. Customs was equally cheery: Stone-faced soldiers with machine guns and bureaucrats in gray Mao suits greeted us as we disembarked on New Year's Day—the western New Year's Day.

Beijing was cold, Nebraska-in-January cold. The air was thick with the smog of a million coal fires. There was hardly anyone on the streets except for the occasional official car doing what official cars always do, speeding along without paying attention to traffic signals, as if the world depended on their making good time. Our first stop, the Beijing Hotel, was a perfect metaphor for the nation. The original section, where we stayed, was old but bore markings of a faded elegance. There was a wing from the early 1950s, built soon after the Chinese Communists took control of the country, and the third wing, somewhat newer, looked like a classic Soviet apartment building (a gray box with windows).

My room was clean though spartan, and not much warmer than it was outside. There was a little burner and a tea kettle so you could fix yourself hot coffee or tea. The shower, which I was much in need of after the long trip, was cold. That night we attended the first of many dinners with endless toasts which meant endless shots of Mao-tai—the national shot-glass filler-upper of China. It's grain alcohol with a mule kick to it. Tasty stuff. It does take the chill off.

After a few days of meetings in Beijing, we took a train to Tianjin, a large coastal city which has been an important industrial center for many years. Not a fun city—even darker than Beijing. Our railroad car was so crowded you could hardly move. It seemed that everyone was smoking and drinking; in one hand they were holding cigarettes and with the other throwing down shots of Mao-tai. However, there seemed to be a lot of camaraderie, probably thanks to the cocktails.

We toured a number of factories and explained cellular telephony to hundreds of technicians and engineers. They were young and very eager to learn. They pored over every manual and brochure for hours, devouring every word, drawing, and diagram. They would jot notes on the blackboard and debate. One thing that became very clear to me was that these people were ready to work hard, and if they were at all representative of their country, China was going to build a strong and dynamic economy.

From Tianjin we returned to Beijing and then went on to Canton (now Guangzhou) via China Air. Canton was a completely different China from what we had seen so far. A fairly modern city, it was located near Hong Kong and it looked like Hong Kong. I began to understand that there was no such thing as "one" China. Each province was different—some very different—with its own culture, food, and dialect. Yes, it was one Communist nation, but very unevenly governed and administered. Although we made no sales during that ten-day trip to China, I learned a lifetime's worth of lessons about China and its people.

I returned to China twice in 1997, this time as a United States senator. The difference was breathtaking. The ubiquitous gray Mao suits of 1984 were gone, replaced by the variety of colorful clothes you would see in most modern-day societies. In fact, the whole aspect of the big cities was modern: neon billboards, traffic; stores full of televisions, computers, and the whole range of electronic appliances; restaurants of every kind—featuring all the cuisines of China, but also McDonald's and replicas of Parisian bistros and Italian trattorias. Beijing in particular hummed with dynamism.

The late Senator John Chafee and I stopped in Beijing in December during the Kyoto Summit in Japan to meet with Premier Li Peng. We also went to Chengdu in Sichuan province to look at some of the environmental and energy projects the Chinese were initiating. Sichuan is a lush semitropical area and the home range of the panda bear. It is spectacularly beautiful. The government, with the assistance of the United Nations and private foundations, was doing very good work on several environmental projects that we visited. We also visited the Three Gorges Dam under construction near Yichang in Hubei province. Once completed it will be the world's largest dam as well as the world's largest hydroelectric station. Energy and the environment pushing and pulling each other, attempting an accommodation:

This was a Chinese version of a similar scenario being played out across the globe. China's immense energy requirements dominate this push and pull. As in all countries across the globe, it must find a balance.

I returned again to China in 1999 and saw a continuation of the remarkable economic progress that I had witnessed two years earlier. China has changed much for the better since my first visit twenty-five years ago, both for the people and for the stability of the nation. My cellular telephone business, and ten thousand other entrepreneurial ventures like it, grasped the early possibilities—and many were successful. What a transformation from the brutal regime of Mao and his Red Guards, when it seemed that the only hope for change was that the population would reach a level of misery that would spark another revolution—and our only hope was to wait for the next emperor to fall.

Economic growth has created a new, more hopeful path in China where it is not misery but prosperity that is transforming society. However, human rights are still a serious barrier dividing our two countries. As the former chairman of the Congressional Executive Commission on China, a congressionally chartered commission that is the result of legislation I introduced in 2000, I am very aware of the lack of significant progress by the Chinese government on the issues of human rights such as child labor and restrictions on religious freedoms. China will not be considered a full and responsible member of the international community, nor will it reach its full potential as a society, until it puts the same focus on human rights that it has on economic development.

Because Chinese foreign policy, once driven by ideology, is now more concerned with the balance sheet and jobs, this new openness has had dramatic effects beyond commerce both inside the country and around the world. For instance, China was selected to host the 2008 Summer Olympics. This is a remarkable and symbolic achievement for a nation so large, with so much poverty, and run by a Communist government. And in 2000, China established the China-Africa Cooperation Forum to help Beijing pursue energy-related contracts, develop trade and investment agreements, expand scientific and technical cooperation, and support greater tourism between China and Africa. As part of this program, China has built railroads, soccer stadiums, and other highly visible infrastructure improvements in African countries. As a result of these efforts, trade between China and Africa has increased at a staggering pace since 2001, exceeding $55 billion in 2006. China has invested heavily in Angola, Sudan, and Nigeria, three of Africa's leading oil producers. It is no coincidence that Africa now provides about one-third of China's crude oil imports.

In Latin America, the same story is being written as the Chinese help develop infrastructure and gain access to energy and natural resources. The image the Chinese are projecting stands in contrast to how America is perceived. According to a June 2007 Pew Research Study, "In general, Africans are more positive than Latin Americans about the growing influence of both China and the United States on their countries. But in both regions, somewhat greater percentages say China's influence is a good thing than say that about United States influence."

We should not be surprised by this. I do not believe that it is something that we could stop, even if we wanted to; moreover, China has an advantage that frees it to extend its largesse where human rights considerations constrain the United States. China has not used foreign assistance and aid to press for the kinds of reforms that America addresses with its foreign aid, such as anticorruption measures and cessation of human rights abuses, as well as democratic and other reforms. Given a choice, countries that receive aid will choose help without "strings" over help with them. Considering the growing Chinese role in world affairs, the next administration will need to find ways to encourage responsible Chinese policies in any way that we can.

This task has been made more difficult by the truculence of our recent foreign policy. Whether viewed in relation to China or in relation to our standing within the larger global community, America has an image problem. Largely because of our misguided venture into Iraq, we are seen in most parts of the world as a unilateralist militaristic giant. This is neither fair nor always true. There is always a certain amount of resentment toward great powers, and we have to factor that reality into our foreign policy and our strategic thinking. But this perception created by the Iraq War opens us to criticism, and often casts us in the role of global bully. That is a difficult position from which to regain trust, and it will continue to undermine our interests in the world as well as our ability to influence the shape and direction of events.

Likewise, the current streak of trade protectionism in America—crying out for retaliation against China—casts America in a confrontational light and actually hurts the consumers and the jobs that we seek to protect in our country. Much is made of the "artificial" exchange rate between the Chinese and American currencies. The argument goes that cheap currency in China represents a back-door subsidy to the Chinese economy that gives it an unfair export advantage while destroying American jobs. As is often the case with simplistic economic arguments—especially those bolstered by nationalism—this does not represent the whole truth, which is more complex and often very different from what it appears to be at first glance.

Yes, we are wearing blue jeans made in China, jogging in Chinese-made running shoes, and using Chinese-made appliances; but the fact is that most of these Chinese jobs did not come purely at the expense of American jobs. South Korea, Hong Kong, Singapore, and Japan are also experiencing job flight because the cost of labor and materials is so much less in China. It is one of the laws of free-market economies that investment and production will seek out the most hospitable environments. Other low-cost producers of cheap, quality goods are also competing with China for the U.S. market. Vietnam, Thailand, Cambodia, the Philippines, Malaysia, and many South American countries are now all part of a global market where the consumer is the biggest winner—especially the American consumer.

If America stopped buying from China, we would still be faced with the same dynamic—a world economy driven by a world market, producing cheap, quality products made in other countries. Note the word "quality." Where China has an advantage in its ability to mass-produce goods at low cost, it has yet to gain the confidence of the world that it can uphold minimum standards of quality and safety. The recent health and safety issues with Chinese imports, particularly toys and pet food, are good examples of problems that centralized economic and trade bureaucracies such as China's face.

Another point needs to be made here. Because we are living in a world market, the components of products may come from many places but they are assembled in one location. For example, much of the clothing that Americans buy that bears a "made in China" label is made with thread from Vietnam, silk from Thailand, and cotton from India, but assembled in China. You might have as many as six or seven items from six or seven different countries woven into the same "Chinese" product. We cannot control the global marketplace. The market is more powerful than any individual, government, or country. The answer to the challenge of Chinese textiles is not more American-made underwear; rather, it is for America to continue to invest in the productive technologies that advanced societies are capable of generating and that an educated, skilled, and trained labor force is capable of manning. This is called being competitive on twenty-first-century terms, rather than trying to roll the clock back to the 1950s. The law of "comparative advantage" always dominates and always wins. We would be much better advised to develop the new industries and jobs required in a high-tech world.

The good old days—which weren't all that good for many people—are gone, just as the cheap oil that powered our giant tailfinned automobiles is gone. If we are looking for openings for the American economy in China, that country's vast and growing need for alternative energy sources is precisely the kind of high-tech challenge that propelled American growth all through the twentieth century. Similarly, the challenge to improve world health by cleaning up the environment is one that China will need to face more and more as it now possesses the largest carbon footprint on the planet. American technology, research, and commerce can reap huge economic rewards from this need.

In many ways, the China–United States economic relationship is critical to our domestic economy. Today, China holds about $420 billion in U.S. Treasury securities. The Chinese have bet on the American economy and the strength of the dollar. In other words, the Chinese have been helping to finance our debt and prop up our currency. Current total U.S. debt held by the public is $5 trillion. Of this amount about $2.2 trillion is held by foreign investors (45 percent). Next to Japan, the People's Republic of China has the largest percentage of ownership of this debt. The time is coming when investment opportunities and currency holdings in other economies around the world will produce a greater return on investment for the Chinese and others than they would receive from American dollars and T-Bills. And you can be sure that the extremely accomplished financial analysts at the People's Bank of China will go where the money is. Literally, we are living on borrowed time and borrowed money. Luckily for us, one of the ironies of the situation is that the Chinese are likely to hold on to their American investments and their dollars longer than we ourselves might be to support one of our creditors. They will do this because we are their largest market and the linchpin of the world economy. If the United States economy weakens, it affects every economy. In late 2007, the U.S. dollar was setting record lows against other currencies. This is a dangerous long-term development and could be a huge problem for America. A devalued currency devalues assets held in that currency and drives up interest rates. A nation cannot build nor sustain a strong economy on a declining currency, and in America's case it would soon lose its indispensable flow of foreign investment capital.

China is a world power. We cannot control it, nor should we try to. Neither should we be shocked when the Chinese decide to spend more on defense. All great powers seek to enhance and modernize their military and strengthen their security. Do we need to be mindful of that? Yes. Do we need to think tactically and strategically about how we might respond to that buildup? Again, yes. But we are far more likely to be able to live peacefully with a China to which we are bound by strong economic ties and mutual interests as an ally and competitor, rather than one that we face as an adversary and enemy.

An example of the way closer ties have worked to our mutual benefit is the role the Chinese have played in negotiating the North Korean nuclear issue. China's leadership and direct involvement in the "Party of Six" talks (United States, China, North Korea, South Korea, Japan, and Russia) have helped move this dangerous issue closer to resolution. A stable North Korea free of nuclear weapons is clearly in the interest of China as well as the United States and the rest of Asia, and the combined diplomatic pressure we have applied seems to be bearing fruit.

Finally, Taiwan will remain a sensitive issue. The strengthening of cross-strait economic linkages has been one of the most positive trends in the region, while on the other hand the buildup of Chinese missiles and other military forces targeting Taiwan generates deep mistrust and increases regional tensions as well as tensions with the United States. Both China and Taiwan need to avoid provocative unilateral signals or actions. The United States must walk a fine but necessary line and continue to support the peaceful resolution of differences between the People's Republic of China and Taiwan, and remain committed both to the "one China" policy and to its obligations under the Taiwan Relations Act.

The bottom line, quite literally, is that our relationship with China is closely interwoven with trade and the self-interests of both our nations, and I see that as positive. Trade fosters understanding and mutual respect; it engages societies, it improves standards of living, and it builds bridges between people. It is an opportunity to help cement a stable relationship in which other issues can also be discussed. But it cannot be an excuse for deferring sensitive issues and differences or excusing unacceptable behavior. Trade cannot mean a lessening of our commitment to human rights and freedom or our willingness to forcefully defend our interests wherever or whenever they are threatened. Trade, like every other factor in international relations, has its limits and cannot solve all nations' differences. However, the most irresponsible thing we could do is create the self-fulfilling prophecy of a hostile China by attempting to isolate it financially. In that regard, trade is and will continue to be an important and defining element of our China policy. It will be central to our overall foreign policy as we direct our gaze to a wider world where the crises are not so immediate but demand our attention if we hope to keep our sometimes wobbly planet on an even keel.

CHAPTER 7

OPTICS

SEEING THE WORLD THROUGH A WIDER LENS

To this point, I have tried to frame America's role in a reordered world in terms of the regions and issues which most urgently demand our attention. While it is both prudent and practical to pay attention to the world's current political stress zones, we must just as surely keep our eyes on the horizon to see what new tempests might be blowing our way. In a world grown increasingly interconnected, it is imperative that we view events through the widest possible lens.

Dealing with the perils, both seen and unforeseen, that confront us demands that we adhere to a few bedrock principles. The success of our policies depends not only on the extent of our power, but also on an appreciation of its limits. We must not succumb to the comforting but misguided distraction of divine mission. It may be our wish—even our destiny—to promote the spread of democracy, but we must be equally careful that our actions are always based on realistic assessments of the needs and dynamics of real countries in the real world and not based on ideological orthodoxy. As Henry Kissinger perceptively noted, "A foreign policy to promote democracy needs to be adapted to local or regional realities, or it will fail. In the pursuit of democracy, policy—as in other realms—is the art of the possible."

Foreign policy is the bridge between the United States and the rest of the world: between the past, the present, and the future, and the best course of action for the future often differs radically from the strategy best suited to the past. For instance, who would have thought in the dark days of 1942 that, as a direct consequence of our greatest foreign policy initiative (the Marshall Plan to rebuild Europe after World War II) we would one day number Japan and Germany among our closest allies? Yet history easily accommodated this course correction.

In order to flourish, America must engage the forces of change; most of all, the power of a restless and unpredictable new generation that is coming of age across the globe. These youthful billions have no memory and little knowledge of the America that helped heal the wounds of the world wars that scarred the first half of the twentieth century. Their concerns are in the here and now and their knowledge of America is often derived from those who oppose us and would sow the seeds of distrust. We cannot let the international perception of America be framed by its enemies, but we can prevent that only if we understand the aspirations and concerns of the nearly three billion people under the age of twenty-one. They are the driving force of contemporary history.

Any foreign policy requires domestic consensus before it can hope to convince the rest of the world. This begins with strong presidential leadership that puts forth a clear vision of our role in the world. It requires congressional partnership, engagement, and support. Without that, a policy will lack legitimacy and sustainability. A lack of consensus at home always means foreign policy trouble abroad. This was one of the lessons of Vietnam, where the United States, divided at home and isolated abroad, failed in what was presented at the time as a noble mission.

Furthermore, building domestic consensus is not merely a matter of effective slogans, persuasive ads, and catchy sound bites. In order to achieve an informed common purpose, it is imperative that we, as a nation, put a genuine emphasis on the lessons of history and of economic realities. To do this, our educational establishment needs nothing short of the kind of kick in the pants that Sputnik provided to the sciences and math fifty years ago. Today the crying need is an additional emphasis on foreign languages, culture, and history. In short, humanity needs to study the humanities.

No single country, including the United States with all its vast military and economic power, can successfully meet the challenges of the twenty-first century alone. Protecting our nation from the threat of terrorism, for example, will require a seamless network of relationships. It is an inescapable fact that our long-term security interests are connected to alliances, coalitions, and international institutions. Our foreign policy must be one that views international arrangements as extensions of our influence, not as constraints on our power. And it must also take the measure of future developments as they are likely to be, rather than as we would wish them to be.

With great foresight, Winston Churchill made this same argument in the 1930s in regard to the impending threat of Nazi Germany. He said that Britain needed to build up a strong coalition of European allies with which to confront this dark and imposing reality. He warned that Britain could not go it alone, no matter how powerful his country was—and it was powerful. But Neville Chamberlain and the British public did not heed his warning. The result came at a very high cost for the British people and the world.

The United Nations can play a central and critical role in forging connections. The global challenges of terrorism, proliferation of weapons of mass destruction, hunger, disease, and poverty require multilateral responses and initiatives. The United States should therefore take every opportunity to help strengthen global institutions and alliances, including the UN. Like all institutions, the United Nations has its limitations and problems. It needs reform. Too often, the UN, especially the General Assembly, succumbs to the worst forms of political posturing. Nevertheless, the United Nations has played an essential role throughout the world in postconflict transitions, supervising elections, providing humanitarian programs and assistance, peacekeeping, and offering international legitimacy and expertise of the kind that have helped stabilize Korea, Haiti, Liberia, East Timor, the Balkans, Afghanistan, and a number of other regions.

Helping bring security to those troubled areas required an immense international effort. Although many of these hot spots are still troubled today, each is more stable than it was, reducing the risk of further violence and regional escalation. More importantly, each has some hope for a peaceful future—although it may take years before that hope is realized. No international conflict is simple or easy to deal with, but each requires attention and the United Nations is the only international organization that can help bring the consensus that is indispensable in finding solutions and resolving crises.

We must strengthen our commitment to the transatlantic partnership with NATO and the European Union so that it remains the central alliance in our global strategy. The end of the Cold War meant a shift in NATO's strategic focus from the defense of Europe to include the Greater Middle East, Central Asia, and Africa. NATO will therefore require a new strategic doctrine for the twenty-first century, and it seems logical that this take place in concert with the EU. In like manner, U.S. foreign policy should treat the EU as a geopolitical force in its own right, distinct from—although connected to—the NATO security alliance. Washington's relationship with NATO would in fact be strengthened through its recognition of the diplomatic and economic significance of the United States–EU relationship. This bloc of twenty-five nations, with internal borders open for trade and investment, constitutes one of the largest economies in the world: EU–United States commerce accounts for more than $1 trillion annually. Leveraging off of this economic leviathan, the United States and the EU can benefit by teaming up to address global issues, particularly those involving the two and a half billion people left behind in the world economy.

As NATO and the EU adjust to the addition of new members and new strategic circumstances, they must simultaneously address gaps in military capabilities and expenditures. The United States cannot be expected to continue to shoulder a disproportionate share of the military responsibilities of the alliance. An example, and a costly one at that, is NATO's reliance on U.S. strategic airlift capabilities when forces need to move over long distances. Our allies will have to redefine and strengthen their commitments to the alliance. Military power will continue to play a vital and central role, but the future success of NATO will be determined in equal measure by its members' ability to deepen and expand their cooperation in all areas of international relations, including fulfilling the massive requirements of economic development and addressing humanitarian crises.

For example, disease—often spawned in the squalor of extreme poverty—now threatens the developed nations of NATO as profoundly as the threat of Soviet missiles did in past decades. Here as elsewhere we must broaden our optics beyond traditional foreign policy concerns. Many of the nations of Africa and Asia are locked in a cycle of violence, poverty, and endemic disease that makes them ideal incubators of avian flu, severe acute respiratory syndrome (SARS), HIV/AIDS, tuberculosis, malaria, and other diseases that lurk in the brothels of Asia or the poachers' camps on the Serengeti Plain. These diseases often make their first appearances in impoverished nations, but from these remote bases, they quickly develop into devastating global epidemics. As the historian William McNeill wrote in his book *Plagues and Peoples*, infectious disease is "one of the fundamental parameters and determinants of human history."

The NATO alliance also requires additional support from other long-standing allies including Australia, Japan, and South Korea. These alliances can continue to enhance and project our own influence and power by adding in the power and influence of our allies. We share common interests and common values, and very often work in common action, like we have done in the Balkans, Iraq, and Afghanistan. The transatlantic alliance will increasingly serve as the foundation of a broader global alliance of common purpose. As global interconnectedness evolves, our alliances will require more attention in order to remain relevant and robust. Moreover, we should be prepared to consider expanding this inner circle of our global partners as other countries prepare to move into the role of responsible citizenship.

Which brings me to a nation with great promise, but one that also must be treated with great care: Russia. Had I written this book twenty years ago, it would have occupied a long and early chapter. From World War II to the early 1990s, the Soviet Union was at the center of all of our international concerns. At the height of the Cold War, it had more than ten thousand nuclear warheads and bombs attached to ICBMs or loaded on Soviet bombers with "special delivery for the U.S." marked on each. The Soviets had tens of thousands more in its stockpile. I grew up with the eerie knowledge that some of those Soviet nukes surely were targeted on the headquarters of the Strategic Air Command in my home state.

Then in 1989, in a remarkable and historic development, the Soviet system, laboring under the weight of its own tyranny and staggering Communist inefficiency, collapsed. But even after the end came to Soviet Communism, America and the West had a difficult time dispelling their long-held vision of the Russians as bad guys, making it a substantial struggle for us to frame and develop a new twenty-first-century relationship with Russia.

So far, Russian democracy has not lived up to our earlier hopes. Remember, though, that Russia is a nation with no history of democratic traditions or institutions. It has never been democratic. When President Vladimir Putin came to power, his nation was wracked with social and economic chaos and, most alarmingly for the rest of the world, still armed with a large and sophisticated nuclear arsenal. Putin brought order and stability to Russia. Granted it was a version of order that we don't like and don't identify with in America, but its implementation was an important step at a critical time. There is still a crackdown on a free press, and restraints on individual rights and on free enterprise in Russia. But parallel to Russia's political troubles, there is also a more positive behind-the-scenes story of investment and economic growth. Russia's economy is much stronger than it was a decade ago. Foreign investment is no longer fleeing; instead it is betting that economic trends will continue upward. More trade and relationship building between our countries can only reinforce these positive developments.

Lest we judge too harshly, we would do well to remember that nations develop in stages—just as American democracy advanced in stages: Less than a hundred years ago American women did not have the right to vote, and until the passage of the Civil Rights Act and Voting Rights Act in the mid-1960s, African American citizens had limited rights. Given our own history we must judge others not only on the basis of the America we know in 2008, but also America as it was in 1776, 1865, 1920, and 1965. We must continue to work together with the Russians toward their own democratic development. It is in the interests of both countries and a more stable world.

Developing more effective bilateral trade with this potentially significant market will ultimately create additional jobs, security, and prosperity for us and for Russia. Its natural resources are immense, and in a global economy where energy is a central factor, those estimated resources include more than sixty billion barrels of oil and natural gas reserves reaching some 1,700 trillion cubic feet. As a whole, EU countries import 25 percent of their energy needs from Russia. It is clearly in our interests to engage Russia as a strategic energy partner and as a stable counterbalance to our continued dependence on oil from the volatile Middle East and other regions. For all these reasons, we have no choice but to deal with Russia constructively. It is my belief that we can exert the kind of influence on Russia that allies respect and respond to, especially if we continue to become vital trading partners.

In building this new relationship with Russia, as with Iran and China, we cannot turn a blind eye to the excesses and abuses of any government. As my friend, Zbigniew Brzezinski, said, "If

Russia is to be part of this larger zone of peace it cannot bring into it its imperial baggage. It cannot bring into it a policy of genocide against the Chechens, and cannot kill journalists, and it cannot repress the mass media."

We have to make clear our disapproval of Moscow's historical tendency toward concentrating power with leaders who are accountable to no one. But I question if provoking Russia with a missile defense system positioned on its border—as the Bush administration has suggested—that has dubious utility to American security, will do anything but strengthen the hand of the hard-liners and further erode our relationship on more important issues like fighting terrorism and Islamic extremism. Cooperating with Russia in rooting out terrorists and Islamic jihadists all over the world is much more vital to our national interests than fracturing that relationship over a questionable missile defense shield on Russia's border.

In recent years, we have worked closely with the Russians on two of the most dangerous problems facing both of our countries and the world—North Korea's nuclear program and the Israeli-Palestinian conflict. Russia and the United States have been close allies in the Party of Six group engaging North Korea on the question of its nuclear capability. We have also worked together as members of the Quartet (along with the European Union and the United Nations) in an attempt to break the cycle of violence between the Israelis and Palestinians and to move the peace efforts toward a two-state solution. These are critically important partnerships for each country's interest.

Successful as this partnership has been so far, this work is far from done. Russia and the United States must continue to work together on these great global challenges. The "Party of Six" and the "Quartet" can serve as models for the Russian-American partnership for attacking other, as yet unforeseen issues of the twenty-first century. We will continue to have our differences, and they will inevitably strain this vital relationship. But those differences must be wisely managed and framed by our larger common interests.

I personally saw the good and the bad, the promise and the portents in December 1998, when Senator Jack Reed and I visited Russia to meet with political and business leaders. Everywhere we went, we had a strong sense of a country struggling with newfound freedoms and institutions. It was a time of great confusion and conflict for the Russian people. We visited the usual tourist stops—St. Petersburg, Moscow, and Siberia—but Jack and I specifically wanted to include a look at the old Soviet radar site in Krasnoyarsk in Siberia, which had been off-limits to everyone, a top secret nerve center of the Soviet defense system.

We took a red-eye Aeroflot flight from Moscow to Krasnoyarsk. I was struck by the fact that seat belts appeared to be optional. Or maybe it was the holdover of old Soviet habits: The authorities pretended that they would enforce the rules and the people pretended that they would obey them. As in my earlier railroad trip in China, my hosts made up for the lack of amenities with nonstop cocktails: that is if your idea of a cocktail is vodka, straight up, in a plastic cup. The meal consisted of meat sandwiches. What kind of meat? Nobody seemed to know. When we walked off the plane at dawn we were met by a Siberian winter wind that stung like needles.

I had been invited to this region by General Alexander Lebed, who I had met in Washington during one of his visits to the United States. He was now governor of Krasnoyarsk *krai*, a province in central Russia. Lebed had the physique of an ex-fullback: well-fed but still quite powerful. With his bull neck, his battle-scarred face, and his steely glance, he didn't just look tough, he was tough. He had come to prominence in 1991 when, as the head of the elite Tula paratrooper division, he refused to support a coup attempt against Soviet President Mikhail Gorbachev. Lebed also brokered a peace agreement between Russian separatists and the new government of Moldova in 1994. He ran against Boris Yeltsin in 1996. When he did not receive enough votes to make the runoff election, he threw his support behind Yeltsin, helping secure his reelection. Lebed was killed in a helicopter crash in 2002.

When I met him in 1998, I found him to be an intensely interesting and conflicted man. On the one hand, one of the true founding fathers of the new, hopefully democratic Russia, and on the other hand—as I later learned—given to the pernicious kind of knee-jerk anti-Semitism that has yet to be extinguished in Russia, a land, like the general, of many contradictions.

One of the noteworthy aspects of our trip and a point that we raised with him was the evidence all around us—everywhere we looked—of the inefficiency and corruption of the former regime and the environmental damage wreaked by its rigid central planning. You could see and feel the legacy of corruption everywhere. It seemed to have caused equivalent damage among the people, hollowing out their spirit. Many seemed lost without the state telling them what to do, providing for them, and giving their lives purpose.

Lebed understood this unhealthy codependency well and explained it to Jack and me over dinner. It would take time, he said, to reorient the Russian people. For nearly five generations, the nation was a society watched over by a benevolent Mother Russia who took care of every need, and made all the decisions. But now, to succeed in the twenty-first century, Russia would have to evolve into a culture where the citizenry took responsibility, for their government and for their own lives. "We need America to work with us on that," Lebed said.

The thought expressed by Lebed—that America and Russia are linked to one another—has stayed with me and I feel it more strongly each time I return and see more of this enormous country that spans eleven time zones. There is an affinity between our two countries born, in part, of the immense wide-open spaces that are common to our heritage and that help to define us. We have our West and Russia has its East—Siberia—a land of forest and steppes. The only place on earth that I have seen that compares to Siberia in raw power and majesty is our Yellowstone region.

In 2005, I spent two unforgettable days in eastern Siberia near Lake Baikal. Set in a boundless forest, it is 365 miles long, nearly as long as Nebraska (430 miles), and is the deepest and the largest fresh-water lake in the world. Standing on its shores, I recalled the words of the great Nebraskan naturalist Loren

Eisley, who said, "If there is magic on the planet, it is contained in the water." Such splendor, which I always seek out in my travels, never fails to move me and to remind me of nature's patrimony and how it binds us all together—Russians, Americans, Chinese, all mankind. It's a backdrop that helps put the political frenzy of the moment in a wider, more humbling, perspective.

Another global hotspot, far south of Siberia's lakes and forest, is the Indian subcontinent. The great danger here is the possibility of military confrontation—nuclear or conventional—between the two giants of the neighborhood, India and Pakistan. The two nations have been ideologically, culturally, and sometimes literally at war for the entire course of their modern existence. In the interest of peace America should maintain a close alliance with both nations. With more than one billion people, mostly Hindu (although its Muslim population is the third largest in the world), India is well on its way to overtaking China in population size. It represents a huge market and a huge reservoir of highly trained professionals. It possesses nuclear weapons. It is also the world's largest democracy.

Like its rival India, Pakistan is an enormous, sprawling, chaotic land. Of its 165 million citizens, almost all are Muslim. In recent decades, it has become a breeding ground and haven for the most extreme and violent jihadists, including Osama bin Laden. Pakistani President Pervez Musharraf has, at the time of this writing, managed to contain this situation with U.S. support and assistance, but the ferocious tiger he rides can turn and devour him at any moment, leaving a sizable nuclear arsenal in the hands of fanatics.

There is no way to turn back the clock and "unwind" the nuclear capabilities of India and Pakistan. They both have the bomb. That is a reality we must face.

Managing competing interests and averting a nuclear holocaust is a constant, improvised, and hugely delicate task, but not an impossible one, as the Cold War, by its very name, proved. With the exception of the Cuban missile crisis, we were never truly close to tumbling over the thermonuclear precipice.

Through the latter half of the twentieth century, the system of test ban, inspection, and disarmament agreements worked. This arrangement was not without its tensions, problems, and cheating, but the point is that, working through the United Nations, with the IAEA, and through other international arrangements, we survived. However, because there are so many more nuclear-capable nations today, the world now requires a new nuclear nonproliferation framework. The United States remains the leading nuclear power, and therefore, we must lead in constructing a new framework, just as Eisenhower and Kennedy did in the 1950s and '60s.

A recent example of creative new thinking along these lines was the 2005 United States–India Civil Nuclear Cooperation agreement. This represented a cornerstone of a deeper new strategic United States–India relationship. In December 2006, Congress passed, and President Bush signed into law, the United States–India Peaceful Atomic Energy Cooperation Act, legislation to implement the July 2005 agreement. I enthusiastically supported this agreement and was one of the first members of Congress to get behind it and help push it through. However, several crucial steps remain before it becomes a workable reality. Unfortunately, there has been severe criticism of the deal within India. This has prevented Prime Minister Singh's government from moving forward on the agreement, and may well end any short-term possibilities for getting it approved in the Indian parliament. I am hopeful that Indian public opinion, reflected by its elected leaders, will clearly see the benefits for India in this agreement and approve it.

This agreement sets up a new framework for India's civil and military nuclear programs, including stronger nonproliferation commitments and access to civil nuclear technology and assistance. In the same way that we found a way to keep the genie of nuclear conflict in the bottle for sixty years, we have no choice but to seek to bring about greater understanding and cooperation among all the nuclear powers. It is important that we never forget the words of one of our great military leaders, General Omar Bradley, who said, "Ours is a world of nuclear giants and ethical infants. We know more about war than we know about peace, more about killing than we know about living." For the world to survive in this century, we must work toward reversing Bradley's strikingly correct observation from the last century.

Looking at the world through a wider lens, we oftentimes tend to neglect the issues, challenges, and opportunities that lie closer to home. In that regard, our relationships with the nations to our south continue to be vital to both our security and our economic health.

Our relationship with Mexico is as critical as any of our foreign relationships. It has nearly one hundred million people and we share a two-thousand-mile border. It is the bridge between North and South America and a strategic pivot for our economic and security relationships in the hemisphere. The United States must continue to encourage reforms there, including the liberalization of Mexico's foreign investment laws, especially in the energy sector. Our support of reform in Mexico should be seen as an investment in our shared security and prosperity, not as foreign aid. This relationship should be a partnership—similar to our relationship with Canada. These two huge neighbors are respectively our largest and third largest trading partners. The strength of our foreign policy is inherently connected to the strength of our relationships with these two neighbors with whom we share almost six thousand miles of common border.

One aspect of this relationship, the North American Free Trade Agreement has provided a very workable and successful template for the economic integration of the entire Western Hemisphere. It extends beyond trade into the equally important issues of energy, transportation, immigration, and security. It helps coordinate efforts between our nations to contain the threats of terrorism, illegal narcotics, and human trafficking.

Critics of NAFTA have failed to appreciate that it represents one of the most important developments of the past decade in

U.S. foreign policy. Since NAFTA's implementation, total trade among the United States, Mexico, and Canada has nearly tripled to an average rate of $2.4 billion per day. U.S. exports to Canada and Mexico have grown by 250 percent over these fourteen years. We need to expand this progress as we have begun to do in agreements with Chile, Peru, and other nations of Central and South America. Even more promising is the possibility this holds for hemispheric integration, which would connect the thirty-four nations from the Arctic Circle to Tierra del Fuego.

Promoting trade does not mean we should ignore the very real problems in Latin America. Hugo Chavez continues to foment discord in this part of the world. He has nationalized Venezuela's huge oil fields and uses the revenues from oil production for anti-American purposes. In Venezuela and the rest of Latin America, large pockets of poverty in the region represent great instability. In order to lessen this danger, we have to focus on addressing the causes and effects of instability through our policies, actions, and words. In particular, ratification of free trade agreements with countries in the Western Hemisphere will begin to bring about economic progress, advances in standards of living, and the kind of stability that helps address the underlying causes of social unrest: the twin maladies of poverty and despair.

American policy does not always recognize these less dramatic but pervasive social problems. We are, by nature, an optimistic nation. History has smiled on us and in the past nothing has seemed impossible. But if the story of the last sixty years has been one of unparalleled progress for America and much of the world, it is equally true that there are huge areas and large numbers of people who have been left behind. In Africa, drought, disease, famine, and genocide have exacted a sad and immense toll in human suffering. Likewise in a crescent that extends from North Africa, through the war-torn Middle East and across the southern rim of Asia, much of the Islamic world has languished under corrupt secular regimes and totalitarian theocracies.

These areas that were left behind bear common burdens: slow or no development, no growth of a middle class, extreme poverty, no legitimate governance. This is a formula that can produce tremendous eruptions with dangerous results. The basic needs for sustenance, shelter, and security drive history. When people are without them, nothing else matters. This is the human dynamic reduced to its inescapable essentials.

The critical reality of our times is that we live in an increasingly interconnected community of six and a half billion people drawn together by a complicated and powerful global economy that rewards many but has left out a significant number. The world cannot sustain this vast productive machine while a third of humanity lives in fear and poverty. Therefore, the greatest task that we face as a global community in the twenty-first century is somehow making a place for two and a half billion people who have been left behind by the advances of the last half century. It is those wretched of the earth who are, and who will continue to be, the main cause of instability and insecurity. We can't fix their problems in the next year or the next five years, but we are going to have to focus on them not only because we owe it to our fellow humans, but because it is essential for our security as Americans. Addressing the despair, hunger, poverty, and injustice that breed violence and unrest can be the centerpiece for a new global policy.

CHAPTER 8

TERRORISM VERSUS TOLERANCE

History's defining events come every fifty to one hundred years. We are living through such a time. As the world reorders itself, we are faced with a monstrous symptom of disorder: terrorism. You cannot talk about terrorism without dealing with its exponentially more lethal and horrifying modern expression: suicide terrorism. It raises such strong emotions and calls forth such primal fears that it is difficult to fashion a rational response or even a reasoned assessment of what can only be called a virulent social cancer. But we must.

Although terrorism is much on our minds in the aftermath of 9/11, terrorism is a symptom and not a cause. It can be traced to a deeper human dynamic that has produced despair and resentment at watching, but not participating in, a world of progress and prosperity. Many governments in the developing world, especially in Africa, the Greater Middle East, and Asia, cannot meet their growing populations' most basic demand for jobs, health care, and security. The combined strains of soaring population growth, lagging economic development, and authoritarian governments have dangerously radicalized the most disaffected everywhere. Exclusion from what appears to be a global feast has fueled the rise of an intolerant and fanatical fringe whose goals and tactics put all of humanity at risk.

Although its place in our consciousness is recent, political terrorism is an older phenomenon. It dates back, at least, to the mid-nineteenth century when the young Russian firebrand Sergei Nechayev first set forth its principles in *Catechism of a Revolutionary*, a title that ominously fused religious imagery with political violence. Nechayev used the theological term "catechism" in a symbolic sense: implying that his devotees were fulfilling a mission as moral as any religious calling. His modern-day descendants, the suicide jihadists, have twisted the theology of a great religion—Islam—and mixed it with the rage and despair of political discontent. The result has been toxic.

Nechayev and his followers, much like bin Laden and his ilk, were mostly sons (and a very few daughters) of the middle and upper classes. They decried the misery of the serfs and peasants but that level of suffering was not part of their privileged and pampered upbringing. Bin Laden is the son of a billionaire. His number two Ayman al-Zawahiri was a successful physician. September 11 mastermind Mohammed Atta was the son of well-to-do parents and was able to afford the cost of living in Germany.

The early Russian terrorists disappeared without achieving their goals, although it bears pointing out that Lenin's older brother was executed for taking part in a bomb plot against the czar. The only lasting thing they achieved was to imbue young

Lenin with a profound and consuming hatred that propelled his march to power. One cannot help but think that without Lenin, mankind might have been spared Stalin, Mao, Pol Pot, and the tens of millions of deaths for which those tyrants occupy the lowest circle in hell.

But if terrorism is, in the end, so unproductive, how can we explain its persistence? What do the terrorists want? In the 1950s in the midst of a prolonged terrorist campaign in Cyprus, the British novelist Lawrence Durrell explained the reasoning, however twisted, behind the actions of the terrorist:

> His primary objective is not battle. It is to bring down upon the community in general a reprisal for his wrongs, in the hope that fury and resentment roused by punishment meted out to the innocent will gradually swell the ranks of those from whom he will draw further recruits.

Misery begets misery. Death begets more death and the vicious circle becomes a spiral which, in our time, presents the very real possibility of the Molotov cocktail being replaced by the nuke.

We are left with two questions, inextricably bound up. First, how do we confront terror in the practical sense of finding, stopping, and eradicating terrorists bent on our society's destruction? The second, more complex, issue is how do we remove the conditions that breed terrorists and terrorism? Arguably, it was in part a desire to seek out and punish the planners of 9/11 that led us, without true cause, into Baghdad in a debacle that created a breeding ground for the next generation of terrorists. We cannot be susceptible to such catastrophic knee-jerk reactions again at the price of young American lives and a further destabilization of an already unstable region of the world.

Dealing effectively with terror requires well thought out actions as part of a long-term strategy. First of all, let's stop talking about a War on Terror—in effect, a jihad against jihad. We must defeat the terrorists, to be sure, but terror is not a country that can surrender, it is not even a clearly defined group of people. Terrorism is purely a tactic in pursuit of other ends. The phrase "war on terror" sounds good, but it is a sloppy, ill-defined term. If we are truly to eradicate terrorism we cannot afford the luxury of sloppy definitions and laziness. The terrorists themselves make no such mistake. They are focused and tenacious. We must be equally focused and no less purposeful.

We should think of terror as a phenomenon that will not simply disappear any more than we can expect to win a war on crime, or a war on earthquakes. As long as there are desperate, ruthless, and deluded malcontents, you can count on there being terrorists. Other nations have endured terrorism for decades: Israel, for example, and Great Britain, and Spain. Does that mean they have lost the so-called war on terrorism because they are attacked? Hardly. As those nations know, there will be no surrender or victory in what we are calling a war, but there can be goals we achieve and milestones we reach. The overarching principle is: If you alter the conditions that spawn terrorism, you will have to deal with it less often.

Meanwhile, we must simultaneously confront the terrorists

who already exist. When Americans are attacked, we will act swiftly and strongly against those responsible. The world's terrorists will have no doubt that there will be no safe harbor. The United States and our allies will hunt down those who harm our citizens.

Stopping terrorists—identifying them and destroying them—is an immense task. The United States has never had to deal with anything quite like this new and unexpected kind of enemy. I wonder if even our greatest leaders could have foreseen it and headed it off. Abraham Lincoln led us through the trying times of the Civil War, but that conflict was building for decades and it came as no surprise to him. Similarly, FDR was aware that a world conflict was coming, even if the Japanese attack on Pearl Harbor was not anticipated.

Without warning, though, 9/11 came as a bolt out of the blue, Indian-summer sky. Perhaps more diligent attention to information in the intelligence pipeline might have tipped us off. That is a point historians will argue. But for the most part, 9/11 was completely unanticipated because for over 200 years, the American mainland has been protected by oceans that buffered it from many of the threats that plagued the rest of the world. We were lulled into a sense of safety. And then we were hit. Now we know to expect the unexpected for, by definition, it is only in the world's back alleys and blind spots—the places where there are no governments to root them out and where anger and despair rule—that terrorists can operate.

The reality is: in dealing with terror, especially jihadist terror, we are constantly improvising as we go along. We are adjusting.

We are responding. We are reflecting. Make no mistake about it: September 11 changed this country forever. It was, in words that Churchill used to describe his era and the rise of Hitler, the "jarring gong" that shook the very foundation of who we are: our personal lives, our professional lives, where we fit in the world, our role, our leadership, our responsibilities . . . everything. We are still working through this, still off balance, and we will be for years to come.

If America is to continue to help build a safer, more stable and prosperous world, then we cannot simply concentrate on securing our borders, shutting down immigration visas, and curtailing exchange programs. That would only isolate us further. Remaking our country into "Fortress America" isn't going to make us safer. This new kind of struggle requires more global unity, not less. We could further undermine our interests if we overreact and allow ourselves to become captive to our fear and insecurity. The plain fact of the matter is that there is evil in the world. The fundamental questions are: How do you deal with it in the short and long terms, and what constitutes the best use of our power? Furthermore, how do you maintain a free and open society while minimizing risk of attack? We cannot remove every threat to our safety while maintaining all of the freedoms we hold dear. Where is the balance and how do we strike it?

The threat of terror is dynamic, not static. Today it may be hijacking airplanes; tomorrow it could be a truck bomb, or a cyber attack on our banking system. Our ability to respond (and better yet, to prevent such attacks) cannot afford to be any less dynamic and agile. Our whole society, but especially our economy and our national security structure, must equip themselves to meet these new challenges. Although intelligence has always been an important tool of our security effort, today it is our most important first line of defense.

The shadowy pockets of terrorist enemies around the world are not easily identifiable, and therefore not easily attacked. The military resources that we can bring to bear are vast, but they are also limited; they must always be deployed responsibly and strategically, and in new ways. Intelligence is the one instrument of power that can unravel plans for terrorist attacks before they are operational. Intelligence can identify these terrorist strongholds and guide us in mounting precise surgical strikes. This, in turn, calls for a transformation of our force structure that would include more special operations capabilities, more mobility, more linguistics specialists, more satellite intelligence and cyber resources. And as it has always been, our most precious intelligence asset, one that we had downgraded and de-emphasized pre-9/11, is human intelligence on the ground around the globe.

Much remains to be done to strengthen, integrate, and improve our intelligence capabilities, although we have come a long way toward making our intelligence agencies and networks more relevant and effective in confronting twenty-first-century threats. Having constructed a newly integrated, accountable intelligence structure incorporating sixteen federal agencies, we are far more capable of utilizing our intelligence resources in real time. For example, in August 2006, British and U.S. intelligence disrupted an al-Qaeda plot to blow up as many as ten passenger jets bound for the United States. In September 2007, U.S. authorities worked with their German allies to disrupt another al-Qaeda-linked plot to attack the U.S. military in Germany. This has been no small task insofar as each of the individual agencies has its own distinct culture and mission. If we are to be successful in combating the greatest threats of the first part of this new century—proliferation of weapons of mass destruction, terrorism, Islamic fundamentalism—then we must rely principally and primarily on seamless networks of intelligence sharing and gathering—not just within our own country but with our allies as well, working in common purpose against a common enemy.

Whatever forces—spiritual, economic, or political—emerge in this new multipolar world, we cannot go it alone. Nobody can. Terrorism is a common threat that requires common actions. It is only through friction-free networks among all nations that we will be successful in interdicting terrorist plots before they are executed. Already, these new coalitions are taking shape and are having an effect. They will self-adjust and shift as terrorist tactics evolve and probe new weaknesses (or perceived weaknesses) in our security capabilities.

In the last chapter I spoke of our increasingly interconnected and reordered world, dwelling on the positive forces that are drawing nations together: economics, trade, environment, and cultural interchange being chief among them. But we are also thrown together by the common problems that confront all of mankind. Diseases like AIDS or avian flu do not distinguish their victims on the basis of their passports. Global warming is altering the environment, with potentially drastic consequences, for developed and third world nations alike. The rapid depletion of petroleum resources will eventually transform the global economy and the distribution of population. And terrorism, as we have seen, can strike in the heart of New York City, at Shiite Islam's holiest place of worship, or on a quiet beach in Bali. The point is: It can strike anywhere and anyone.

All of humanity is in this together.

Each nation is different. Each nation has its own unique pressures and problems, strengths and weaknesses, based on its singular history and heritage. A border crossing in a mountain pass in Pakistan is different from a checkpoint at a Spanish railroad station. A deceptively placid beach on the Gulf of Arabia requires different security than the subterranean passageways of the London underground. Each nation comes at the issue of terrorism from a different starting point.

Terrorism can strike any nation, at any time, for any reason, and therefore all nations have a stake in responding to the threat of terror. But adjusting to a new system of international security does not require abandoning national sovereignty. To the contrary. Strong sovereign nations are critical pieces of a world mosaic. But even the mightiest sovereign state must share resources, intelligence, and assets in order to most effectively protect itself and its allies. The terrorists recognize no borders and we cannot let borders hamper our pursuit of them. This is not a prescription for unilateral action, but instead for coalition and consensus-building.

This will require leadership, patience, understanding, and

vision. It is not without risk. We must recognize the immense complications in dealing with terrorism, and know that it will take an alignment of many nations with competing interests in order to confront this insidious evil. Whatever our differences with China or France or any other nation, those differences must be weighed against the urgency of dealing with the most important challenge to our way of life since World War II. The evolution of a coordinated global response to the threat of terror will be imperfect, but it must nevertheless be undertaken.

Dealing with the conditions that breed hatred, despair, resentment, and intolerance—the recruiting grounds for terrorists—requires a more long-range strategy. Terrorism has its roots in the broad sweep of history and, at the same time, in the frustrations and pathologies of individuals. The aimless young men, without work, without hope, whom I have often seen glaring at the armored personnel carriers on the West Bank all shared the cold, hollow stare that invites ruthless demagogues to sow their seeds of hatred.

Where does the hatred come from? In part, America is its target because we are the sole great power in the world, and, as the preeminent representation of the West, we are reaping the accumulated resentments of centuries of colonialism. In this connection, you will recall that for hundreds of years, most of the countries of Islam were ruled and exploited by European powers. In a culture where honor and shame count for much, generations of Muslims felt degraded by the actions of the West. Their feelings of impotence turned to rage. It became easy for the most disaffected Muslims to connect their personal misery with the subjugation of their people and their religion. Look at the Palestinian territories today for the clearest example of this rage and hatred.

The fact that many Islamic countries suffered under corrupt, brutal, and backward regimes did little to counter the perception that it was the West that was the source of their troubles. In many cases, blame for the survival of these oppressive regimes was placed on the West.

We should not let the jihadist perversion of religion mislead us into a fear of religion as a progressive force. Former German Chancellor Helmut Schmidt once told me he believed that Poland was the only country under Soviet control that was not stripped of its spirituality and its soul because it retained a strong attachment to its faith. The church was the spiritual anchor for the people of Poland and they never let go of it. The strength of the church in Poland enabled that country to lead in the downfall of Communism and in the relatively rapid rebound of a moribund social structure.

Clearly, Islam and the West have misunderstood each other's values and cultures going back one thousand years to the bloodshed and ill-will occasioned by the Crusades. The West may speak with the noblest of intentions of the virtues of liberty, for surely it is liberty that has been the source of many of our achievements as a people. But the word Islam itself means submission: submission to God's will. Liberty, in that frame of reference, is often taken to mean license and immorality—that is, defiance of God's will.

This seems strange to our way of thinking, but ours seems

no less strange to many devout Muslims who see our civilization running on petroleum—in many cases the rich bounty of their otherwise barren lands—and they feel excluded from the benefits of modern civilization and disrespected by those who are enjoying it.

We cannot try to make Islam into the image of suburban America or cosmopolitan Europe any more than we would agree to live under an Islamic caliphate. At some basic level, all peoples of the world must learn to respect all religions and our neighbors' rights to be different.

I am reminded of the very wise words of Benito Juarez, who was president of Mexico at the same time that Lincoln was president of the United States. You can see his famous phrase wherever you go in the Mexican republic he helped establish and nurture. *El respeto al derecho ajeno es la paz:* Respect for the rights of others is peace.

We would do well to remember this in dealing with the ideals and cultures of Islam and all religions. So yes, we must confront the terrorists and eradicate them with unrelenting purpose. But we must also recognize that the way of life we have chosen may not be what our neighbors choose, and that we can only prosper to the extent that we live in a world of understanding and tolerance. In the end, understanding and tolerance will allow good to triumph over evil, but until it does, America must always be prepared to defend herself with her incomparable citizen soldiers.

CHAPTER 9

WHO SPEAKS UP FOR THE RIFLEMAN?

The great German military theorist Carl von Clausewitz said, "War is the continuation of diplomacy by other means." What he left unsaid, and what is perhaps more to the point in terms of human consequence, is that war represents the complete failure of diplomacy.

War has its own dynamic. It favors neither democracy nor tyranny. In all wars men and women die—both combatants and innocent civilians. Nations and individuals who know war are never again the same. Having been a foot soldier in an ill-conceived, poorly prosecuted, and unsuccessful war, I believe we would do well to heed the words of one of our greatest warriors, Douglas MacArthur, who said, "The soldier above all other people prays for peace, for he must suffer and bear the deepest wounds and scars of war."

Having witnessed these hard truths firsthand, I am, like many veterans, changed forever by the experience of war. That is why I am so vocal and so fervent on the issues of war and peace and the well-being of our soldiers. It is the responsibility of every elected official, especially those who have seen combat, to assure that any policy that sends men and women into war is worthy of the sacrifices that we ask of them and their families. If it is not, then it is the wrong policy.

Some say that speaking out against a policy—even a failed one—in times of war is somehow not supportive of the president or our soldiers. That is untrue and unacceptable. My colleagues and I are representatives of the American people and it is the Constitution that we swear to uphold and protect. Our oath is to America, not to a president or a political party or a policy. Congress is Article 1 in the Constitution. The country comes first: not a party or a president.

According to the Veterans Administration, there are over twenty-three million veterans in America today. By virtue of their service to our country, every one of them has earned the right to have his or her opinion heard on issues of war and peace. I would go further and say that we have the obligation to speak out. In public debate and in the media, the fighting man and woman is often referred to in reverent tones, but I wonder how many of us here at home actually picture the grunt in the mud and grime with the cold stench of death hanging over him, with improvised explosive devices underfoot, with snipers, and incoming mortar rounds and rocket fire raining down. Too often we tend to think of these quiet heroes in abstract terms: "our troops." But because I have been one of them, they are not an abstraction to me. Each one is someone's son or daughter, dad or mom, brother or sister.

To fully comprehend this article of faith, you should understand something of the bond between soldiers. We each learn it in our own way, but I have never known a soldier who didn't feel it. It's a tradition that gets handed down. It starts in basic training and once you are under fire it is welded into your soul. I think the first time I began to feel it with clarity was at the conclusion of my basic training at Fort Bliss, Texas. My drill sergeant was Sergeant First Class William Joyce, who had been in the army for twenty-two years. He was a quiet guy—which sounds like a contradiction in terms for a drill sergeant—but underneath the bluster of the barracks, most of them were quiet, serious professionals. When Sergeant Joyce talked, you listened, not because you had to but because you knew it was important. He had that air about him. He was a soldier to his core, the kind of guy people think of when they say, "He bleeds Army olive green."

He always spoke in terms of "this man's army," as on the day he said, "This man's army can do amazing things for people. It's done amazing things for me."

He was from a poor family in Alabama. "My only way out of there was the army," he told me that same day. That was the first time I had ever heard him say anything remotely personal. We were driving into El Paso to the Chamber of Commerce luncheon where I was to receive the American Spirit Honor Medal, as the outstanding trainee among the G.I.s in my basic training cycle. I have never been prouder of any achievement in my life. I still have that trophy and medal in my library.

I had always thought of Sergeant Joyce as the classic tight-lipped noncom, a tough character. I wasn't so much in awe of him as really respectful of him. I had never met anybody quite like him. We connected. On that trip into town he opened up a little. He said he had once landed in trouble with the army. As a result he was busted and lost a stripe and had to work his way back up.

"What did you do, Sarge?" I asked.

"Doesn't matter," he said. "The point is, we all do stupid things, but failing the army, well, don't you ever let that happen. The important thing is, you must never forget, there's always redemption. It's never too late to start over: make your life right."

Then he said the words that I will never forget. It put things in a perspective that has helped shape my life. "I'm doing what I do for you, but I'm also doing this for more people than yourself. And you've got to understand this: You've got to be the best and give your best because people are going to rely on you. They're going to depend on you if you go to Vietnam. They're going to rely on you throughout your life. You're special because you've got this training. You can never let those people down. People's lives will depend on your abilities, training, and judgment."

I've seen coaches who have that effect on players. They can change kids' lives with just a few words. Teachers, too. But this guy had it more than any coach or teacher I'd ever known. Then, in the way these things often happen in life, I lost track of him. After I left Fort Bliss I went to Fort Ord, California, to take advanced infantry training and then to White Sands Missile Range in New Mexico where I was in the first ever Red Eye Missile Gunner class. (It was a very top secret weapon; the first shoulder-fired heat-seeking missile in the army.) I called Sergeant Joyce one day when I was in New Mexico and we talked briefly.

That was the last time I heard from him. He was going back to Alabama and he was going to retire. I hope he did and that he caught the biggest bass in the state and then, just for good luck, he threw him back. He would have done that.

"People depend on you. They'll always depend on you." That about summed up the most important lesson I ever learned. There's nowhere that you feel that more than in the heat of battle. I believe that combat is a furnace that can destroy you, or it can forge you into something better and stronger than you were before. Never let your buddies down, always cover their backs. Years, even decades have gone by, but I've always felt that bond with the men and women I served with and every person in a military uniform. I stay in touch with a few of the guys my brother Tom and I served with in Vietnam. We always pick up where we left off—no matter how long it's been since we saw each other. Those friendships were truly battle-tested. They are uniquely strong.

How Tom and I came to be fighting side by side is an interesting bit of family history wrapped up in some military history. Ever since the five Sullivan brothers from Iowa perished together on the same ship in World War II, the policy of the Department of Defense has been that two members of the same immediate family would not serve in the same war zone at the same time.

However, there were exceptions, as in the case of Tom and me. We both had received orders to go to Germany, but both of us volunteered to go to Vietnam. I arrived first (Tom came six weeks later) and was assigned to the Ninth Infantry Division in the South, while Tom joined the Eleventh Cavalry Regiment (which was under the command of Colonel George S. Patton III, the son of General Patton of World War II fame) in the North. Tom put in for a transfer to my unit and I applied for a transfer to his unit because we wanted to serve together. His transfer came through so Tom joined me and the rest of the Ninth Infantry in the Mekong Delta for the remainder of our tours in Vietnam. For ten months we were truly brothers-in-arms, side-by-side.

I remember the first time I saw combat. It was just before Christmas 1967. We were on patrol in the jungle. It was quiet one second and then, in the next, all hell broke loose as the Viet Cong (VC) opened up on us. The bullets were whizzing through the thick underbrush and trees; you could hear and see them tearing the leaves a few feet over your head. The guy in front of me was hit, then the guy next to me, square in the chest. And I thought to myself, "This is it." And then, a voice within me asked, "What is this about? What is this about?" But there was no time for philosophical reflection. The training kicked in, Sergeant Joyce's words, "You just go do your job."

A few months later, March 26, 1968, Tom and I were walking point—that is, at the head of our reconnaissance patrol. After a few hours we were rotated to the back of the formation. As it turned out, this probably saved our lives. No sooner were we there than the guys up front stumbled on a trip wire crossing a stream, igniting Chinese Claymore mines hung in the trees. Exploding mines full of shrapnel fell all around us.

One member of our unit, Corporal John T. Summers III, fell dead: He was the first guy I saw killed in action. He was a tall thin kid from Baltimore, an African American kid who had been drafted, no more than eighteen or nineteen years old, quiet and well liked. A piece of shrapnel tore into my chest. I dropped, dazed and bleeding. Tom, who also took some shrapnel in the arms and shoulders, tore my shirt open and wrapped bandages around my chest. The jungle was so dense and thick that our patrol had to wait a long time until the medivac helicopters could locate us and hover overhead to lower baskets down to retrieve the dead and most seriously wounded. After we evacuated those who could not walk out of the jungle, Tom and I took point again to machete our way out. It was getting dark and we all knew that the night belonged to "Charley" (the term we used for the Viet Cong). All of a sudden Tom yelled, "Stop, don't move!"

There was a trip wire in front of me, attached to a grenade hanging in a tree. We disarmed it. That made it twice in one day that my brother probably saved my life.

Less than a month later, I got the chance to repay the favor. Our unit had moved into a village where intelligence reported that the VC were visiting every night, storing armaments, confiscating rice and fish, threatening village elders, and taking hostages. We went in around midnight, cleared the place out and took a few prisoners. The armored personnel carrier (APC or "track") that carried Tom and me was the lead vehicle into the village, which meant that we were the last ones out. I remember listening to Armed Forces Radio and the song that was playing was Linda Ronstadt's "Different Drum." I loved that song. Then boom! We hit a land mine and the VC opened up on us with machine guns.

Tom was on the .50-caliber machine gun wearing the standard radio operator helmet, and when I saw him knocked senseless, I thought he was dead. Acting out of instinct, I threw Tom and the others off our track, because I knew with all of the ammo we had on board, it was going to explode. I took some shrapnel, my eardrums burst, and the left side of my face and body were burned from the blast. They say burn wounds are the most painful of all injuries. All I know is, I had never felt such pain before in my life.

The Viet Cong opened up on us with small arms fire from the tree line. There is nothing so dark as a moonless night in dense jungle and there is nothing so bright as the night lit up by incoming tracer fire. We returned fire and held the VC off until the lead tracks in our patrol made their way back to pick us up. Tom and I were medivaced out of the area around three in the morning to a field hospital where we spent a couple of days being patched before being sent back to Bravo Company, Second of the Forty-seventh Infantry in Bien Phuc.

From that day on, I was a changed person. I remember a strong resolve coming over me, as our chopper climbed over the glistening green canopy of the jungle and I watched the steam rise above it in the morning light. I made myself a promise that if I ever got out of that place and was ever in a position to do something about war—so horrible, so filled with suffering—I would do whatever I could to stop it. I have never forgotten that promise. I made it to myself but also to everyone who answers the call to serve their country. I think of it every day, because once you set war in motion, its consequences are often the ones least intended and they are always uncontrollable.

As a political leader, you can never predict how war will turn out, only that it will be worse than you thought or planned for. You better be damned sure of your reasons for getting into it. You better know what and why and how you intend to pursue your objectives before you take a nation to war and commit its citizens to the sacrifices, suffering, pain, and losses that are inevitable.

That's why, years later, I asked so many questions before we went into Iraq and why I continued to raise them. Why are we going to war? Is Saddam really a threat to America? Who will govern after Saddam? How are they going to govern? What is our role going to be? How would Iraq be stabilized after the invasion? Why are so few U.S. troops going in? What does this have to do with terrorism? How is this going to affect the Middle East? I was criticized for this intense probing. I was called unpatriotic. But criticism should not stop us from questioning. As the historian Henry Steele Commager said, "Men in authority will always think that criticism of their policies is dangerous. They will always equate their policies with patriotism, and find criticism subversive."

In my mind, patriotism is about asking the tough questions, not avoiding them. It is unpatriotic *not* to question a government's policies before the first life is lost. Of course I want our country to "win," but we must ask precisely what does "winning" mean and we need to ask that question before the first shot is fired.

You can question and criticize my judgment—or any elected representative's judgment. You can question my votes, but we should never let our decisions about war be held captive by political ideology or partisan agendas. All who have the privilege and responsibility of serving this great nation fail our country if we allow politics to prevail over clear thinking. All Americans wearing the uniform of our country deserve a policy worthy of their sacrifices. That is the responsibility of every elected official. Partisan considerations must always come last in matters of war and peace. America's interests must always come first.

The debacle of Vietnam was as much the fault of the Congress as any one institution. The Congress was essentially silent for years, except for a few courageous voices: J. William Fulbright, George McGovern, Mark Hatfield, Wayne Morse, and Ernest Gruening. The rest didn't ask the tough questions. And if the people's elected representatives don't have, or won't find, the courage to probe war policy, then who will?

Who will speak up for the rifleman?

CHAPTER 10

OUR SWORD AND SHIELD

One of the most enjoyable and valuable traditions in our Nebraska congressional delegation is the weekly breakfast that we host for anyone from our state who happens to be in Washington on any Wednesday when Congress is in session. These breakfasts are a wonderful exercise in grassroots democracy. It's a tradition that goes back to 1943, and somewhat surprising to me, Nebraska is the only state that does this. I learn as much from these visitors—sometimes more—than from many of the closed-door policy briefings I receive in Congress. The briefings from the policy professionals give you an important view, but it is top-down and sometimes heavy in abstractions. The breakfasts, by contrast, take you to ground level, to the front lines of public debate with real people. In politics, as in war, that "foot soldier's" point of view is invaluable. If you truly know how one infantryman feels about battle, or how one widowed senior is affected by her medical bills, you are on your way to being a more effective—and better—representative.

So here is what I learned one morning at a recent "frontline" Nebraska breakfast. As we do every week, Nebraska's members of Congress take turns introducing our fellow "Huskers." Then, customarily, each guest tells a little bit about himself or herself, what brought them to Washington, and whatever is on their minds. One woman got up to speak. Originally from Nebraska, she now lives in Alaska, the most recent posting of her husband, a U.S. Air Force colonel ready to retire.

"I have concern for our military," she said, in a voice that was both quiet and firm. "The concern isn't for my husband and me. We've had our time. The concern is for those who will follow us and ultimately, for our country."

At this point I could see tears welling up, but she never wavered, and kept on speaking her piece. "We are letting our military, our proud American military, be decimated, not only by the war in Iraq, but by the stress that the extended tours, uncertainty, and lack of clear goals have put on military families. It's hard for me to say this but for the first time in my life, I would not encourage anyone to join the military. It used to be a wonderful career but it's different now. To be honest, I would actively try to dissuade anyone from this career. I am truly sorry that I have to say this but I have to."

She didn't say anything specific about the war in Iraq. Her speech wasn't pro-war or anti-war. It was pro-military. She said that this country is asking a very few people, the military and their families, to bear all the burden, and make all the sacrifices, while the rest of America gets tax cuts and is not asked to make any sacrifice for their country. She wasn't bitter or self-righteous in the way she said it, but her remarks were damned poignant. She's right. This is something that has been working on me for some time. How do we fix this social imbalance? Because we must fix it if America is to continue its indispensable world leadership.

Our military has been pushed beyond the breaking point. The commitment of a large number of forces—but not enough to prevail—in an ill-defined mission in Iraq has produced lower levels of recruitment both in the regular Army and the Army National Guard. This trend was no doubt aggravated as low recruitment levels forced the armed forces to extend tours of duty and redeployments to Iraq for a second, third, and fourth time. I saw the effect this was having on our soldiers during one of my recent visits to Iraq. In my own private survey, I posed a question to ten enlisted men and women from Nebraska: Is any of them considering staying in the military? Half of them responded with an emphatic "No!" Two said yes, three said they hadn't yet decided but were leaning against reenlistment.

Their answers did not surprise me. We are doing tremendous damage to our army and marines because of the wars in Iraq and Afghanistan. Many active duty and retired generals and senior officers have told me it will take a generation to build our force structure back to where it was before Iraq. Captains and senior NCOs run an army. They're the company commanders and company sergeants who lead troops at the ground level, and who have the experience and expertise to lead effectively. But now, to meet the shortfall, the army has had to put second lieutenants, fresh out of West Point and Officer Candidate School and with no experience or street savvy, into vacant senior captains' positions.

Unquestionably, we are pushing our armed forces to the redline. As the Iraq Study Group put it in what is referred to as the 2006 Baker-Hamilton Report:

> America's military capacity is stretched thin: We do not have the troops or equipment to make a substantial, sustained increase in our troop presence. Increased deployments to Iraq would also necessarily hamper our ability to provide adequate resources for our efforts in Afghanistan or respond to crises around the world.

In 2007, General Peter Pace, who was then chairman of the Joint Chiefs of Staff, reported to Congress that there is now a "significant" risk that our military will not be able to respond to an emerging crisis in another part of the world. And appearing before the House Armed Services Committee, Pace was asked whether he was comfortable with the preparedness of the army units in the United States. His answer could not have been more direct: "No . . . I am not comfortable."

The effect of the Iraq War on U.S. forces, materiel, and ordnance has been staggering. The Army and the Marine Corps sank more than 40 percent of their ground combat equipment into Iraq and Afghanistan. As a result we are looking at repair and maintenance costs of tens of billions of dollars—for years to come—which we are not now funding and I fear never will. The

2007 Pentagon budget had $17.1 billion to "reset" army equipment damaged in noncombat situations, with a separate fund of $13.9 billion in emergency funds to replace or repair gear damaged in combat. During this time, National Guard Bureau Chief Army Lt. General H. Steven Blum told the Commission on the National Guard and Reserves that it will take $40 billion to re-equip the Air and Army National Guard. He also told the Commission that 88 percent of the guard units in the United States are "poorly equipped." We are decimating the most powerful fighting force the world has ever known—and we are only beginning to understand the astounding costs and the time it will take to rebuild it. This is a force that was designed to defend our country and its interests, not one that could occupy whole countries and build nations in multiple theaters.

Throughout history, militaries have had to adapt to new threats, new weapons, new dynamics, new geostrategic realities. Those that did not, could not, or would not adapt were defeated, and disappeared. The security of our nation is not a Democratic or Republican issue, it is an American issue. We must be steely-eyed and clear-headed when setting our security strategy.

Saying yes to every appropriation is not the way to develop the kind of judgment and purpose required for an effective modern military. In fact, just the opposite is often true. Bloated budgets and lack of effective oversight and review are symptoms of a deeper, structural inadequacy in our military posture. President Eisenhower pointed out dangers that lay along this path in his farewell address to the nation in 1961. If you haven't read that famous speech in its entirety, you should. It is a profound, incisive, and humane document from a man who led our armies in war and our nation in peace. Here is a little of what he said:

> Until the latest of our world conflicts, the United States had no armaments industry. American makers of plowshares could, with time and as required, make swords as well. But now we can no longer risk emergency improvisation of national defense; we have been compelled to create a permanent armaments industry of vast proportions. Added to this, three and a half million men and women are directly engaged in the defense establishment. We annually spend on military security more than the net income of all United States corporations.
>
> This conjunction of an immense military establishment and a large arms industry is new in the American experience. The total influence—economic, political, even spiritual—is felt in every city, every State house, every office of the Federal government. We recognize the imperative need for this development. Yet we must not fail to comprehend its grave implications. Our toil, resources, and livelihood are all involved; so is the very structure of our society.
>
> In the councils of government, we must guard against the acquisition of unwarranted influence, whether sought or unsought, by the military industrial complex. The potential for the disastrous rise of misplaced power exists and will persist.

We must never let the weight of this combination endanger our liberties or democratic processes. We should take nothing for granted. Only an alert and knowledgeable citizenry can compel the proper meshing of the huge industrial and military machinery of defense with our peaceful methods and goals, so that security and liberty may prosper together.

It is worth pointing out that Ike was not talking about an evil conspiracy of war profiteers and corrupt generals. He was speaking of something much more subtle but, over the long run, equally ruinous to our security and our democracy. Instead of being the servant of the Republic, the potent alliance of the military and corporations can become so large and powerful that it controls the decision-making process, thereby effectively dominating national security policy. The Republic becomes the servant of the insatiable needs of a bloated and distorted military economy.

Great concentrations of power always threaten free societies. A government's highest responsibility is the security of its citizens. We must do whatever is needed to protect our citizens and provide our men and women in uniform the best policies, leadership, training, equipment, and technology available. And we must invest heavily, but smartly, in intelligence. It is the first line of defense for our country.

There are many aspects to a nation's security: economic, energy, intelligence, border protection, and geopolitical strategy.

The military is the ultimate guarantor of our security. But a nation must strategically employ all instruments of its power—diplomatic, military, and economic—to defend its interests. There is no substitute for a nation's wise use of its resources and capabilities.

Our Department of Defense (DoD) is the largest department in the federal government. Its Fiscal Year (FY) 2008 budget is $648.8 billion, including the additional supplemental appropriations for Iraq and Afghanistan. DoD is the largest consumer of oil in the world. In fact, according to the 2006 CIA *World Factbook*, there are only thirty-five countries in the world that consume more oil per day than the Pentagon. It is a mammoth institution with millions of military and civilians working in it. A government unto itself.

This kind of immense concentration of power is not a natural ally with, nor conducive to, accountability. Too often, this gargantuan machine's resources are used as economic development projects for states and congressional districts. Senators and representatives earmark special appropriations for their pet projects under the mask of defense spending. This cheats real defense requirements—whether by keeping an obsolete base open that provides very little national security to our country, or by financing politically connected private companies through complicated, shadowy no-bid contracts that are useless to our national defense. It is wrong, wasteful, dishonest, and dangerous. We have become captive to the interests of the large military industrial corporations. All that President Eisenhower warned about in 1961 is disturbingly true in 2008.

We need to root out this unaccountable, fraudulent, and wasteful activity. That is why in 1988 the Congress set up the Base Realignment and Closure Commission (BRAC). It was the only way to pry this kind of nonsense out of the iron grips of members of Congress. BRAC can't do it all and often succeeds only about half the time with its recommendations, but it is the only outside force that has any leverage to try to change this careless misapplication of taxpayer resources. We need to do better. The United States cannot sustain the kind of large budget numbers we will need to finance our long-term national security requirements by continuing to allow this kind of selfishly motivated government.

A very disturbing development in our government today, one that Ike never saw, is the outsourcing of security to private contractors. This trend was made disturbingly clear in October 2007, following an incident in which Blackwater employees killed seventeen Iraqi civilians. This event sparked an explosion of national outrage in Iraq, which had been building ever since we invaded and which was formed by a decision of the American proconsul, Paul Bremer, that gave American contractors immunity from prosecution under Iraqi law. For years contractors operated in a legal and moral gray area, unaccountable to Iraqi or American officials. In October 2007, relatives of Iraqi victims from the September incident resorted to suing Blackwater in American courts in hopes of achieving a measure of justice.

The Iraqi government moved to establish its legal authority over all contractors and told the U.S. government that they wanted Blackwater out of Iraq. One of the lasting legacies of America's experience in Iraq will be the role played by these contractors in the shadows of America's national security policy.

Why we have turned to these private security contractors is understandable—we do not have a large enough force. But in effect relying on mercenaries cannot be and has never been a cost-effective or reliable policy. Remember the Hessians whom the Europeans hired for their security and armies and whom Washington defeated in our war for independence, or the Germanic tribes who manned the Roman legions until they figured out they didn't have to work for Rome when they could just as easily conquer it. Our military feels equally uneasy about today's increasing reliance on contractors who are not bound by a code of conduct that has helped ensure that our military has been the finest and most professional fighting force the world has ever seen. The loyalties of hired soldiers are not to nations or causes, but rather to employers and employment contracts. Is that who we are? Is this what our great democracy has come to?

This trend is clearly seen in Iraq. According to a July 2007 *Los Angeles Times* report, a census taken by U.S. Central Command (USCENTCOM) found that the United States is paying for one-hundred-eighty thousand private contractors in Iraq (one-hundred-eighteen thousand were Iraqi, forty-three thousand were non-U.S. foreigners, and twenty-one thousand were Americans). According to a May 2007 Government Accountability Office report, more than $32 billion of DoD's obligations on services in FY 2006 were for professional, administrative, and management support contracts. The same report found that DoD's obligations on service contracts rose 78 percent from 1996 to 2006. In March 2007, the Special Inspector General for Iraq, Stuart Bowen, said that lines of authority and accountability in Iraq reconstruction were unclear because most of the oversight for reconstruction work had been turned over to contractors. This is a mind-numbing snapshot of the incredible waste, fraud, and abuse of this process paid for by American taxpayers. Maybe it's intended to be mind numbing, in the hopes that the people will not pay attention to it.

There are many patriotic people working for these firms, but, in the final analysis, their relationship to their job is financial and they owe their allegiance to their employers and to their own self-interest, not to their country. While you may be able to count on paid security guards, you cannot put your faith in them in the same way that you can rely on a member of the U.S. military. There are many areas where outsourcing is practical and warranted, but it needs comprehensive congressional review.

I have been a strong supporter of the current all-volunteer force ever since 1973, when President Nixon signed it into law. It was the right thing to do for the right reasons, chief among them that it enabled us to create a more nimble professional force of highly trained specialists. The wars of the twenty-first century will probably not, for the most part, involve massive numbers of troops. Instead, they will require a force structure that can respond to all levels of challenge. A professional fighting force is more clearly suited to this range of responsibilities. This policy toward force structure has produced the best-led, best-trained, best-educated, and best-equipped and motivated military in the world. It is made up of individuals committed to a lifetime of service to America.

If it proves to be the case that the all-volunteer force finds itself unable to meet the present and future manpower needs required to maintain America's security, the nation must be prepared to act to correct that dangerous possibility.

But that's no reason to undo the all-voluntary army. We shouldn't have to go back to the draft; however, we do have a serious manpower problem and we probably will continue to have this problem. In military terms, it is a force-structure problem. We created this problem through ill-advised and shortsighted policies based on abstractions and a concept of quasi-divine mission. However, we can renew and energize our forces and reconstruct our force structure through wise leadership and policies. The core of the problem is readily apparent. We are overcommitted around the world. We are in 140 nations and yet we have the smallest standing force of any time since World War II. Our force capability does not match our mission requirements.

We are breaking our army and marines.

If missions keep expanding, I do not believe that we can long escape a national debate about reinstituting some kind of universal military service. It would be the only fair way to spread the responsibility, privilege, and burden of citizens for defending our country.

I do not believe that the way to fix this and attract the kind of soldiers that we want and must have is to rely on offering more and more bonus money for signing up and reenlisting. In 2006, the military spent more than \$1 billion on incentive recruitment and reenlistment bonuses. Money is important, but is not and should not be why men and women join the army. Money is not what motivates them. It is, has been, and will be duty, honor, and country that commit them to a cause greater than their own self-interest. If we have to resort to accepting people in our military who are there only for the finances, we will destroy the spirit, soul, quality, and professionalism of our army and weaken the fabric of the all-volunteer force.

We must assure the bright and patriotic young men and women who join the military that they will be fairly remunerated, trained, and treated like professionals, and that they will be given opportunities for career and personal enhancement. Most importantly, they have to be assured that their families will be taken care of. Anything less will be insufficient and directly impact the quality of the people we want in our armed forces—and whom we must have in our armed forces.

Our military is an indispensable element of our power, our sword and our shield. But overreliance on military power is a misguided and dangerous policy. It is irresponsible to place burdens upon it which it cannot carry and objectives it cannot achieve. Only enlightened leadership and a united people can ensure a strong military. America's policies must always be worthy of our military men and women, their families, and their sacrifices.

PART II

CITIZENSHIP, SERVICE, DEMOCRACY

CHAPTER 11

"ALWAYS SHOULDER THE WHEEL"

I n my years in the Senate, and before that as a businessman, a government official, and a soldier, I have seen a lot of this world. The more I have traveled, meeting with world leaders and everyday people, the more I marvel at our system of government. There is no way that the Founders could have known that the Constitution they put in place would lead to a society of unlimited productivity and opportunity. How could they? There was no precedent. What they did know was that freedom under the rule of law is the basis for a society that is both just and dynamic. Over the course of 230 years, we've needed amendments to the Constitution they created. It has always been a work in progress. That is one of its great virtues: not as an iron law, but rather as a framework through which we can address our times.

It's no accident that the Constitution starts with the words "We, the people . . . " When we consider the achievements of American democracy, we often think of our great leaders, and more often than not, the leaders who come first to mind are the great presidents: Washington, Lincoln, Jefferson, both Roosevelts. While it is true that these extraordinary men exemplify what is best about America, they didn't do it alone. Without the participation and support of ordinary citizens—"the people"—we would not have triumphed in our revolution, kept the Union together through a horrendous Civil War, joined together to build the transcontinental railroad, won two world wars, or sent our intrepid astronauts along the uncharted path of space exploration. By definition, democracy since its birth in ancient Athens has only flourished with the participation of the *demos*: the people.

Simply by being born in the United States, Americans enjoy certain rights, but the act of birth alone does not make us citizens. It is only those who actively participate in our democracy who are, to my way of thinking, deserving of the honor of being called citizens. The more widespread the participation, the more vital the democracy. Conversely, sitting by and passively enjoying the privileges of citizenship in a free society without in some way serving the common good is the first step down the path to the decline of any republic. We are put on this earth *to do something*, or, in the words of Edmund Burke (one of the founding fathers of modern conservatism): "All that is necessary for the forces of evil to win in the world is for enough good men to do nothing."

If our democracy is to thrive and survive, what must we do to engage our countrymen and women in the responsibilities of citizenship? For it is only by accepting those responsibilities that we can preserve the system that has unleashed the fullest human potential in history.

Citizens are made, not born, and in my experience, it is only through service that we create the bond of citizenship that ties us to our communities and our nation. We are failing ourselves and our country if we do not teach our young people that it is good to serve and that service brings with it the reward of feeling that you are part of something bigger than yourself. Imparting that knowledge to a generation held captive by digital distractions will take engaged encouragement by parents, teachers, and the nation. In short, our kids won't know what we don't teach them.

I feel fortunate that I grew up in a time and place where service was never a question. It was expected of you and, in turn, you expected to serve. Back in the 1950s and '60s, in the little towns of Nebraska, much of the life of the community centered around the American Legion or the Veterans of Foreign Wars (VFW). There was a pervasive spirit of patriotism that we all felt and which defined us. It was assumed that one day you would put on a uniform and you would serve your country. It was as automatic as going to school or church. It was a commitment to a cause beyond self-interest . . . it was part of everyone's life. Observers from other lands have remarked on this special, altruistic aspect of the American character. In his classic *Democracy in America*, Alexis de Tocqueville said, "There is no nation on earth, ever has been a nation on earth, that has service to others and voluntarism as a very central part of its society."

I owe much of my concept of service to my parents. They did

what most parents did in those days—or at least that's the way things were in the prairie towns where I grew up. Towns like Columbus with its lovingly kept football field, its Main Street where you could find whatever you needed when the stores were open every Thursday night, and its two well-maintained cemeteries (including the one where my father is buried). Its classic town square in front of an equally classic midwestern courthouse, green and comfortably shady on steamy summer afternoons and especially magical on the Fourth of July when the flags and the red, white, and blue bunting made it as festive as a Christmas tree heavy with ornaments.

All the grown-ups participated in the life of the town. Some people were volunteer firemen, or they helped out at the hospital, or coached Little League, or visited shut-ins. My dad was commander of the American Legion and VFW posts, active in the Knights of Columbus, and vice president of my high school athletic booster club, The Shamrock Club. He was on the school board when I was very young and we lived near the South Dakota border in Ainsworth. He felt it was one of the most important things you could do because it had such an effect on the future. Mom was always busy doing charity work and church work with the Catholic Altar Society wherever we lived, and she was president of the Women's Legion Auxiliary more than once. She did all of that while she raised four high-spirited boys in the close quarters of little houses.

Dad was absolutely committed to the idea of elections and the responsibility to vote. Every time I close the curtain in a voting booth, and just before I pull the lever, I think of my dad telling me, "Chuck, the right to vote is a responsibility and a privilege." You could write those words in a movie and somebody would accuse you of being hokey, but that's the way he felt and the emotion was real. I have never forgotten my father's words. He never missed voting in an election during his thirty-nine years of life.

The first election I can recall—quite vividly, actually—was the 1952 race between Dwight D. Eisenhower and Adlai Stevenson. I was just a little kid, and life seemed exciting with the banners and posters and campaign buttons everywhere. I knew something was up when posters of Ike started to appear in the store windows down the street from my grandfather's lumberyard in Ainsworth. Ike's face had just the trace of a smile. He looked like somebody's grandfather—a nice man with a happy glint in his eye who might bring you baseball cards or candy bars when he came to visit. Mostly, he looked like a man you could trust.

My father and grandfather were keyed up about the election. They liked Ike—a lot, partly because as a World War II veteran, my dad revered Eisenhower and his war leadership. The Korean War was on and everybody knew somebody who had a friend or a relative serving in the first of the Cold War's shooting conflicts. In fact, my dad had been called back into service, as many World War II veterans had been, to help address manpower shortages in Korea. They eventually sent him home because he was married with three children at the time. Before that happened, though, he had to report, and I remember him leaving on the Greyhound one morning and my mother and grandmother crying.

People whom I had never heard raise their voices or express

a sharp opinion argued pretty heatedly during the 1952 election: at the barber shop, at the confectionary, and at Spearman's IGA where we shopped for groceries. There weren't all that many arguments, since Ainsworth was about as rock-ribbed Republican as any town could be, but when arguments did happen they never ended with one person convincing the other to change his or her mind. You might as well have had a Protestant minister and a Catholic priest debating which church had a more direct line to God: Nobody ever convinced the other guy and probably they didn't expect to.

On election night, Grandma and Grandpa Hagel came over to join my parents as they listened to the returns on their Philco radio. My mom said if I brushed my teeth and put on my pajamas I could join them for a few minutes as they gathered round the radio and listened. My pajamas were the kind with feet in them; it was cold in north-central Nebraska in November. State by state the results came in. Dad and Grandpa Hagel reacted the way I had seen them respond to the score of a ball game when their team won. They were elated as the newscaster announced that it appeared the Eisenhower-Nixon team was headed for a big win.

I caught their enthusiasm—not because I understood it all, but simply because everyone in the house was happy and I felt good when that happened. I also liked the fact that I could stay up a little later. This election was going more to their liking and would turn out better for them than the one four years before when Truman beat Dewey on November 2, 1948. Coincidentally, that was the same day that my brother Tom was born. Interestingly, Tom has always been the one Democrat in the family—and very proud of it. Dad and Grandpa Hagel would feel that they were failures today because of Tom's apostasy. And Tom's middle name is Leo—after Grandpa Hagel!

At the age of six I didn't yet have any plans to run for the United States Senate, but looking back, that's when I developed an interest in elections, or at least the excitement that went along with them. I knew that for some reason they were important.

Citizenship back then was always present, just like the air we breathed. I think that brought a certain dose of reality to all of us. Everyone was affected by national and community events, and did their part for their country. Boys registered with Selective Service when they turned eighteen, and girls recognized that their sweethearts would go into the military one day and go away just as their dads and brothers had. Once you've been in the service or once you've waited for someone dear to you to come home (and these days it's not just men who go away, but women, too) you understand that the serious problems in the world will impact all of our lives, and that you cannot hide. You need to be part of the solution.

Although, for reasons outlined in earlier chapters, I believe the all-volunteer force is the right answer for our country, I also believe that national service of some kind is an idea that needs to be explored by our society and it needs to happen soon. Our young people should be invested in being a part of their community and their country. National service helps do that. Many of the kids in my children's generation have grown up insulated by computers, iPods, cell phones, television, and the comforts of the suburban cocoon. Most have had little exposure to or experience with sacrifice and the real world. Through no fault of their own, many lack any sense of what it takes to assure peace and prosperity for a society.

The Iraq and Afghanistan wars have not resonated with this generation the way previous wars did with other generations—largely because most Americans are disconnected from the burden and sacrifices of these wars. Less than 1 percent of our population is carrying all the burden, making all the sacrifices, and doing all the fighting and dying in these wars. There is no draft—no direct link to these wars for the other 99 percent of our population.

Life goes on pretty much the same way as it has been going on for most Americans. We expect others to do the things we are too busy to do for ourselves. Somebody who was born in Latin America picks the peaches, mows the lawn, and roofs your house. In some back office in Bangalore, an ambitious young person tells us how to reboot a frozen computer. In the alleys of Baghdad, somebody else's kid walks past ruined houses that might conceal snipers or past a parked car packed with high explosives. Let somebody else do the heavy lifting or the unseemly work. It's called outsourcing. But you cannot outsource citizenship. Citizenship is all about responsibility.

Since 2005, the effect of Hurricane Katrina has moved young people in a way that I haven't seen in a long time. This tremendously destructive killer storm nearly annihilated one of the crown jewels of American culture, New Orleans. The government response—at every level—was atrociously inept. All of a sudden my kids and their friends saw on television a great American city reduced to a level of squalor and misery that wasn't ever *supposed* to happen here. Sure, that kind of thing happens in the rest of the world, in cities and countries whose names we can't pronounce—but not here in America.

And then, in the fall of 2005 and on through the winter and spring of 2006, thousands of high school and college students descended on New Orleans. My wife, Lilibet, took our then-sixteen-year-old-daughter, Allyn, and her seventeen-year-old cousin Sophie to New Orleans on a church-sponsored mission where they put on gloves and boots and worked for three days, mucking out houses that had been flooded and cleaning up the wreckage of the Lower Ninth Ward. In the fall of 2007, over Columbus Day weekend, Lilibet and Allyn went back to New Orleans with my fifteen-year-old son, Ziller, and Allyn's high school friend Alex to again help clean up homes. Remarkably, there is still much work to be done. Both of these efforts were sponsored by St. John's Episcopal Church in Washington, DC.

What they learned is that the young generation can help, and what we can all learn is that those young people will want to help if given an opportunity. These kids came to understand that there is something bigger out there than their busy lives and the distractions of the moment.

Did this turn their lives around? Probably not, but it has planted a seed. Scientists tell us that there is actually a genetic tendency to altruism, that sometimes a human being will look beyond his or her own immediate interests and perform an action that serves the group, sometimes at a cost to the individual. In the big scheme of things it makes sense. If it's all about ensuring the survival of our DNA, then if the group cannot survive, what chance does the individual stand? I think that explains, at least in part, why we feel better about ourselves when we serve others. Time and again I have seen this transformation in young people. They do some good and it does them good: They start to get a sense of the country and responsibilities and how we get from where we are to where we need to be.

I had an occasion recently to give it some further thought when a group of twenty-five Stanford University MBA candidates came to see me. These were very bright, very motivated young people. They were in Washington for a week's worth of meetings with regulatory agencies, newspaper editors, government officials, and some members of Congress. I spent an hour and a half with them, answering their questions. Early on in the session a young woman asked, "Senator, how can I contribute to society? What can I do to help make a better world? What's your advice to us?"

Big question. I thought about it for a moment. "This country has given each of you incredible opportunities," I told them. "I know you've all worked hard to be in a position to make something of those opportunities. That's wonderful and it's to your credit—but if the opportunities weren't there, if they had not been enhanced and preserved and built upon by past generations . . . then do you honestly believe you'd be in the same situation?

"You need to be informed and active in your communities. That doesn't mean you all need to run for office but you need to help somehow . . . put something back into the community. Mentoring, public advocacy, weekend clean-ups in the park. It needn't take a lot of time but it all adds up. Trust me on this: The more you serve, the more connected you will be to the world. You will be better for it."

As I reflected further on this meeting it struck me that here were these motivated, smart, and capable people in their early twenties and they really didn't have much of an idea about how to serve. They were actually asking questions about citizenship. They wanted to be engaged but didn't know how. We must live by strong principles but we also need to apply them every day in real ways in the real world if we hope to make a difference in people's lives.

The Stanford MBA students were not really any different from most of the young people I meet with from all over the country. They want to be involved—they want to contribute— they have something to say and believe strongly and care deeply about their world. We need to help them express all of this in meaningful ways. I see this same potential with each new group of interns in my office. I see it each time I have the privilege of addressing graduates and their families at college commencements across this country. I watch these magnificent young people— brimming with hope—walk across the stage to accept their diplomas. I listen to their wonderful stories. Nothing chokes me up more than witnessing and participating in their sense of pride and accomplishment, their high hopes and the love of their families and friends. These are the things that are real and important in life. Our society must never forget these feelings.

It is easy to say, and I believe it is true, that individuals have an obligation to prepare themselves for citizenship, but as in all important life skills, doesn't the older generation and society at large also have a responsibility to pass along the values of citizenship and democracy to help prepare the next generation? Our educational system has not done a very good job with this responsibility. How many schools have civics courses in their curriculum anymore? How many teach the most basic elements of government, the role of government, the structure of government, or how government works? Or citizenship and service? Not very many. We know that citizenship is more than just what you learn in school. But laying an informed foundation through our educational system is a big part of it.

We may all be born with "certain inalienable rights" but none of us is born knowing how to be a citizen of a democracy. If we are doing our job properly, service and citizenship shouldn't be seen by our young people as chores or some special add-ons to their lives. They should be tasks that they want to take up willingly because they will enrich their lives and their country. Robert E. Lee expressed it well: "Duty is the most sublime word in our language," he said. "Do your duty in all things. You cannot do more. You should never wish to do less."

If citizenship grows out of service, how can we as a society, instill this for the good of us all? As I said earlier, the draft certainly had this effect on past generations. But compulsory military service is not the only way to serve one's country, especially in these times that require a professional army made up of skilled specialists. If not military service, then should we look at some other kind of national service for young people?

There are public service jobs out there waiting to be done. During the Depression, the Civilian Conservation Corps and the Works Progress Administration put the energy of hundreds of thousands of people to good use. During that era, the last of the major job initiatives of the New Deal was a project near and dear to Eleanor Roosevelt called the National Youth Administration. Over the course of a decade it provided part-time jobs to nearly two million boys and girls. It was a sort of giant pilot program for the idea of work-study grants that are a common part of financial aid packages for college students. Interestingly, the head of the program in Texas was an ambitious young man named Lyndon Baines Johnson.

We still visit the parks they helped create, and use the electricity from the dams they built. We listen to the recordings they made, and through the photographs they took, we see how the generations before us lived. Of course, this is a different time and different circumstances dominate our world today, so Depression-era programs would not necessarily fit our era. However, isn't there some way we could capture the energy and patriotism of young Americans and apply it to the social good of our country? Don't our parks need refurbishing, don't our vacant lots need cleaning, wouldn't our senior citizens welcome some help and company, don't our disadvantaged youth need coaches and counselors? Can't the millions of documents in the Library of Congress and the National Archives be digitized so that the poorest kids in the most remote schoolhouses in Appalachia have access to the same resources as students in Ivy League schools? Wouldn't the poor and sick and hungry in the parts of the world left behind by the economic surge of the last half-century benefit from a reenergized and expanded Peace Corps, and wouldn't that improve America's image and influence all over the world?

I don't have all the answers on how we could help to prepare our next generation of Americans for citizenship and service. I do know that we can't legislate or impose these responsibilities or values. We must teach them, demonstrate by example and, in so doing, lead our young people to them.

When considering questions of service, citizenship, and democracy, I recall what one of my favorite teachers wrote in my 1964 St. Bonaventure High School yearbook, *The Venture*. I still have it in my office. The note was from my English teacher, Mildred Herrod. She was quite a remarkable woman—two master's degrees and volumes of wise advice and uncommon knowledge. Through her I first met those back-stabbing senators (literally) who did in Julius Caesar, and Rhett Butler and Scarlett O'Hara, and two midwestern boys with whom I identified: Tom Sawyer and Huck Finn.

She wrote next to her picture in my senior class album, "Chuck, always shoulder the wheel." It was her way of saying always take responsibility. I took this to mean that you should always try to get the best out of yourself, not because others expect it but because you do. It's advice I give anyone who wants to take it: Compete with yourself. If you compete honestly with yourself, you will be your own fiercest competitor and critic and you'll never be up against anyone tougher. When you're better, everybody around you is better. You can offer more; you can contribute more; you can do more and be more effective for the bigger causes. Most importantly, you can make a better world.

Four words that I have always tried to live up to: "Always shoulder the wheel!"

CHAPTER 12

CRABS OR PRAIRIE DOGS

POLITICS AND PARALYSIS

There are two descriptions that I sometimes find useful in explaining the behavior of us politicians in today's brutally negative political environment: crabs and prairie dogs. Take your pick.

First, crabs. If you ever put a bunch of them in a bucket you will notice that they just sort of flex their pincers and flop over each other rather clumsily. Occasionally one of the more intrepid crabs will try to climb up the side of the bucket in an attempt to break free. He'll get partway up the side and then the crabs left behind will reach out and pull the escaping crab back down into the pile. Politics is like that. Granted, the floor of the U.S. Senate is a more majestic setting than a crab bucket, but the behavior of the inhabitants is often quite similar. If you run up against the common wisdom, whether it is questioning an ill-conceived war or cutting back on entitlements that we will be unable to fund for the long term, you can be sure, the other "crabs" will reach up and try to pull you back into the false security of the bucket. Of course all of the crabs—even the intrepid ones—end up in the cooking pot, and similarly my colleagues and I often are in danger of leading the nation into very hot water.

Now, consider the prairie dog. I have never seen a more nervous fellow. If you pull up alongside a prairie-dog town and wait for a few moments, a prairie dog will stick his head out of one of his tunnels. It's a very tentative movement. He looks this way and that, very jittery. If you cough, or open the car door, or make any sudden noise at all he ducks back underground right away. Sometimes, when he thinks the coast is clear, the little prairie dog will summon up all his courage, pop out of his hole, and run for dear life to the next hole. He doesn't want to leave himself exposed for a fraction of a second more than necessary. The similarity to a politician who will often do anything he can to avoid taking a stand is unmistakable.

Whether you are a crab being pulled back down into the bucket or a prairie dog afraid of his own shadow, the result, as I have seen in many years in Washington, is that we often play for the lowest (and safest) political common denominator. At best we nibble around the edges of many big problems rather than confronting them head on.

Very few of us come to Washington with the intention of being either a crab or a prairie dog. In fact, quite the contrary. It has been my experience that the people who run for office believe in democracy, believe in trying to improve the lives of all Americans and making our world a better place. But they must overcome the massive inertia that the system imposes on them and the obstacles (or temptations) thrown in their way by special interests with seemingly inexhaustible resources.

When paralysis sets into the political system, it grinds down the democratic process and impedes governance. This conflict has always been part of democracies but its piercing whine is loudest of late because of the voracious appetite of more and more media outlets requiring controversy and political fireworks in order to build ratings. In a divisive partisan environment, you rarely break with your party on any issue for fear that you will alienate your base and find yourself politically isolated. Worse, you may be vulnerable to partisan retribution. Then—the horror of it all!—you could lose reelection because you actually believe in something and are willing to act on those beliefs. In politics, self-preservation is a very effective motivator and it conditions one's positions and tempers one's boldness. Political leaders have always used fear, intimidation, and exclusion as tools for keeping party discipline. The message is not new in politics: Go along to get along.

Instead of seeking common ground and consensus, which is what defines democracies, we end up trying to beatify our side and demonize the other guy's. For example, Republicans believe that they represent responsible and wise governance and that Democrats are unprincipled users of power. Democrats, not surprisingly take the opposite view. The result quite often is that nothing gets done; but our sound bites ricochet around the media and add to our files of press clippings and Web site hits. The political fringes are happy, television and radio talk shows don't have a second of dead air, blogs hum away with incendiary sloganeering, and America's problems are deferred. You have to respond to every attack and the attacks are never ending. Politicians use the media and the media use politicians and we continue to neglect America's most pressing problems. The result is few tough stands are taken, fewer difficult votes are cast, and the public becomes increasingly distrustful of the process. A Gallup poll from September 2007 found that trust in the federal government is now lower than it was during the Watergate era.

One of the consequences of extreme partisanship is the trivializing of political debate. That's a shame. In ancient Athens, it was soaring and inspiring rhetoric that made Demosthenes and Pericles synonymous with the birth of democracy. In our own country, thoughtful rhetoric was once the mark of an able leader. Think of Lincoln, who managed in the magnificently brief 272 words of the Gettysburg Address to complete the definition of freedom that Jefferson and Madison began in the Declaration of Independence. Or think of such giants of the Senate as Daniel Webster and Henry Clay: men with a golden tongue in the service of a sharp mind, who could move their colleagues to action. In more recent times, we think of Robert Dole, Daniel Patrick Moynihan, Howard Baker, Mike Mansfield, Everett Dirksen, and Nebraska's George Norris. They forged consensus on issues— which is the essential objective of legislators and leaders. They were able to bring together people of differing opinions in order to move forward with the nation's business. They accomplished this by the strength of their arguments and the power of their logic.

The *Oxford English Dictionary* defines rhetoric as "the art of using language so as to persuade or influence others." When was the last time any speech in the Senate changed any minds? A better question is: Was anyone even listening? Instead most speeches are reiterations of positions frozen in place before the first words of a debate are even spoken.

That is not the way I imagined it would be when I had my first understanding of the power of political speech in high school.

It was in November 1963, but none of us knew at the time that on the twenty-second of that month, John F. Kennedy would fall to an assassin's bullet and that my generation would collectively end its innocence in one afternoon. In the beginning it was like every other November in the Midwest. Some days were Indian summer–like in their clarity and some bore the first bone-chilling winds southward from the Dakotas and parts north. In the protected hollows and valleys, some oaks, maples, and cottonwoods still wore their fading autumn colors. Football season was winding down. I checked the antifreeze in my 1946 black Willys Jeep. And, as they did every year, the juniors and seniors in Tom Sheridan's civics and history classes at St. Bonaventure High School participated in the school's mock United Nations. With the whole school in attendance, the seniors played the role of UN ambassadors for all different countries. I gave myself a challenge and picked the Soviet Union. I thought it would be interesting to see things from the bad guy's point of view, and advocate for the Communists.

With Mr. Sheridan's guidance, by researching each nation's position on issues, and through reading newspapers and magazines, we all studied the issues we would have to speak on. As "the Evil Empire," I spoke on the menace of NATO, nuclear weapons, colonialism, and capitalism. I asked rhetorical questions and made counterarguments when the other "ambassadors" questioned or cornered me—and I liked it.

I have thought about that mock United Nations many times over the years. The experience of working through the democratic process with my peers, the sense of satisfaction from thoroughly knowing the issues, and making an effective case was exhilarating. I began to understand that in the public forum, words can matter, they have meaning—and they produce consequences.

Unfortunately today, rhetoric often means "empty of meaning" or "just going through the motions." Or, alternatively, it signifies oratorical ballistics that border on demagoguery. Too many opinion makers who control the megaphone of public discourse in the media seek to inflame passions rather than encourage dialogue. They are rarely called to account if they are careless with the facts and reckless with the reputations of others. Such people are not legislators. They are not educators. They are not problem solvers. They are entertainers.

Right alongside them, kind of like backup singers in a rock group, we have the pundits. They are supposed to be sage fonts of political wisdom; just ask them. When they are not shouting at one another, they are little more than partisan mouthpieces who have learned their talking points by rote. Collectively these "chattering classes" create a hostile, venomous atmosphere, raising the temperature until any politician with a sense of moderation and balance risks appearing as a wimp next to these high-octane blowhards. But reasonableness doesn't push ratings, and low ratings hurt the bottom line of the media corporations. The result is that at the root of much of the poisonous rhetoric that colors current political discourse one does not find principles, but rather ratings and money. All of us have to take some responsibility for this current state of affairs. We who are the practitioners of politics have allowed our system to slide into this ditch of dysfunction.

The distorting influence of money is found not only in the way it shapes the priorities of media. Special interests have always used money as a tool to exert influence on politicians on both sides of the aisle. They finance our conventions; they finance our campaigns; they pretty much finance everything we do. Labor, business, and every special interest in Washington have corrupted the political process. Both political parties are in the grip of these special interests.

How then do we break this financial stranglehold if it means committing political suicide at the same time? Until we find a way, we will rarely engage the great challenges that face our nation—especially long-term challenges such as entitlements, health care, and immigration reform. Special interests are not, in and of themselves, bad. We all are part of special interests. And the right of special interests to be heard is enshrined in the Constitution. But who lobbies for or represents the general good of America to the Congress, or in the fifty state capitals of America? Where is the battery of paid lobbyists and attorneys working on behalf of the common interest?

It is up to the elected representatives to represent the overall interests of our country. Each of us who is privileged to hold office swears an oath to the Constitution—not to a political party or a president. We may have reached our positions thanks, in part, to the support of many legitimate interests—corporations, industries, and lobbies among them. When the time comes to vote for the national interest, it can be painful but proper to say no to a corporation, industry, or lobby when you believe their interests at that moment are not as important as that of your state or country. As a result, you always run the risk of losing support and bearing the brunt of negative advertising campaigns directed against you for voting for what you believe is in the best interests of your country!

At the end of the day, we politicians and the people are jointly responsible for the kind of political system we have, its maintenance, preservation, and integrity. But how are we to do the job we were elected to do when faced with the prospect of endless and financially ravenous campaigns? Campaigns are obviously important and necessary. They help educate, inform, and motivate. They are intrinsic to the vitality of democracy. However, they never seem to end.

As I write these words, America is already six months into a presidential campaign with the election still fifteen months away! If we are spending most of our days preparing for the next election, when do we find the time to govern, to deliberate, to seek consensus so that we can find answers to our problems? We seem to have reversed the proper order of a public servant's priorities. One runs for office in order to serve. Instead, it seems that the system is set up so that we hold office primarily to prepare for the next election—with the goal of perpetuating ourselves in office. The campaign is a never-ending cycle. We run harder and harder taking more and more time away from studying the issues and taking action on our judgments. The need for more money grows ever greater as we base our campaigns on beautifully crafted, very expensive, thirty-second feel-good commercials that we hope will vault us back into office each election.

But even the most feel-good commercials cannot undo the reality of war, health care, and energy demands, or the impending fiscal shipwreck that looms on the horizon. Where I think we have failed ourselves and the people we serve is that we are always glancing over our shoulders before we speak, to make sure it is safe. We are rarely looking ahead, providing leadership in taking on the most difficult, intractable, and politically dangerous issues. We're constantly focused on those all-important poll numbers. But governing by timidity and fear of giving offense to special interest groups and sources of money is unacceptable, and I think it begins to explain the disenchantment with the political process that people are feeling today.

Too many of us in politics are concerned with making sure that we are always absolutely "consistent," as if changing your mind based on new facts or informed judgment were evidence of a character flaw. That's prairie dog behavior. Events change, issues evolve. Not ever changing your mind or acknowledging a mistake, or at least not being open to the possibility of a mistake or misjudgment, is dangerous. It closes down options that can only result from bold new thinking just when the nation needs it most. Public figures are too often overly cautious and timid about saying anything really new or provocative, especially if it means being painfully honest. Teddy Roosevelt was right on target a century ago when he said, "A typical vice of American politics is the avoidance of saying anything real on real issues."

I ran straight up against this in the spring of 2000 when commentators from the right and the left played out a heated rhetorical tug-of-war over the fate of a young Cuban boy named Elian Gonzalez. You may recall that Elian had fled Cuba on a small inner tube with his mother and others on their way to Florida. His mother (along with ten others) died during the voyage and Elian was taken in by distant relatives when he arrived in America. People lined up just about how you would have predicted given their politics. Those who hated Castro wanted little Elian to stay in America. Those less doctrinaire about isolating Cuba and its dictator decried the motives of his family in the United States in keeping him here. It was all about the politics and very little about the boy and his father who, even though he lived under Castro, still loved and missed his son the way any father anywhere would have felt. Elian had become a political object. In trying to put this into perspective, I wrote the following in an op-ed piece for *The New York Times* after the hotheads on both sides came out in full cry following Elian's forced removal from the custody of his Florida relatives.

The images of Elian Gonzalez being seized from the home of his Miami relatives were indeed horrifying. But before we react with hurried congressional hearings, casting blame and fanning the emotional flames, we should step back, cool down, and apply some perspective.

The Elian Gonzalez case has become a passionate debate over Fidel Castro and Cuba. We need to have that debate, but not under these circumstances, and certainly not by using this six-year-old boy as a pawn on a political chessboard. Over the last five months we have lost the real focus: what is best for Elian Gonzalez.

To me, this case has always been fundamentally about a father-son relationship. Elian lost his mother in a tragic way. By all accounts, Elian and his father have had a loving relationship. By United States law, the boy should have been placed in the custody of his sole remaining parent as soon as his father, Juan Miguel Gonzalez, arrived on American soil.

The alarming photographs from Saturday's operation by the Justice Department obscured the point of the raid—to reunite Elian with his father when those housing him had repeatedly refused to hand him over. The boy is where he belongs, and the case is in the hands of the courts. Now Americans should trust the judicial process and allow it to work. After the legal process has concluded and Elian's fate has been determined in a dispassionate, legal, and humane way, it may be appropriate for Congress to hold hearings, examining all events since last Thanksgiving.

Holding congressional hearings now would only further politicize this tragedy, further inflame the passions, and do nothing to resolve the future of the child. We are a nation of laws and family values. We should allow the legal process to work without overshadowing and complicating it with the protracted public drama of congressional hearings. We should not allow this situation to degenerate further into which political party can benefit the most. Americans have made it clear that they do not want to see this issue politicized.

This is not about Fidel Castro or Cuba. This is about a young boy, his father, and his future.

This simple commonsense position in favor of a father being with his son brought me no end of criticism—some of it quite belligerent and vituperative from the "family values" side of the political spectrum. This made no sense to me but it makes all the sense in the world when everything a politician says is passed through the prism of political point scoring. Sometimes you have to forget the politics, and their consequences, and just say and do what you think is right. Politics may be a fact of life in our system but it certainly is not all there is to life, nor should it ever be the overriding factor in any decision that affects people's lives.

America has always gravitated toward leaders who talk straight, who refuse to constantly calibrate their responses based on the advice of political handlers, polling, and focus groups. Harry Truman, Dwight Eisenhower, John Kennedy, and Ronald Reagan were leaders who simply and straightforwardly spoke the facts as they saw them. To be sure, these presidents were far from political innocents. They had their consultants and advisors and they were very mindful of the power of the press and later of television, and of the need to present the right image. But when the times called for it, they also had the capability and the courage to put all the handlers and consultants aside and speak plainly to the heart of the matter. The American people expect this of their leaders. We have had too many years of "gotcha" politics that produce more sound than light. We need leaders who can articulate a vision of where we want to take this nation and then lead us there; honest, competent, accountable leadership is what has always mattered most.

Politics only mirrors society. It reflects our world, the hopes, dreams, fears, and expectations of our people. A nation's leaders are not only found in politics and government. Educational, scientific, religious, medical, business, labor, military, media, and cultural leaders also shape a nation—its values, standards, and future. It is the responsibility of all our leaders to put the general good and interests of their nation first. Individual interests must be balanced with the nation's interests. America has done this as well as any nation in history. I've always believed this great accomplishment was because of the multifaceted fabric of our society. The differences in our society have been woven together in a brilliantly colored fabric of Herculean strength. This is America's greatest asset, and we must constantly tend to it.

Like many Americans, in and out of government, I am often frustrated and disappointed at the gridlock in our political life. But I am also encouraged, because I have every confidence that we will break through this roadblock and put our country back on track—because the American people will demand it.

How will we do it?

Each time in American history that our nation has required adjustments to our political system, change has occurred. Watershed political years such as 1994, 1980, 1968, 1932, and 1854 (when the slavery question gave birth to the Republican Party) all had one thing in common: The political party in power was thrown out because the people saw it as irrelevant and incapable of leading America. In fact, six years after the Republican Party was born, it elected its first president, Abraham Lincoln. Events force change. Democracies are the most finely tuned and receptive to change of all forms of government. They always find a new "governing center of gravity." We are living at such a time: the reshaping of the American political landscape as we start the twenty-first century.

CHAPTER 13

BEYOND GRIDLOCK

A NEW ELECTORAL SCENARIO?

The two-party system as we have known it since the Civil War era has been a durable and valuable feature of our democracy, but it is worth pointing out that political parties are not mentioned in the Constitution, Bill of Rights, or any other founding documents of our republic. Nevertheless, political parties help us to frame fundamental questions and a philosophy of government: What should be the role of government? What do we want government to do for us? How much government do we want and how much government are we willing to pay for? To a great degree, the two major parties have offered a forum for the resolution of these questions. But the paralysis and partisanship in Washington of recent years call into question the role of the current party system.

Any thoughtful review of American governance must include a focused look at political parties. Their future effect on our government's ability to help solve the nation's problems, and successfully address the challenges of a larger and more complicated society in a more connected world, demands our attention. There are many signs that the electorate has already begun to shift allegiances and party affiliations. The will of the people, like the irresistible force of the tides, is moving. It is up to the politicians to respond to these forces that are carrying us to new shores. This is as it should be in a democracy, because in most instances it is the people who first see problems developing in a very real way in their daily lives.

Recent elections and polling data suggest that the American body politic could be in the process of realigning itself away from the two-party system. The parties eventually must embrace this new reality, or if not, the reality will embrace new parties.

For evidence of this shift, look at the increase in the number of registered independent voters, bearing in mind that rising percentages in one slice of the electoral pie always means declining ones in another. According to Gallup in August 2007, 37 percent of the voting age public in America called themselves "independents," while the Democratic and Republican parties got 32 and 29 percent respectively. In other recent polls, the numbers aligning themselves with the two parties are even lower than Gallup's numbers. In nearly every state in the Northeast, for example, independents now outnumber Republicans and Democrats. People are not leaving the traditional parties because voters particularly like the unknown. In fact, just the opposite is true. There is usually a comfort level in going with what you know, and it is a truism of American politics that people tend to vote for the same party their parents voted for. But now, even those parents are deserting the traditional parties.

I believe the explanation for this is as obvious as it is irrefutable. People are leaving the Republicans and Democrats because the parties are doing such a lousy job of addressing their voters' problems. From fiscal responsibility, to health care and Social Security reform, to education, to immigration reform—nothing seems to get done. There is plenty of passion but little action as Congress and the president cannot get beyond flame-throwing speeches instead of building a consensus of purpose to address big challenges.

Likewise, on the talk shows, in press conferences, in committee hearings and debates in the Senate and House, there seems to be an inability to put aside pre-scripted political talking points in order to get down to the hard work that results in solving problems. Equally disturbing, on a number of the more urgent issues, leaders and opinion makers try to play it safe politically rather than coming forward with the bold responses required for solutions to long-festering problems. For example, on the potentially crushing entitlements crisis (unfunded obligations to Social Security, Medicare, and Medicaid), the two parties have ignored this political hot potato. But complex social problems cannot be solved by deferring them or engaging in dueling sound bites.

It is therefore understandable, amidst the hot air and inaction, that there is a move in the electorate toward nonaffiliation with any party. In the multiple-choice test of political life, more and more Americans are choosing "none of the above." On close inspection, what we are seeing may not be so much a case of the people leaving their parties as it is of the parties deserting their people. Think about it: Who speaks for the GOP—the Republicans who represent the most rigid conservative positions and single-issue voters (the much vaunted "base") or those who have a wider view on political issues and are less likely to actively participate in caucuses and campaigns? Likewise, are Democrats best represented by those who will not accept any discussion at all on the Second Amendment or *Roe v. Wade* or by those who are no less concerned than their Republican friends about terrorism or the future of Social Security?

Both parties have moved closer and closer to narrow ideologies and interest groups that will neither compromise nor seek common ground to build consensus. A direct result of this is that the party enforcers demand undeviating allegiance to the party line. This puts any legislator in a difficult position when their sense of duty as a representative of the people and their best judgment conflict with the policy of their party or their president.

At a recent Republican event in Nebraska, former House Republican Majority Leader Dick Armey raised this issue. He said he had recently asked a number of House Republicans why they had voted the way they had on a couple of big votes in Congress. Their votes didn't seem to add up to him. These congressmen explained that they had been told that they owed the president their votes and they owed their leaders their votes. Armey was incredulous at their response. He asked them, "What do you owe yourself . . . and more to the point what do you owe those you represent? . . . What do you owe your country!" As Edmund Burke said, "Your representative owes you not only his industry but his judgment as well; he betrays rather than serves you if he sacrifices it to your opinion."

For nearly six years (that is, before we even went into Iraq), despite holding one of the Senate's strongest records of support for President Bush, I have seen my standing as a Republican called into question because of my opposition to what I believe has been a reckless foreign policy undermining American interests in the world, one that is divorced from a strategic context. "You are expected to support the president," I am told, because I am a Republican. My answer is that I am first an American—then a Republican. The Founders of our nation and authors of the Constitution conceived a beautiful, workable, and accountable system of government called "checks and balances." Sometimes we must check in order to balance.

As every American history student knows, the courts and Congress are coequal branches of government with the president. Article I of the Constitution saves pride of place for the voice of the people, the legislative branch. The judicial branch is the arbiter that decides when either the legislative or the executive has overstepped its constitutional bounds. These three branches of government are equal partners in governing our country, each with its own responsibilities. Members of Congress take the same oath of office that the president does: to uphold and defend the Constitution of the United States, not the president's (or anybody's) poll numbers. We all carry sacred constitutional responsibilities to find solutions together, govern together, and protect America's individual liberties enshrined in the Constitution.

That is the way the Founders intended things, but, too often, the best way to survive in politics is not the best way to govern. Your party leaders expect you to be loyal and unquestioning, especially when there is a world of pressure and rewards out there that reinforces this distortion of our democratic system. I have seen it happen and grow to alarming proportions throughout my years in Washington. Not every politician is defined this way. But most are. Independent-thinking senators like the late John Chafee and Pat Moynihan, as well as John Breaux, Mike DeWine, Bob Graham, and Bob Kerrey defied this standard. John McCain, George Voinovich, Olympia Snowe, Joe Biden, Chuck Grassley, Dianne Feinstein, Dick Lugar, Ben Nelson, and Jim Webb are among the most independent thinking in the current senate. And we currently have two senators (Joe Lieberman and Bernie Sanders) who are registered Independents.

It may be that a new party or independent movement will be required to break the partisan stranglehold on our country's interests and priorities. Political parties are like all institutions: If they do not stay vital, they will become irrelevant, and, ultimately, they will disappear. In the current impasse, an independent candidate for the presidency, or a bipartisan unity ticket with a president from one party and vice president from the other could be appealing to Americans. It wouldn't require the death of either major party, and it could help to rebuild American consensus because finding common ground is the only way such a ticket could govern.

How would a politically independent administration govern? In the first place, its allegiance would not be to party or special interests. It could only govern with the support of a bipartisan consensus in Congress as well as the nation, free of much (but not all) of the paralysis brought on by entrenched forces within both political parties. I don't know if any of this is likely or, in a practical sense, possible. But the world is not static, and we know that dynamic systems, institutions, and actions will always be required to meet evolving challenges and to solve new problems. Politics, like all things in life, finds its own center of gravity.

The fact that there are so many newly registered independents—more than at any time in our history—clearly means that a political reorientation is under way. This has happened in the context of an electorate with unprecedented access to information. The Internet and the blogosphere have made ringside political pundits of us all. This new technology has transformed the political process more than anything since the advent of television. Ultimately, I believe, the Internet will have an even more profound affect on politics than television did. YouTube had a tremendous impact on the political races of 2006 and will have an even greater effect on the presidential and congressional elections of 2008.

Given the shifting political sands and the connectivity of the electorate, it is becoming increasingly clear that one of the things that needs to find its new center of gravity is the way we select our presidential candidates. A nation of 300 million people with over 200 million eligible voters requires a coherent electoral primary process. The chaos we have now is based on the whims of the state legislatures and political power brokers, each trying to be first in the spotlight by, arbitrarily moving primary elections up earlier and earlier. This is insane.

The personal interaction between the candidate and the voter in Iowa and New Hampshire has been an important element in electing our presidents, but it is being overwhelmed by the chaos of the current system, which is dominated by the show business of the media and the Internet. We need a national process. For example, establishing four multistate regional primaries, each a month apart beginning in March of the presidential election year. Regions could rotate their positions (earliest and latest) every four years. I have cosponsored a bill in Congress that addresses this issue. We're now having caucuses and primaries almost a year before the general election.

The news media, especially television, also bear some responsibility for this mess. Let's stop the superfluous "pretend" debates. The American people, as well as the candidates, deserve better than a perpetual media circus. Serious issues deserve serious attention by serious candidates in serious debates.

We will never recapture the special spirit of American democracy without a public that is committed and engaged, and leadership that inspires us. There are no great nations without great leaders.

PART III

SENSE AND DOLLARS

CHAPTER 14

COMPETITIVENESS

STAYING IN THE GAME

Any of my Senate colleagues would be very pleased if he or she introduced a piece of legislation and within hours every newspaper, news station, and talk show clamored for an interview. We would be gratified by the interest shown in our work because it validated the effort we and our staff had put into addressing an issue of great national importance. It is more often the case that years of hard work, research, and careful drafting of a proposal are followed by a speech to a nearly empty Senate chamber, a couple pages in the *Congressional Record*, and a sparsely attended news conference.

Last year, Connecticut's senior senator Chris Dodd and I introduced legislation that we expected would attract little notice. The number of journalists at our press conference would barely have constituted a quorum for a round of gin rummy. The date was August 2, 2007. Five hours later, we were deluged with phone calls from the press seeking our comments. The event that precipitated this interest was not the way we would have liked our legislation to gain notice.

Our bill, the National Infrastructure Bank Act of 2007, hadn't changed in those few intervening hours. Certainly Chris and I hadn't been transformed from two earnest legislators speaking on infrastructure funding policy into spellbinding leading men (although Chris was gathering notice as a Democratic candidate for president). What had happened was that at five o'clock that afternoon, at the height of the evening rush hour, a forty-year-old bridge in Minneapolis had given way and crumbled into the Mississippi river, sending cars, trucks, and a school bus full of kids crashing down in an avalanche of concrete and steel. This moment of terror and destruction resulted in thirteen deaths and many injuries.

It captured the attention of the nation not only for the empathy we all felt for the victims and their families, but from the chilling knowledge that we all shared: This could have happened to any of us. I would go so far as to say that with one-hundred-sixty thousand bridges in America today in need of serious repair, you can be sure it will happen again with no less devastating consequences. America's infrastructure—our roads and bridges, electricity grids, railways, subways, airports, ports, water and sewer systems—are the vital organs and arteries of our nation. Our very sustenance moves along them. But like a human body that is neglected and out of shape, this great system constructed over the course of the last century is in a desperate state and in need of vital reconditioning.

What a change from the hope and promise I felt as a young boy when my dad and my maternal grandfather Joseph Patrick Dunn drove me to see the wondrous highway that was being built across Nebraska just outside Grand Island. Stretching from one horizon to the other, four lanes of graveled and graded roadbed were becoming Interstate 80.

"This road is going to go from one coast to the other," my dad said with a mix of wonder and pride. "Three thousand miles east to west and two thousand miles north to south! It'll connect America. It's amazing." President Eisenhower made this happen because he was so impressed with the autobahns that the Germans had built in the 1930s and '40s, and wanted to give America the ability to move its military as well as its people and commerce as easily, efficiently, and quickly as the Germans had. In 1955, Eisenhower said, "Our unity as a nation is sustained by free communication of thought and by easy transportation of people and goods." One year later he signed the Federal-Aid Highway Act of 1956, which created our interstate highway system that I saw taking shape before my eyes.

I was too young to comprehend how long three thousand miles was, but I did know that it was 180 miles from our home in Ainsworth to Grandma and Grandpa Dunn's house in Grand Island and that it took a long time to drive, so we were talking about a very long stretch of highway under construction across America. The earth-moving equipment, the sounds of front-end loaders going back and forth, dumping their loads of sand and cement, teams of men in hard hats, the line of sand pits now filled in with runoff to become a gleaming ribbon of sky blue lakes that paralleled the course of the highway—it was all so big and impressive to a young boy, like pictures in books of the thousands of workers building the pyramids. You could see, hear, and feel the power and the promise of America out there on The Plains in the 1950s.

A few years later during the summer between my junior and senior years in high school, I had the opportunity to make my own small contribution to the highway system. I shoveled wet cement from daybreak into the night building a highway bypass around Norfolk, Nebraska. I learned three things on that job: the importance of highways; a new and colorful vocabulary; and the desirability of a college education.

Within just a few years, the national system of interstate highways—the largest public works project in the history of any nation—had linked the resources and people of the United States in ways that spurred growth and transformed our lives. How far we have come, I have since reflected, since the days when my great-grandfather, Herman Christian Hagel, earned his living as a dray man, hauling dry goods in his horse-drawn wagon from the railroad station in Rushville up to the U.S. Army fort on the Pine Ridge Reservation at the turn of the twentieth century. It was twenty miles of bad road, just a wagon rut. It took him a whole day for his round trip. Today you can make the drive to Pine Ridge in fifteen minutes. It is so amazing to me that in the space of one family's living memory, life could have changed so much for the better.

Now, a half-century from that morning with my dad and Grandpa Joe, it is no less apparent to me that in the same way that I need to pay more and more attention to maintaining my mind and body in reasonably good functioning order, so it is with the great but aging edifices of American society and prosperity. We can no longer take it for granted that our country will automatically continue to prosper if we do not plan for significant and wise investment to maintain the capabilities of our people and the infrastructure that has served us so well. This should have been obvious to all of us—especially to our national leaders. After all, our infrastructure, as well as America's unique free-market economy, was built through investment. Without constant attention to that infrastructure, our power and position in the world will diminish while others will inevitably step into our place.

The costs of fixing and maintaining our nation's infrastructure will be enormous. A power grid that redlines every summer during peak demand; major municipal water and sewer systems that average over a hundred years in age; hundreds of thousands of bridges, most of them built over fifty years ago; 48,876 miles of interstate highways and hundreds of thousands of miles of roadways bearing heavier traffic loads and less maintenance—all add up to an infrastructure that will require hundreds of billions of dollars to maintain, let alone improve. It is a cost beyond the financial reach of government alone with all of the other obligations we have, especially the trillions of dollars in unfunded liabilities for our entitlement programs and the giant price tag on our Iraq effort.

Where will the money come from? After two years of study, and thanks to the efforts of scores of experts, Senator Dodd and

I proposed the National Infrastructure Bank Act where U.S. government bonds would attract private sector funds to take on projects in excess of $75 million. Not only would this put private capital in the service of the most pressing infrastructure needs, it would also create hundreds of thousands of new jobs that would pump money into the economy and tax revenue back to the treasury so that a large proportion of the infrastructure bonds could be retired simply through the growth stimulated by the proposed Infrastructure Bank.

Our initial proposal for this public-private venture was $60 billion in tax credit bonds. The eventual cost of infrastructure maintenance and modernization in America over the next twenty years will be well in excess of a trillion dollars. But if this idea works out—putting private investment funds to work on behalf of public projects (where they can have the most positive effect on the economy)—then it could serve as a financing model for future public-private partnerships.

Addressing this and other challenges will not turn the clock back to a world where America is and remains the only economic superpower. But it will return us to the promise that I saw everywhere in the America that I grew up in, a society that had hit upon a golden formula much sought after by the rest of the world: hard work + creative thinking + risk/reward incentive + free-market opportunities (+ some good luck) = success. From the older capitalist economies of Europe to the newly ascendant giants of Asia, the American system has been the model that sparked the growth of a true global economy. The raw numbers are astonishing. In 1850—when technological change began to provide liftoff for many economies—the total global production of goods and services was something like $553 billion. A hundred and ten years later, in 1960, with the advancement of transportation, communications, and industrial technology, the number was $10.5 trillion. In 2006 the total global output of goods and services was over $48 trillion.

What explains this historic rate of economic growth? There are at least four major factors: an open (that is, not overly regulated) financial system that allowed for the free flow of capital; a global trading regime that succeeded in proportion to how closely it adhered to a policy of free trade; an international infrastructure that speeded the flow of goods, services, and energy resources; and huge advances in productivity, which were the fruits of an educational system that provided the underpinning for massive research and development.

We are now competing in a bruising global marketplace. For America to remain the largest and most productive economy, we must continue to pay close attention to all of the factors that helped keep our economy the world's most powerful for over a hundred years. You may be sure that our competitors are paying attention. By using the term "competition," I don't mean to imply that the international economy is an elimination tournament with one "winner." The fact is, the more countries that do well economically, the more people there are to buy each other's goods and services. Standards of living go up, allowing for more purchasing power by an expanding middle class. This presents more opportunities for more people, leading to more stability and security and less conflict. So for example, while the fall of Communism has posed a competitive challenge to our system by unleashing a vast low-wage labor pool of bright and motivated new workers, it has also created three billion new consumers, all of them potential customers. Seen in this light, competition is a process that enables all who engage in it to sharpen skills, improve services and products, and enlarge the overall market, to everyone's benefit.

So although it is not instructive to think in terms of a single winner, it is important to remember there are losers. Countries that close down their trade opportunities, that do not uphold the integrity of their financial system, that allow their infrastructure— both material and human—to atrophy will lose.

America must focus its resources and attention. Our first priority should be our human capital. As a recent bipartisan study (the congressionally commissioned Hart-Rudman Report) put it clearly and soberingly, "the inadequacies of our systems of research and (K–12) education pose a greater threat to U.S. national security over the next quarter-century than any potential conventional war that we might imagine."

Every reputable observer of economic affairs will tell you that part of the reason America rose to and maintained its position of economic predominance over the last hundred years was our huge investments in research and development and in an educational system that produced the scientists and engineers whose vision and labors gave us advances so regularly that we took progress for granted. There was so much of it, we came to assume that progress grew on trees rather than in the dreams, hard work, and capabilities of our fellow Americans. The enhanced productivity that came with breakthroughs in technology in America accounted for nearly 50 percent of U.S. growth since World War II. We have always been the leaders in research, in advanced degrees in the sciences and engineering, in generating the investment funds to realize the promise of new technologies. But recent history gives us cause for concern.

The extent of the problem was put starkly and simply by Erskine Bowles in his 2006 inaugural address as the sixteenth president of the University of North Carolina. "Think about this," he said, "in the past four years our fifteen schools of education at the University of North Carolina turned out a grand total of three physics teachers. Three."

That's three physics teachers for the whole UNC system, the same state where the Wright brothers took flight in the first airplane and thereby founded an industry that has transformed modern life. U.S. universities and colleges had twice as many bachelor's degrees awarded in physics in 1956 as they did in 2004.

While U.S. freshmen and sophomores in high school ranked near the bottom one-fifth in applying math concepts to the real world, a recent survey found that American youngsters spend more time watching television than they do in school. Or consider this pair of facts: In 2005, six of the top ten corporate patent recipients in the United States were *not* U.S. companies. At the same time, according to a study commissioned by the National Academy of Sciences, the National Academy of Engineering, and the Institute of Medicine, "the combined U.S. investment in research in the physical sciences, mathematics, and engineering equals the annual increase in U.S. health-care costs every twenty days." It has not taken long for the consequences of that decline to be felt in our economy where in the space of a decade, the U.S. trade balance in high-tech goods and services went from a positive $50 billion to a negative $50 billion.

Eager and ambitious students from Korea, Ghana, Pakistan, Brazil, Poland, Egypt, Israel—every nation on earth—came to America to study and stayed on to teach in universities or to work in private industry. For a time, then, we have been able to bridge the "research gap" by importing scientists from other lands. More and more it is these foreign-born scientists who have been at the forefront of computer technology and biotech, accounting for 59 percent of all science and engineering degrees. They have been drawn by the promise of America and we have benefited from their contributions.

For sixty years, an enlightened immigration policy attracted the best and the brightest to our shores. Now, when our educational system is falling farther and farther behind and we find ourselves in critical need of more scientists and engineers, the U.S. Congress has yielded to xenophobia and the demagogues who thrive on it, to restrict the visas that enable these foreign-born scientists to work in America and contribute to technological progress here.

If we continue to keep our doors closed, these capable and valuable people will find a welcome sign in research institutes and industries in other nations. Moreover, although I favor liberalized immigration practices that would attract such valuable people, it is not a substitute for revitalizing our own educational system. Relying on an unending infusion of foreign brainpower is akin to our financial institutions and our government relying on foreign investment capital to compensate for our unwillingness to save and invest. Today's individual savings rate in America is at an all-time low and our personal debt is at an all-time high. Just the opposite holds true for most emerging economies in the world, like China and India, as well as developed economies like Japan. Eventually capital of all kinds will find new opportunities outside the United States and the brainpower that drives innovation will follow the money.

The need for this country to continue to lead the world in innovation—which is the only way we will remain competitive—can be addressed only if we invest the considerable resources required by our educational system. We must promote the sciences through public-private partnerships, grants, loans, tax credits, scholarships, and other incentives. We must encourage our best, most talented and most idealistic citizens to embrace teaching as a noble and necessary profession.

If the next generation is to remain competitive, it is not good enough to say we will maintain our current level of skills. As history has clearly shown, it is inevitable that as a society progresses and an economy matures, it will require a higher level of skills for its labor force to prosper. We will not advance in the twenty-first century by training our labor force for twentieth-century assembly-line jobs. Automation and other technological advances have ensured that there will continue to be fewer and fewer jobs in the global manufacturing sector and many of them will continue to be taken by lower-paid labor in developing countries. That is the direction of the world, and the era of the four o'clock whistle with millions of American workers, carrying their lunchboxes as they stream out of manufacturing facilities, fades more and more into the memories of a simpler time.

This dynamic is not confined to the United States; it is happening everywhere. The same technologies that have enhanced productivity in America's manufacturing sector, as well as in all sectors of our economy, are employed in the manufacturing sectors of other countries. The trend we see in manufacturing is the same one that we experienced over the past century in agriculture as mechanization replaced human labor. One hundred years ago, 35 percent of Americans worked on a farm or in agriculture. Today, because of dramatic increases in productivity due to improving agricultural technologies, science, and research, that number is 3 percent.

The workforce, both at home and abroad, has no choice but to learn new skills. That is why protectionism will not create jobs. We need instead to discover the means to enhance the skills of our workforce and to develop new markets here and abroad to allow our workers to compete effectively in the global marketplace. The market will demand that companies invest in human capital in the same way that they invest in more tangible assets. Smart companies will make this investment because it is in their interests.

Where will we find the new jobs to employ a more highly skilled workforce? The free market always outruns the professional prognosticators and economists. The record of America's economy is one of unpredictable and volatile changes that the most sophisticated long-term models could not predict. In 1982, when I cashed my insurance policies and sold my Buick and sank the proceeds into a cellular telephone start-up company, the cellular phone market worldwide was essentially zero. Today it is approximately $3 trillion.

Although I thought I was going to be a part of an important new technology, neither my partners nor I had any inkling of how truly revolutionary this technology would be. Or, to cite another example, thirty years ago if I said the words "operating system" you would have been excused if you guessed that I was talking about surgical procedures. Who would have thought that Bill Gates would generate hundreds of billions of dollars of business solely on the basis of what amounts to a digital rule book that tells computers how to go about their work? And then there is the most revolutionary technology of all—the Internet. If there has been one recent innovation that has transformed the world in every way in almost everything we do, it is the Internet. However, like all great technological leaps forward, it also comes with new challenges. How do we prevent it from invading our privacy, holding our lives hostage, compromising our finances, and spreading hatred?

There are a number of critical areas where there is now and will continue to be a need for a highly trained workforce, chief among them the energy sector. It is by now generally accepted that it will be more rather than less expensive for an increasingly ravenous global economy to consume carbon-based energy sources at the rates currently projected. The world produces and consumes eighty-six million barrels of oil a day and America consumes more than twenty million of these barrels. Today America depends on foreign sources for almost 70 percent of its daily oil requirements, and this percentage continues to increase each year. The unpredictability of cost and availability of oil will continue to affect the world economy and America's competitive position in it. The cost of oil rose to nearly one hundred dollars a barrel in late 2007. A significant amount of that black gold is supplied by countries in troubled regions of the world, such as the Middle East, Africa, and South America. As humanity consumes record amounts of oil and fossil fuels we continue to deepen our dependency on carbon-based sources of energy.

Affordable, accessible alternative and renewable energy sources are a requirement for our future. The urgent need for new energy technologies and sources, and the ability to deliver this energy, are probably the two greatest economic challenges and opportunities of our times. The answers will come in many ways as we develop new conservation technologies and new energy sources. Wind, solar, hydro, small-scale nuclear power, renewables such as ethanol and biodiesel, and technology-driven advances in clean coal technology all open up economic vistas as far-reaching as any that John D. Rockefeller contemplated in the infancy of the "age of petroleum." While China, to cite the most obvious example, is occupied churning out basic industrial products using older technologies and requiring large amounts of dirty coal and great quantities of oil, it behooves America to unlock the future energy sources to which the Chinese and other emerging nations will have to turn to sustain their new economies along with environmental accountability in coming decades. I say it behooves us because we have the labor pool, the infrastructure (if we maintain and modernize it), and the tradition of innovation within an economic system that facilitates and rewards entrepreneurship and risk taking. As Livy observed two thousand years ago, "There is nothing man will not attempt when great enterprises hold out the promise of great rewards." I can think of few enterprises with greater rewards than those waiting for whoever can meet these global energy demands.

The energy issue brings me to a related area—the environment and the question of global climate change. The debate revolving around who is for and who is against the environment is a false one. I have yet to meet anyone who is "against the environment." The more serious division is between those who merely decry the present and those who want to address its problems so that we have a brighter future. Again I see tremendous opportunities for which an economy like our own is supremely suited. It is relatively easy for an emerging economy to foul its air and water while heedlessly churning out mass-produced items. The pall that hangs over the new cities of China and Southeast Asia offers daily lung-clogging and eye-stinging evidence of this truth. On the other hand, to utilize energy cleanly, to conserve it through more efficient methods, to scrub the emissions and effluents of industry, to find economical ways to recycle the mountains of waste that accompany production and consumption—every one of these challenges represents huge economic opportunities that will require robust research and development and a skilled workforce.

Partnering with developing countries to assist them with their energy, economic, and environmental development will be the most critical and practical actions we can take to help these nations (representing most of mankind). Technology has always driven progress, so sharing technology with these developing countries in order to short-circuit their cycles of pollution-driven growth is a key to global environmental success. We cannot separate a nation's economic and energy needs from its environmental responsibilities.

Turning to another area of great promise, we live in a time when more people are living longer, healthier, and more active lives than ever before. Fulfilling the health-care needs of a graying demographic that is so much larger than in the past will require a new and innovative regimen of both prevention and treatment. Casting the net even more widely, the health-care needs of all generations will continue to bring huge financial rewards to those who develop new drugs and bring new well-care techniques to market, to cure the sick and to preserve good health through preventive medicine and the promotion of healthful lifestyles. When good health, or at least its possibility, is offered in the marketplace, the economic potential is enormous. Like they used to say about some chocolate milk product when I was a kid, "it's good and good for you."

Seen in this light—that is, that developed economies

and skilled workforces have their own unique and exciting opportunities—we may lay to rest a bogeyman and expose it for the chimera that it is. I am referring to "outsourcing," a perennial red-meat issue right up there alongside immigration. It's great fodder for cable news and radio talk show commentary, but the facts are not in favor of the knee-jerk outrage that the word conjures up. As we have seen, the jobs that have been lost, are, in large part, jobs that would have been lost in the long term anyway. America can't make cheaper wind-up toys or produce less expensive socks than the Chinese or the South Americans, nor are such products where our future lies.

Outsourcing of some manufacturing operations has in fact resulted in lower-cost goods for U.S. businesses and consumers, and more and better choices for both. I pay about the same for a pair of Levi's today as I did fifteen years ago. There are few other basics in life about which I can make the same claim.

Outsourcing cannot be understood as simply the number of jobs shipped overseas. It is more complicated. Companies can save and profit through the reduced costs gained by outsourcing some jobs. With expansion and additional revenues, more U.S. goods, services, and equipment are purchased to support outsourced industries. This also contributes to innovation, growth, and, over time, better and more jobs for America's most competitive industries and technologies. At the same time, economic growth in other nations creates markets capable of purchasing American goods and services. Ultimately, people's willingness to work—wherever in the world that may be—has never hurt the global economy or the American economy. It has strengthened it—even with the displacements, adjustments, and challenges of a global marketplace.

Our security and prosperity cannot be separated from our pre-eminent position in the global economy. As the largest, strongest, most flexible, and most sophisticated economy in the world (the 2006 U.S. gross domestic product [GDP] was $13.2 trillion—next closest was Japan's $4.3 trillion, and world GDP was $48.2 trillion), it remains the case that one cannot conceive of global prosperity that does not go hand in hand with a healthy U.S. economy. We are so vital to every other economy that the rest of the world has nearly as big a stake in our economic well-being as we do. Because of that interconnectedness, we need to remain open to the world marketplace.

Unfortunately, there is a protectionist streak in America today that is reflected by legislation in Congress and the deliberate slowing of and difficulty in ratifying trade agreements. Protectionism is a false safety net. It never helps long-term interests. While it may bring some immediate relief to endangered or declining sectors of the economy, it always has an overall injurious effect. Time and again we have seen this insular political impulse lead to isolationism at home and instability abroad. The free marketplace of ideas, goods, and services always wins.

After World War I, America pursued an isolationist foreign and trade policy that resulted in a weakened international order. While it was not the only underlying cause of World War II, it is also true that economic instability contributed to the rise of fascism which, in turn, unleashed the hounds of war. In contrast, after World War II, America's leaders laid the foundation for the World Trade Organization (WTO) and a new global political and economic order by creating such structures as the General Agreement on Tariffs and Trade. As a result, America and much of the world have enjoyed historic peace and prosperity for more than sixty years. Although this period was far from serene and trouble free, in comparison to the first half of the twentieth century, when we experienced two devastating and bloody world wars and the Great Depression, the time between 1945 and 2007 were spectacularly successful years.

All through these decades, trade—the daily flow of commerce between nations—has been the engine of growth, innovation, wealth, and job creation for America. A free and open global trading system has proved its remarkable power in raising standards of living, building a more peaceful world, and increasing individual opportunity. Although numbers can sometimes be mind-numbing, the sheer size of the growth of world trade is hugely impressive. Between 1948 and 2001, world exports rose from $58 billion to almost $6 trillion, and—not coincidentally—protectionist tariffs fell from an average of 40 percent to 4 percent. Between 1984 and 2004 American exports of goods and services rose from $291 billion to over $1.2 trillion. In those same years, U.S. employment figures rose from around 105 million workers in 1984 to nearly 140 million today.

Trade-stimulated growth brought the reconstruction of a war-ravaged Europe, and it is leading to higher standards of living today from Bangor to Bangkok and from Kamchatka to Capetown. Trade has brought new, more affordable products to our shores and at the same time has opened up unprecedented opportunities for the sale of U.S. products and services, as more prosperous people around the world seek out quality American goods, services, and agricultural products.

Like all real-world phenomena, world trade is not without its problems and challenges. Health and safety issues, unfair trade practices like dumping (selling goods in mass quantities below market price), intellectual property rights violations, and currency manipulation are all very real and objectionable parts of the global trading system. But we have been able to negotiate our path through these difficult issues in the past and we can in the future. That's why a world trading regimen like the WTO is so critically important. No institution or system is without its flaws and imperfections—just like human beings. And just as we do as individuals, we have to work at these issues and resolve them. They are man-made issues capable of man-made solutions.

Americans should welcome this new era of global competition, not cower from it. Since the era of the clipper ships, when our traders sought out the beckoning markets of Asia, international trade has been an essential part of our prosperity. It will be—must be—even more so in the future.

To lead in the twenty-first century, America needs to combine fiscally responsible policies with a commitment to trade. Our economic policies will influence and affect the shape and direction of America's domestic policies and programs, as well as political reform and change throughout the world. Now is not the time to retreat from our commitment to free trade, market economies, and democratic reforms. Free trade promotes stability and democracy in other nations. By pursuing free and fair trade, and by encouraging business and investment practices that contribute to more open societies at home and abroad, we can establish partnerships with developed and developing nations that contribute to peace while building prosperity.

Hopeful and well-fed peoples, while they may still covet their neighbors' riches, are less likely to stir themselves to war as long as there is the possibility of prosperity and progress at home. Nations that have vigorous trade relations are less likely to cause mischief abroad because the nations of the world trading community are shareholders in an enterprise that binds us all together and we all have a stake in its success. Global prosperity through free and fair trade will result in a reduction of our security commitments abroad, allowing for decreased expenditures required for peacekeeping, nation building, and force protection, in turn saving dollars and, more importantly, American lives. As other nations prosper they will take on new responsibilities and commitments to assure and enhance the security of a strong and vital global marketplace. It is the only way they can assure and protect their own self-interests.

Despite its marvels, trade is not a guarantee. It is an opportunity to be seized, not a prize to be claimed just by showing up. It requires an economy unburdened by crushing debt and confiscatory taxes, unshackled from investment-dampening regulation, and unthreatened by a legal culture of crippling and costly litigation. These four factors play a huge role in dampening the competitiveness of our capital markets. While it is true that worldwide prosperity is fostering the growth of new and deeper capital markets outside the United States, the historical primacy of Wall Street, by virtue of the strength, flexibility, and size of the American economy, can continue well into the future if we address the challenges that face it today.

Recent developments, though, can temper the enthusiasm of the most energetic America boosters. Look at the trends in international initial public offerings (IPOs)—one of the bellwethers of financial markets: In 2000, the United States had 50 percent of the total valuation of all global IPOs; in 2005, the United States had only 5 percent. In 2001, 57 percent of all global IPOs (valued at $1 billion or more) were listed on Wall Street. Five years later, in 2006, only 16 percent of all global IPOs were listed on Wall Street.

Or look at the equity markets. A total of $41.2 billion was raised on the Hong Kong Stock Exchange in 2006 compared with $37.3 billion in London and $29.3 billion in New York. Do these numbers mean that America is no longer a good investment bet? I don't think so. In part they are a reflection of increased opportunities all over the world, and this is good. It is part of an historic global diffusion of economic power—industrial, technological, agricultural, and energy-based.

America is still the core of the world economy; however, the rate of change occurring in every marketplace is rapid, intense, and challenging. We must address the deficiencies in our laws and tax and regulatory codes which, instead of attracting investment, can drive up the cost of doing business in America, making it much less attractive to foreign investors upon whom we have relied over the past few years to finance our large national debt.

Turning to health, anyone who has noticed the disappearance of the local family doctor or specialists such as ob/gyns in our rural areas is already familiar with the way in which skyrocketing malpractice insurance has impacted health care. This is just one aspect of the epidemic of litigation that afflicts our economy. In 1997, a mere eleven years ago, class-action settlements totaled $150 million. By 2006 they had risen to over $10 billion. This is not to say that all class-action suits are frivolous. They are not. Some address very real oversights, if not outright illegal and immoral actions. But at the same time, the fact remains that we have fostered a culture of litigation built on the premise of striking it rich in the class-action lottery. The result has been a chilling of the investment climate, giving pause to foreign companies contemplating investment in the United States

Equally chilling is our corporate tax policy. Corporate citizens should, of course, contribute to the national treasury just as private citizens must, but in order to remain competitive, we need a level international playing field. That is not where our current tax structure puts us. In the United States, federal and state governments combine to take an average of nearly 40 percent of taxes from corporate income. Compare that to other countries with fast-growing economies: Ireland has a corporate tax rate of 12.5 percent; Hong Kong's is 17.5 percent. These countries have seen investment and employment rise dramatically without harming their tax revenues.

Our high tax rate also affects our ability to compete in the global marketplace. Our current top individual capital gains tax rate of 15 percent puts us in the middle of the pack of the thirty nations within the Organization for Economic Cooperation and Development (OECD). China completely exempts domestic investors from capital gains taxes and recently extended that exemption to foreigners. Furthermore, the 39 percent U.S. corporate tax rate (including state corporate levies) is the second-highest tax rate among the thirty OECD member countries. Only Japan has a higher corporate tax rate. As other developed countries have lowered their tax rates, the United States has been transformed from a relatively low-tax country in the 1980s to a relatively high-tax state today. Germany, France, Japan, and Britain are moving toward corporate tax reduction, while China already has moved on a large corporate tax reduction. As U.S. Secretary of the Treasury Henry Paulson wrote last year,

> Maintaining our competitiveness in today's global environment requires us to think comprehensively and act prudently. As Europe's biggest economies and developing nations around the world move to reduce corporate taxes and gain the benefits for their workers that U.S. workers already enjoy, now is an opportune time, when our economy is in a position of strength, to consider ways our business tax system can be improved.

He's right.

Capital gains taxes place another layer of tax burdens on American companies. These taxes affect our global competitiveness by making the United States a less attractive place for foreign investment. They discourage growth, investment, and savings, and undermine the entrepreneurship and risk-taking that are the foundations of our economy's success.

These issues of tax and regulatory policy and tort reform, though politically charged, must be addressed by a Congress and executive with the courage to exert leadership, whatever the political consequences. Likewise, the challenges of infrastructure, workforce skills, and new industries are no greater than those we have faced in the past. America has always found the inner strength to rise to any test. That is all to the good, because the biggest challenge is one that we have been unwilling to confront and constantly put off in hopes that it will go away. It is a greater drain on our economic well-being than any foreign competition. I am speaking of the heavy, dark, and ominous cloud that hangs over future generations—entitlement programs.

CHAPTER 15

ENTITLED?

n an October 19, 1998 letter to my fifty-four Senate Republican colleagues during the Fiscal Year 1999 Budget Debate, I wrote the following:

> Our most basic responsibility as elected public officials is to be accountable to the people. We should have the courage and the honesty to put our judgment and careers on the line and vote on how we intend to spend the taxpayer's money . . . I don't believe the Founding Fathers ever intended for a few members and staff to make closed door, arbitrary decisions on almost one third of the federal budget and then sneak it through on a voice vote . . .
>
> The American people turned over the Congress to the Republican Party four years ago. I believe they did so because they were fed up with the arrogance and corruption that often overtakes large institutions. Congress

is no different. We promised the American people that we would be different. We would be accountable, honest, and straight-forward. We would cut government spending, taxes, and regulations . . .

We in this Republican-controlled Congress run the risk of squandering the opportunity America has given us. Leaders lead through the force of trust, honesty, credibility, and confidence. We must show America that we can lead and govern and do what we said we would do. If we don't, we will be cast aside as the Democrats were in 1994. The American people will find a government as good as they are—even if it takes years of bobbing up and down with different Congresses. America deserves better . . .

Why are we in the United States Senate? To accomplish what? The easy votes? The lowest common denominator of government? These are the questions each of us must ask ourselves. If we are unwilling to make the tough decisions, then who will?

I was moved to write that letter because of my growing concern for the way that government was bankrupting the future of the nation. It occurred to me at the time—and often since then— that if my congressional colleagues and I were corporate officers, we could very well be indicted and convicted for a straightforward case of cooking the books. While commentators often take the American people to task for not saving enough, how can you expect people to save when their government functions by piling up debt upon more debt, endlessly deferring the difficult decisions that will be required to prioritize our national obligations and resources?

The money Congress spends is not the government's money. It's the people's money. They earned it. They worked for it. It's up to us to spend it wisely and responsibly. That means that we who have the privilege of leading this nation also have the responsibility to look ahead, preparing and planning for the strategy and the means to take on the great challenges that will face us over the next generation.

The impending retirement of the seventy-seven-million-strong "baby boom" generation—my generation—will impact every aspect of our economy, government, and society, including health care, the workforce, and our competitive position in a community of nations with young and eager workers. In 2007 the nation's first baby boomer applied for Social Security benefits. Here we go!

The next generation of Americans will respond to these challenges as every generation has responded: with innovation and hard work. However, my generation has a moral obligation to ensure that this next generation is not saddled with financing crushing entitlement burdens that will affect their ability to compete. That is why we must reform our entitlement programs, starting with Social Security, which is based on a 1935 model trying to operate in the twenty-first century. It will soon be incapable of delivering the promises and resources that it was built to provide.

Over the years, former Federal Reserve chairman Alan Greenspan and I would often meet for breakfast in his office at the Fed. These were instructive and engaging opportunities to exchange ideas with one of the most incisive and wide-ranging thinkers of our time. Plus, I like Greenspan and enjoy his company. A topic we discussed at almost every breakfast was the need for Congress to act on modernizing entitlement programs "sooner rather than later." Greenspan has consistently warned that unless we act now to confront the huge unfunded liabilities facing our entitlement programs, our nation will inevitably face "severe" economic consequences. He is right.

America's largest entitlement programs, Social Security, Medicare, and Medicaid, are on a trajectory that cannot be sustained. For FY 2007, the Congressional Budget Office tells us that 62 percent of the $2.7 trillion budget will be obligated to mandatory spending (of which 44 percent is for these three programs). Those are tax dollars that are committed, money that cannot be used for anything else. Each year the percentage of the budget obligated to funding entitlement programs grows larger and larger. The current unfunded liability for Social Security over the next seventy-five years is almost $5 trillion. Medicare's unfunded liability during this same period is nearly $34 trillion, and Medicaid faces an $8.5 trillion shortfall. That's an unfunded total of $47 trillion. This is an unfathomable amount of money and the American people are obligated to pay it. Add to that America's current total national debt of almost $9 trillion.

We have dug ourselves into a very deep hole.

One entitlement in particular, Medicare, is growing faster than any other government program. As all health-care costs continue to rise, coupled with the growing number of retirees, there will be enormous pressure on our federal budget to divert money from important discretionary government programs like defense, research, intelligence, education, roads, parks, housing programs, etc.

Another entitlement, Social Security, is not in crisis today, but there is clearly a crisis on the horizon. It is within our power to preserve the social safety net of this nation. It has been done before. The Greenspan Social Security Commission presented their recommendations to fix Social Security in January 1983, and Congress enacted many of them three months later. As part of the reform, Congress accelerated a scheduled increase in the payroll tax, phased in a raise of the retirement age, added federal and nonprofit workers to Social Security (they were not subject to Social Security taxes before), and delayed a cost-of-living adjustment.

Now, twenty-five years later, we are faced with need of reform once again. The earlier we confront this reality, the more options we will have to come up with a sustainable course of action. President Bush made Social Security reform the centerpiece of his domestic agenda following his reelection, but was never able to muster support for it because he only put forward "principles" for reform that emphasized personal accounts. This allowed opponents of reform to cast the debate as being about the privatization of Social Security, rather than the solvency of the Social Security system.

Because of these entitlement programs and runaway federal government spending in other areas, America, with the world's largest economy, paradoxically finds itself in long-term financial trouble. Our national debt held by the public is over $5 trillion. About half is held by foreign investors and governments. Every day, just to make our interest payments on this debt, someone—the Saudis, the Chinese, the Europeans—must invest $2 billion to $3 billion in our Treasury bonds and notes. This is a critical line of defense for America, because as a nation we have no private capital reserve to draw from.

How could this have happened? Although the numbers are stunningly large, the math could not be more simple. The most recent budget (FY 2008) is about $3 trillion. Here's where the money goes: 63 percent is already obligated to pay for interest on the national debt, government retirement plans, veteran's benefits, and the three big entitlement programs (Social Security, Medicare, and Medicaid). That leaves almost a third of the Federal budget, so-called discretionary funds, or about $960 billion for the president and Congress to decide where it goes. All other federal government spending not mentioned above must come from these discretionary funds. Worse still, as the cost of entitlements goes up every year, that discretionary percentage of the budget gets smaller, and within the discretionary market basket the defense percentage keeps growing, crowding out all the other important requirements for our country. One of these days there will be no money for anything but war, debt, and entitlements.

You might say—and many have suggested—that all of this is happening because we are undertaxed: supposedly we could raise enough money by rolling back tax cuts for the wealthy. The fact is that we are currently collecting record tax revenues. The more fundamental problem is that we continue to spend more than we're taking in. Still, taxing the rich is a very popular theme whenever campaign season comes along. You go after the "fat cats" who are said to be swimming in vaults full of greenbacks like Donald Duck's Uncle Scrooge.

The tax-the-rich solution is not that simple. While I strongly believe that people who do better should pay more, I know that you cannot tax at a rate that inhibits capital formation. If we're going to compete globally, then we're going to have to be competitive tax-wise. The main reason that investors are willing to put their money in U.S. companies and bonds is because America rewards risk takers and has the most stable economy in the world. John Kennedy, who was far from the shrink-the-government school of leadership, was a strong advocate of tax cuts because he knew that a free-market economy constantly required new investment for jobs, research, and technology, thereby fueling the engine of progress: productivity.

So our fiscal plight is not due to taxes being too low. Instead, I would suggest that we have a lack of presidential and congressional fiscal discipline and leadership, and a failure to prioritize our goals and resources. The world financial community has taken notice of this lack of discipline and will respond accordingly.

Here's what I mean by lack of discipline and leadership. Look at the way we have accounted for the Iraq and Afghanistan wars. When you review the total budget, more than half of the discretionary money is obligated to the Department of Defense. You tell yourself, "That's okay. We're fighting two wars and war is costly." True enough, but of the $10 billion a month being spent in Iraq and another $2 billion a month for Afghanistan, most of that money does not appear in the budget (although our creditors are well aware that we have taken on those financial obligations).

Why is it not a liability on America's balance sheet? Because it is considered "supplemental" or "emergency" spending.

Supplemental spending is not counted in our budget process; it is not carried as a budget liability—it's like magic money! For example, since 2001 President Bush has sent ten emergency supplemental appropriations requests to the Congress, totaling $820 billion. We have been financing the wars in Iraq and Afghanistan through these sleight-of-hand appropriations, not through the regular oversight process in congressional hearings. No wonder our budget and fiscal policy is in shambles.

But the money does come from somewhere and still has to be accounted for. The administration and Congress have been very clever with smoke-and-mirror tactics like "forward funding" and "thirteen-month budgets." It allows the president to use the terms "balanced budget" in his State of the Union. At the very same time that he makes this claim, the president sends up billions of dollars in off-budget supplemental emergency requests. Although none of these supplementals has been included in the budget, each of them has added more to our national debt than the combined national deficits of the first 170 years of the Republic. (As a point of reference, the United States first surpassed the $100 billion public debt level in 1943—at the height of World War II.)

Where does that money come from? Who pays? Ultimately, the American people will have to pay. Such trickery is no different from the accounting practices of Enron, WorldCom, Tyco, and Qwest. That's why those swindlers are in the penitentiary making license plates.

The duplicity doesn't end with defense spending. For example, Social Security is off-budget, meaning we don't account for it or pay for it in our annual federal budget. Payroll taxes fund Social Security. In this way, Social Security is essentially a transfer payment system. The payments into the system from current workers are transferred as benefits to retirees. The way we got to a so-called balanced budget in 1998 and the big budget surpluses of the last two years of the Clinton administration was mainly due to a surplus in the Social Security trust fund. We counted those surpluses as part of our annual federal budget—which they are not.

The Social Security actuaries tell us that by 2017, more money will be paid out of the trust fund than has been accrued as surplus. As we continue to draw down those surpluses, by the year 2041 there will only be enough money in the fund to pay 75 percent of what we're obligated to pay for the seventy-seven million baby boomers and their children who will be going on the entitlement rolls over the next few decades. We are on an actuarial course that cannot be sustained.

But the problem can be fixed.

We would do well to go back to the words of Franklin D. Roosevelt when he signed the Social Security Act of 1935. "None of the sums of money paid out to individuals in assistance or insurance will spell anything approaching abundance. But they will furnish that minimum necessity to keep a foothold; and that is the kind of protection Americans want."

Over the years we've drifted from the original intent of Social Security and, in many cases, framed it as the main or sole means of retirement. No matter how we choose to restructure Social Security, we need to reenergize the idea of individuals taking some personal responsibility for their own retirement. We need to create a system that encourages and incentivizes people to save and to build their own personal wealth.

In other words, Social Security was not designed to be, and cannot be, the sum total of our seniors' retirement funds. It was meant as a safety net from destitution and ruin. As is the case with many American families, Social Security has been very important to my family, particularly my mother's parents. My grandfather, Joseph Patrick Dunn, was a small farmer outside of Wood River, Nebraska. He was an Irishman, and anybody with any Irish blood in him knows we like our spuds. He often told me that many times in those hardscrabble years of the 1930s when he was struggling to save his farm, dinner consisted of baked potatoes. When my brothers and I would spend time with Grandpa and Grandma Dunn, I marveled at the way he would surgically engage that magnificent Irish staple. He celebrated that big white hunk crowned with butter, salt, and pepper, and he made it last as long as a gourmet meal, which it was to him.

Not unlike many of the farmers of his day, he didn't have much, and was eventually forced to leave the farm. The family moved to Grand Island. Joe and Katie Konkolewski Dunn had six daughters, my mom being the fourth. Grandma and Grandpa rolled up their sleeves and found work in real estate, nursing, and other jobs to support their family. All six Dunn girls worked during high school, and my aunt Amelda eventually went to college for two years. As my grandparents grew older, Grandpa Dunn took sick and couldn't work. Social Security allowed them to keep their home.

Years later my mother, brothers, and I were beneficiaries of Social Security. On Christmas morning 1962, when I was sixteen years old, my mother woke me up. "Something has happened to your dad," she screamed. I ran into their bedroom where I found my father dead of a heart attack. Later that morning, after the ambulance had taken my father away and our neighbors, the Murphys, had returned to their home across the street, we found ourselves suddenly alone—now there was just my mother and her four sons. She said to me, "Chuck, you're going to have to be the man of the family now. I'm going to need your help to raise your brothers." Fortunately, she had some other help too, in the form of the Social Security Old Age Survivors and Disability Insurance Program.

My brothers and I all worked in different jobs during school. I worked at Frank Murphy's Texaco station and junkyard, Tom Riley's Chevron station, and the Jack and Jill Grocery Store. In the summers I worked on highway paving crews for Gerhold Concrete Company, and for Cornhusker Public Power, cutting trees and trimming power lines. My brothers, as they grew older, also had jobs like working all-night shifts at local manufacturing companies and driving eighteen-wheelers. Mom's job was at Cornhusker Public Power District. Even with all of us pitching in, though, I don't know how my mother would have been able to keep the family together with a roof over our heads without those monthly Social Security checks. You could see the terrible strain go out of her face each month when she opened the brown government envelope with the green check inside.

So I understand that Social Security is one of the best things to come out of the New Deal because my family and I are grateful products of the program. Today, Social Security provides benefits for families who find themselves in the same straits that my family and I did in 1962. Monthly benefits are paid out to more than six and a half million spouses and children of breadwinners who died prematurely or became disabled.

There is no escaping the fact that Social Security is necessary, and there is also no escaping the fact that something needs to be done about the future of Social Security. We need to preserve, protect, and improve it.

In the 109th Congress and again in the 110th Congress, I introduced legislation (the Saving Social Security Act of 2005) that addressed the future of Social Security. Fundamentally, it was based on simple demographics. When Social Security was first enacted in 1935, the average life span for Americans was sixty-three; today it is seventy-seven, and in 2041 it will be eighty. In addition, in 1935 there were many more young workers than retirement-age seniors. In 1935 there were forty-two workers per retiree; in 1950, there were sixteen workers per retiree; in

2007 there were 3.3 workers per retiree; and in 2041 there will be just 2.1 workers per retiree. So to boil it down to the basics, there are more older people and they are living longer, at the same time that there are fewer younger people in the workforce. In terms of the present Social Security system, these numbers do not compute.

In the simplest terms, the solution I proposed took cognizance of today's demographic realities. Let me preface this by saying that I am well aware that many Americans are already far along in their working lives, making contributions to Social Security in the expectation that they can retire at full benefits when they are sixty-six . . . gradually increasing to age sixty-seven for those who turn 62 from 2017 to 2022. It would be unfair to change the rules of the game now that they have advanced so far. In my bill, for those workers forty-five and over, Social Security would remain exactly as it is today. We made a commitment to those people and we should honor it.

The changes that I am talking about would have begun to take effect for those who turn 62 in the year 2023. Retirement at full benefits would be moved up a year, from sixty-seven to sixty-eight. Workers could still take early retirement at age sixty-two, but at a benefit level of 63 percent rather than the current 70 percent of full benefits. Significantly, for the first time in the seventy-three-year history of Social Security, benefits would have been calculated and adjusted according to life expectancy. Social Security never altered its benefit calculations based on this factor. By factoring increased life expectancy into the base benefit calculation, the payout could be adjusted. In other words, because people are living longer and collecting longer, the monthly check would be a little bit less.

Workers currently under the age of forty-five would slowly be eased into this re-engineered system. They would also be given the opportunity—the option—to invest part of their Social Security payroll taxes (less than 33 percent) in well-defined mutual funds. This arrangement is modeled on the Federal Thrift Savings Plan through which Federal employees—including every member of the House and Senate—receive their retirement pensions. These investment funds would come under the oversight and careful stewardship of a board of directors that would include the secretary of the treasury, the chairman of the Federal Reserve Board, the chairman of the Securities and Exchange Commission, and two Senate-confirmed appointments, nominated by the president.

It is true that there is no guarantee with such market-based investments: however, the historical success of the market is not a theory. In no fifteen-year period in the past eight decades has the growth of stocks ever been negative; in no twenty-year period has the average growth been less than 3 percent, which exceeds the rate of return on present Social Security assets.

Under my plan, Social Security is guaranteed to remain solvent for at least seventy-five years as scored by the Social Security administration. Granted, that's not forever, but it's much better than going broke by 2041, which is where Social Security will be if we don't make some changes. Dealing with this problem now means facing less dramatic and difficult choices down the road.

The earlier we confront the reality of this impending crisis, the more options we will have to come up with a responsible and sustainable course of action.

The other two big entitlements, Medicare and Medicaid, are more difficult problems to solve because they have become so deeply interwoven into our country's health-care system. Health-care costs are growing faster than any other sector in our economy. Hence, Medicare costs are growing faster than any other government program. As we see health-care costs continue to rise, coupled with the growing number of retirees, it will only continue to put more and more pressure on our federal budget, threatening the funding of other important discretionary government programs. As a senator, I hear about the rising cost of health care every day. It is an issue that touches the lives of all Americans.

Medicare drives health care today and, like Social Security, it is on an unsustainable trajectory. Over the next seventy-five years, the Medicare Part A trust fund (hospital insurance) faces a nearly $12 trillion unfunded commitment and will be exhausted in 2019. Medicare Part B (supplementary medical insurance) faces an unfunded commitment of $14 trillion; Medicare Part D (prescription drugs) faces an $8.5 trillion unfunded commitment. And during this same period Medicaid faces an $8.5 trillion liability.

I think an experience that is shared by every American—and one that throws this health-care crisis into bold relief—is the sticker shock that sets in when you see how much a particular drug costs. The solution is not, however, as some have proposed, to put the drug companies on the price-control leash that countries with national health plans have them on. Think about it. Yes, drugs cost a lot, but at least we have them to gripe about while they are saving and bettering our lives. Have pharmaceutical companies been well remunerated for this? Yes, they have. Unfairly? Well, that's a debatable point. But we have to be very careful in whatever action we take so that we don't dry up sources of risk capital that will be required to continue to help our society find cures for our most dreaded diseases and produce the research and drugs that will help accomplish this. Before you scrap the current system, I would urge you to step back for a broader look. If you consider the assortment of drugs available today to the average American citizen, even people on Medicaid (at the bottom of the income ladder) have the latest drugs available to them.

An additional factor driving costs is the expectation in this country that we're all entitled—every one of us—to the newest technologies, medicines, and treatments no matter the cost. Is it every American's birthright to have access to every medical possibility no matter the expense or who pays for it? It would be nice if we didn't have to worry about costs and who pays the bills. It would also be nice if, as Merle Haggard once sang, "We'll all be drinking that free Bubble Up and eating that Rainbow Stew." The real world doesn't work that way. What we can do, and need to do, is find a way to guarantee every American accessible, affordable, quality health care. There can be no caste system when it comes to health care, which is why we must fix the problem now—or affordable quality health care will be priced beyond many Americans' ability to pay for it. We must not allow this to happen.

These health-care problems are exceedingly complex and will not be solved with slogans or any single legislative "magic bullet." But we will never make any inroads until we devote the leadership, time, discipline, and resources to fix things. That is why, along with Democratic Representative John Tanner of Tennessee, I introduced in both the 109th and 110th Congresses a bill to create an independent, bipartisan commission charged with making recommendations on how to preserve our entitlement programs.

In 2006, I empaneled a health-care commission comprised of fifteen health-care professionals from across the state of Nebraska and the country. The commission's mandate was simple. I asked them to review the current state of health care in the United States and present recommendations for developing an accessible and sustainable system for the twenty-first century. Over the course of a year, the commission met eleven times with experts and organizations from every sector of health care. In February 2007 they presented me with a comprehensive set of recommendations.

I used their recommendations as the basis for legislation I introduced later that year called the Federal Health Care Board Act of 2007. The board would serve as a nonpartisan framework and mechanism to address the looming heath-care crisis. This board would be an independent federal government agency modeled after the Federal Reserve Board. It would do the following:

1. Establish a national standard for a basic health plan to cover all Americans. This would be a basic minimum policy and would have a set regional cost.
2. Establish a national protocol and standards for secure and universal individual electronic medical records.
3. Implement a structure for the disclosure of pricing from providers and payers through an informational clearinghouse.
4. Establish a national standard for public health services (safety net providers).
5. Create loan forgiveness and scholarship programs for providers in underserved areas.
6. Establish a model for mandatory dispute resolution for malpractice claims.

I expect that there will be more panels and more legislation offered before we get our arms around the entitlements question. What is inescapable is that America needs and will demand a president and a Congress committed to enacting entitlement reform. There are few higher priorities for the future of this country. It will have a defining effect on America's capacity to compete in the marketplace of the twenty-first century.

It will require America to summon what is needed most, when it is most needed.

Leadership.

PART IV

LEADERSHIP

CHAPTER 16

MY MOUNT RUSHMORE

mong the things I have most looked forward to as a United States senator were the occasional visits of former heads of state like German Chancellor Helmut Schmidt. As part of his annual world tour he would often stop in at Room 248 of the Russell Senate Office Building (my office). He singled me out for a house call, I think, because he knew of my interest in world affairs, and also because we liked one another and I always listened closely to what he had to say. He was in his eighties the last time I saw him, bent with age but still sharp as ever. He would always come with a couple of handlers—serious young men in dark suits from the German embassy.

No sooner was he seated in my "no-smoking office" than he would pull out an elegant cigarette case and select what appeared to be a fancy, unfiltered cigarette like James Bond used to smoke (back in the days when smoking was still glamorous). Invariably my assistants would register a look of total shock. Smoking in the

Senate Office Buildings and in particular the senator's personal office? Verboten.

"Please see if we can find the chancellor an ashtray," I would say, and my assistants would scramble for a make-do ashtray for the chancellor. He would light up, take a long drag, exhale contentedly and, with the air of a man who had just finished an excellent meal, ask for coffee: black—no cream, no sugar—the sturdier the better. We would exchange pleasantries until, having finished the cigarette part of his performance, he would tide himself over with a pinch of snuff. He would whip that stuff out and sniff it down in a blur. I never saw anybody move faster.

Finally, having established his zone of comfort, he would sit back and opine. "Vell, Senator," he said the last time I saw him. "We are living in one of those dreary times in history when there are no great leaders. The last time the world had leaders was the early 1980s: Thatcher, Mitterrand, Kohl, Reagan, Gorbachev. They were all significant leaders. Look at what we have today . . ." His voice trailed off. He raised his eyebrows and spread his arms. "No leaders."

I remember this particular conversation very well: not only for its candor, but also because, echoing the chancellor's bleak mood, the sky had grown very dark. The aftermath of hurricane Isabel was bearing down on Washington. Schmidt's aides looked nervously at their watches, anxious to catch the train to New York before the storm stranded them. Everyone else had cleared out of the Senate buildings, but Schmidt would have none of it. He roared at his aides, "Ach! Nein!" and dismissed their concerns with the kind of disdainful grimace that does not invite further comment.

He wanted to make a point. "There is a vacuum waiting to be filled. It will be filled, but whether it will be filled by good leaders or bad leaders—that is the issue."

Over the years, I have thought long and hard about the question of leadership. It's one of those things that is hard to define but we all know it when we see it. It's an instinctive recognition. It is much more than the words leaders speak or how they deliver them. Many politicians have a gift for language and eloquence, but they are not necessarily leaders. Nor does it have to do with just brainpower. Granted you need to have some intelligence, but there are many more intelligent people than there are leaders. Leaders are people with whom we connect on a gut level. For whatever reason, we decide, "this is a person I trust—I connect with—I agree with—and I like."

This is not to say that people don't make the wrong decisions about leaders. The history books are full of examples of leaders who brought their nations to ruin. They abused the trust people put in them—but the critical fact is, they were able to gain that trust to start with.

Part of the bond of trust between leaders and followers is the sense that the leader genuinely believes in something. If he doesn't, he will surely be found out when events test him (for the sake of brevity only, I'm using the word "him"). That bedrock belief—at the core of any leader—is the soul of leadership. That doesn't mean that you can't change your mind, or that you won't listen to and evaluate differing opinions. You are limited if you don't. But fundamentally you must have a core belief rather than trimming your sails and zigzagging to and fro as polls and advisors trend one way or the other. You've got to be directed, motivated, and anchored to something far greater than the next set of polls or even your next election. If you do not have the courage to do that, you're not worthy of being a leader. The essence of leadership starts at the core of the individual. My dear and trusted friend and a man I admire immensely, John Becker, once reminded me of the often quoted but nonetheless brilliant advice of Polonius in *Hamlet*: "to thine own self be true."

Leaders, like everyone else, are products of a certain time and place. In that regard, their personal experiences help form the vision by which they lead. Take President Lyndon Baines Johnson, for example. Right now, I'm looking at a book on my desk, *A Tale of Two Quagmires: Iraq, Vietnam, and the Hard Lessons of War* by Kenneth Campbell. History remembers LBJ for his wrongheaded prosecution of a war that could not be won. But on the domestic side of the ledger, there was another, far-reaching side to his presidency.

Johnson's upbringing was very Lincolnesque. He lived in homes with dirt floors and no heat. The Depression hit him very hard. He had a visceral understanding of what it means to live without the most basic necessities. Having come up from the bottom, he had a natural feeling for the disadvantaged. The tenacity and drive that it took to rise from those circumstances served him well when, as president, he took on the problems of poverty and discrimination. That's what propelled him in the two great achievements of his term: Medicare and the Civil Rights Act. They redefined the social and political landscape of the nation.

His advisors, including Jack Valenti and Georgia Senator Richard Russell, told him that civil rights would cost him his political future. They told him that his stance on this issue would permanently lose the South for the Democratic Party. They were half right. His political career collapsed, but because of Vietnam, not civil rights. And the once-solid South did become Republican "red" on the electoral map. Still, his vision, courage, and foresight on health care and civil rights, as well as his superb tactical knowledge of Congress, enabled him to hammer these historic pieces of legislation through the House and Senate. Had Johnson come from a different background, I doubt that he would have been driven to attack these issues. When he spoke, most Americans trusted him, because we believed he spoke the truth, from the heart.

John F. Kennedy embodies a more classic example of leadership: leadership born of privilege and tempered by a strong sense of public service. During the Cuban missile crisis, which was a defining moment for so many in my generation, Kennedy stood alone at a moment of peril unlike any faced by an American president, as our country and the Soviet Union teetered on the brink of nuclear conflict. Had Kennedy given in to the pressure to move either more harshly or more timidly than he ultimately did, he could have unleashed a series of events that could have obliterated our world and humanity along with it. Instead,

Kennedy followed a steady, creative, and ultimately successful diplomatic course.

Kennedy, like all Presidents, had his failings. But over the course of the thirteen days that made up the Cuban missile crisis, he provided a measure of leadership that cannot be overstated. As I have studied this conflict, I believe that it was Kennedy himself (Kennedy the man, the complete person: life experience, judgment, personality, faith, leader, politician, father) who made the difference between nuclear holocaust and a responsible and peaceful settlement. History might have taken a very different course had it been another president making the decisions for the future of mankind in October 1962. He had the strength of character and confidence of purpose to shape events, rather than be helplessly swept up in the tide of events. It is interesting to note that through this entire time he had the added strength and steadiness of his brother, his most trusted advisor.

Nearly fifty years after he became president, Kennedy still personifies political inspiration and leadership. In more recent times, a Republican who similary inspired his countrymen was another American of Irish heritage, Ronald Reagan. I don't know where Reagan will come out on a list of good and great presidents. History must sort things out a bit more before that verdict is handed down.

Like many other presidents, Reagan was a product of tough times. His father drank too much, and the Great Depression hit his part of Illinois as full-on as any place in the country. In effect, it pulled the rug out from under the small-town, neighbor-helping-neighbor way of life that epitomized the values Reagan would always strive to recapture. Those were the roles, epitomizing old-fashioned American values, that were most meaningful for him as an actor. But eventually he realized that reading somebody else's lines for imaginary characters was not enough.

Thus the actor entered public service. He always knew what he believed in and he was a master at sharing that vision with others.

His great contribution was that he did not fail the country, or the world, at a time when he was needed. He helped America begin to believe in itself again. Communism did not fail because Ronald Reagan called it evil. It failed because it was flawed from the start. Reagan, speaking from the heart, and from his gut, was steadfast in his opposition to Communism, although this never stopped him from engaging the Soviets and negotiating with them.

Perhaps a less forceful president would have kept the Soviets thinking that they could somehow hold on and eventually prevail. Reagan was not a philosopher nor, on the other hand, much of a detail man, but he was unflappable and immovable on the question of "Communism versus freedom." He knew who he was and what he believed. As Nicholas Lemann, writing in *The New Yorker* observed, "The world does not change according to anyone's plan. Reagan's relation to the fall of the Soviet Union brings to mind Tolstoy's maxim in *War and Peace*, 'It is only unself-conscious activity that bears fruit, and the man who plays a part in a historical drama never understands its true significance.'"

Although I don't agree with every aspect of his political philosophy, it is nonetheless hard to overlook, in a chapter on leadership, the president who led us the longest—helping to lift us from the dark cloud of the Depression and inspire us through one of America's greatest challenges, the Second World War. Through the New Deal, Franklin Delano Roosevelt effected profound changes in the social contract between the government and the governed. Like his cousin, Teddy, he was a child of wealth and privilege, but there must have been something in the Roosevelt family's DNA that allowed them to understand the trials of the common man struggling to make ends meet. I have always thought that one of the reasons FDR was able to come to grips with the needs of the broad mass of the American people, and especially those who were in some way seriously disadvantaged in life, was because of his own very painful and difficult struggle with polio. When he spoke, people felt his compassion and depth of understanding of the human condition. Without Social Security, which he brought into being, I probably would not be where I am today. And without the great public works of that era we would not be the same nation we are today. As much as he felt the needs and touched the hearts of Americans, he also moved their spirits. FDR's Four Freedoms, first enunciated before Congress on January 6, 1941, encapsulated the promise of America as succinctly and fully as any statement of national purpose I ever read.

In the future days, which we seek to make secure, we look forward to a world founded upon four essential human freedoms.

The first is freedom of speech and expression—everywhere in the world.

The second is freedom of every person to worship God in his own way—everywhere in the world.

The third is freedom from want—which, translated into world terms, means economic understandings which will secure to every nation a healthy peacetime life for its inhabitants—everywhere in the world.

The fourth is freedom from fear—which, translated into world terms, means a world-wide reduction of armaments to such a point and in such a thorough fashion that no nation will be in a position to commit an act of physical aggression against any neighbor—anywhere in the world.

That is no vision of a distant millennium. It is a definite basis for a kind of world attainable in our own time and generation. That kind of world is the very antithesis of the so-called new order of tyranny which the dictators seek to create with the crash of a bomb.

All of the leaders I have mentioned stepped into their roles based on their ability to inspire trust. In this regard each leader's background and life story is important if we want to understand why they were who they were. Not as the subject of a teary-eyed campaign film to be shown at a national political convention, but rather as a glimpse into the character of the men and women who would lead us. Personal history imprints an outlook on the world that helps define where each leader hopes to take the country and how he or she will assess our needs.

For example, for generations our national leaders knew and understood the profound and terrible tearing of the social fabric brought on by war. Having seen war's horrors firsthand, leaders who were veterans helped steady the country's course and calm the passions of the moment before sending our youth into the fire of battle.

This is not to say that you have to be a veteran to be a smart, wise, or strong leader. But it does mean that we are all products of our experiences; we are products of our environments; we are products of where we come from. Regardless of jobs or philosophies, we all are shaped and molded by our early experiences. If a leader goes to war or talks about committing a nation to war, leaders who are veterans are very careful because they understand, as I have said before, that it is very easy to get into a war, but so terribly difficult to get out of one. Veterans also understand that sometimes there is no other alternative, but it's their searing personal experiences that help them to look at the totality of the picture before taking the fateful first step into war. So to put a spin on common political wisdom, while it is true to an extent that "all politics is local," it is equally true, if not more so, that leadership is always personal.

Insofar as leadership is personal, every leader takes his cue from people he has known, people who have inspired him. Some of them are well known to history and some barely known outside their family or circle of friends. We don't always choose the people who influence us. The words and actions, and above all, the examples that role models set, help make us who we are. In that respect, each of us has his or her own personal Mount Rushmore, representing people who inspired and influenced us.

Before telling you who I would add to that magnificent South Dakota mountain, let's first look at the leaders whose faces currently peer down from Rushmore.

George Washington—it is thanks to his example that our system of checks and balances has survived to this day. He could easily have claimed for himself the title of king or emperor or president for life. They were all offered and he declined them. He could have remained president for as long as he desired. It was Washington who set the framework and the political culture for our country by walking away from limitless power and stepping aside when his term was up: a rare action in the annals of history.

His farewell address, like many subsequent sign-offs from our presidents, was a big-picture document. I recommend that you read it. Even if you have read it before, read it again now. Its wisdom, gained from the experience of setting up a new government founded on new principles, is as valuable today as it was in 1796. It is a document of lofty ideas, but just as much it is a document full of practical recommendations. In it he warns of the danger of parties, factionalism, and political conflict.

Perhaps even more memorably, his view of America's role in the world bears rereading in light of current events. His advice to stay clear of "foreign entanglements," rather than being the call for isolationism that some have taken it to be, reflects a clear assessment of the relations between nations. "There can be no greater error," he wrote, "than to expect or calculate upon real favors from nation to nation. It is an illusion which experience must cure . . . " This, in my understanding, is a prescription for a foreign policy based on reality rather than wishes or divine mission, and it is advice that our leaders would have done well to heed before venturing into Iraq.

Abraham Lincoln—one of our greatest leaders, perhaps the greatest, in part because no American president was ever tested the way that he was. Had he been president in another time, without the question of slavery and the inviolability of the Union on his docket, he might simply be remembered as a compassionate and wise man. But those two historical tests, and his ability to lead, inspire, and accomplish, raise him above all the others. Character, courage, and competence, the three indispensable qualities in any leader, were never more clearly on display than in his tortured but ultimately triumphant administration. If it is true that the Declaration of Independence set forth the principle of the rights of all men, Lincoln's Gettysburg address—a monument of clear, noble, and compelling political language—sealed the bargain, securing those rights for every citizen, black and white, northerner and rebel.

Thomas Jefferson—a brilliant man. He penned the Declaration of Independence. Jefferson dreamed very big dreams, but he had the ability and strength of leadership to make them come true. The Louisiana Purchase was probably the single most important factor in the transformation of a string of ex-colonies into a nation whose Manifest Destiny would extend across the continent.

Teddy Roosevelt—a strong, bold, and visionary president.

Roosevelt came to power because the McKinley machine selected him as McKinley's running mate. That role would have guaranteed that as vice president, instead of being a party reformer and a problem for the Republican Party bosses, he would rarely be heard from again. He would have no power, no role in Republican and national politics and therefore, no future. Of course, the GOP power brokers didn't anticipate McKinley's assassination and Roosevelt's move into the Oval Office.

From the very first moments of his presidency, T.R. truly sensed the moment of American greatness as we moved into a new century. Although it took time for us to comprehend the fact that we were no longer a nation of small farmers, when Roosevelt took office, America was in the process of becoming the number one economy in the world. He understood that this was a turning point in our history. He believed deeply in the promise of this transformation and he embraced it with all the "bully" of his being. I seriously doubt that a "stand-patter" like McKinley, or any of the presidents of that era, could have seized this moment on the world stage the way that T.R. did. His personality, intellect, and drive fit the times. The naval armada known as the Great White Fleet, which Roosevelt sent around the world, was a grand display of America's new might and America's eagerness to show it off.

Domestically, T.R.'s willingness to take on the trusts did much to assure that this country wouldn't eventually become an oligarchy run for the benefit of the rich and by the rich. And his role in preserving our great natural wonders and open spaces is a priceless legacy, as anyone will tell you after visiting the national parks that he put aside for America's future generations. A fundamental principle of his, in particular, has always guided me. "The one indispensable requisite for both a nation and an individual is character," he said.

Clearly, those leaders already in residence on Mount Rushmore belong there. Now let me tell you who I would add to my own Mount Rushmore: three individuals who shaped the world differently, who, through their own distinct personalities, character, abilities, and moment in time left a better world than they had found.

One leader whose historical contribution is now clear and who I would put up on my Rushmore is President Dwight D. Eisenhower. Like Reagan, he was a son of the Midwest. One of seven brothers, Dwight Eisenhower was born during the family's temporary sojourn in Texas. They had moved there because the only work his dad could find was cleaning locomotives in Denison, Texas. Eventually, looking for a new life with new opportunities, the family moved to Kansas. The six Eisenhower boys (one had died) all made it through high school in Abilene, and Dwight reached West Point, where he played football but wasn't a particularly good student. Knocking around from army post to army post, for nearly sixteen years he languished as an army major with his career seemingly going nowhere until his command of detail and his ability to plan on a massive scale caught the eye of General George C. Marshall. Marshall tapped the heretofore neglected reservoirs of judgment and logistical genius that would ever after characterize Ike and change the world.

From commanding the world's largest invasion force on D-Day to steering our nation away from the peril of nuclear holocaust, and doing much to lay the foundation for a post–World War II world, Ike led by quiet example and calm self-assurance. Although LBJ receives due credit for the Civil Rights Act of 1964, it was Eisenhower's sense of duty and political arm twisting that pushed through the Civil Rights Act of 1957. This was the first such civil rights legislation since Reconstruction. Adam Clayton Powell Jr., who was New York's only African American member of Congress, said of that landmark legislation, "After eighty years of political slavery this was the second emancipation." Also it was Eisenhower who took the politically courageous act of sending in the 101st Airborne Division to integrate Little Rock public schools and uphold the 1954 Supreme Court decision, *Brown v. Board of Education*.

Through his firm support for the United Nations and the North Atlantic Treaty Organization, he brought U.S. power and prestige to bear in creating an international order that, for the most part, kept the peace and defused—or at least contained—great crises for two generations. He had the ability to comprehend many factors at once and to synthesize them into clear, simple, and compelling ideas. Although his farewell address to the nation in 1961 is most famous for its warnings about the military industrial complex, there is another passage that puts forward the most even-handed prescription for understanding and preserving our system of government I have ever read. It doesn't have the ringing phrases of the Gettysburg Address, nor the Olympian detachment of Washington's farewell, but its wisdom and pragmatism accurately captures the day-to-day realities, which, over time, make up the historical process and the destiny of man. "Crises there will continue to be," Eisenhower wrote.

In meeting them, whether foreign or domestic, great or small, there is a recurring temptation to feel that some spectacular and costly action could become the miraculous solution to all current difficulties. A huge increase in newer elements of our defense; development of unrealistic programs to cure every ill in agriculture; a dramatic expansion in basic and applied research—these and many other possibilities, each possibly promising in itself, may be suggested as the only way to the road we wish to travel.

But each proposal must be weighed in the light of a broader consideration: the need to maintain balance in and among national programs—balance between the private and the public economy, balance between cost and hoped for advantage—balance between the clearly necessary and the comfortably desirable; balance between our essential requirements as a nation and the duties imposed by the nation upon the individual; balance between actions of the moment and the national welfare of the future. Good judgment seeks balance and progress; lack of it eventually finds imbalance and frustration.

Not exactly a battle cry, but the most realistic summing up of what government can and cannot do. So Ike goes up on the mountain.

If I had to pick one legislator with whom I served for my Mount Rushmore, it would be the late United States Senator Daniel Patrick Moynihan. There has probably not been as well-rounded and multitalented a person in public life since Benjamin Franklin. In addition to his military service in World War II, he served in the Kennedy, Johnson, Nixon, and Ford administrations. That is a wide spectrum of politics, and yet he had the intellect, ability, range, and finesse to succeed in important jobs in these four totally different political machines. He was our United Nations ambassador in the Ford administration; our ambassador to India in the Nixon administration; and assistant secretary of labor in the Johnson and Kennedy administrations. He also found time to author over a dozen books and hold down a full professorship at Harvard—plus he was an excellent bartender. Not a bad list of accomplishments for a New York City kid from a church mouse–poor Irish family with few prospects or opportunities.

I remember the time that he and I were part of a planeload of U.S. senators making up the official Senate delegation headed up to Rhode Island for the funeral of our colleague John Chafee. I sat next to Moynihan going and coming. I noticed that he was reading a very large book on Greek architecture. Now, you'll have to take my word on this, but you will rarely if ever see a U.S. senator poring over a book on Greek architecture. But Moynihan was an original. He was very outspoken about preserving some of the most beautiful and most endangered historic buildings in Washington, DC (such as Union Station and the Willard Hotel).

When Moynihan spoke out on something, you could be sure he had done his homework: hence the architecture book. He told me more about Ionic columns and Doric capitols and plinths and friezes than I ever thought existed, certainly more than I ever thought I would know or even want to know. The amazing thing about it—and this was pure Moynihan—he was able to connect this rarefied knowledge with the solution to a real-world problem, and he could make it fun, to boot. In his view, the human record, even thousands of years old, has things with which we can still connect. The basics don't change.

As a senator, Moynihan's force of intellect, personality, and political savvy, combined with his razor-sharp wit and charm, attracted support from both sides of the aisle. This is a testament to the power of his arguments and his ability to make common cause with senators from different states with different interests. He did this in a very gentlemanly, civil way. He could sell you something before you even knew you were in the market to buy. People always felt good when they were dealing with him. America has had great senators, both Republican and Democrat, who have been very effective, but no one quite like Moynihan.

From a more personal perspective I have one more addition to my mountain: my mother. People don't often think of their parents as great leaders. But I can't think of a more significant responsibility for a parent than to provide leadership for your children. By that measure, my mom was a tremendous leader. Leaders lead by example, not words. In times of trouble, or when people we knew just needed someone to talk to in order to get their thinking straight, they would go to my mother. Whether it was my aunts, our neighbors, friends, members of the American Legion Ladies' Auxiliary, or the Catholic Altar Society, they would all come to her asking, "What should we do?" or "Betty, what do you think?" In her own quiet way, my mom always had an answer. She never thought about herself as a leader, but people sought her out. It was not so much a case of force of personality but strength of character and courage that attracted people to her. Because she had a strong inner compass, she always had the sense of confidence that one looks for and trusts in a leader.

My mom was a very direct person, but also very kind and considerate, and always took responsibility for her actions. She held herself to a higher standard, and she demanded that others be held accountable, too. That is a leader. She hit things straight up. She didn't wallow in her problems or use them as an excuse. When my sixteen-year-old brother Jim was killed in a car accident, I think it hit her even harder than my dad's fatal heart attack. Burying a child is devastating. My mom started to drink—way more than was good for her. She eventually checked into rehab for six weeks and never took another drink for the rest of her life. That's what I mean when I talk about facing life head-on.

My mother didn't move the world in great ways like the other Mount Rushmore leaders. But she never squandered a moment or missed an opportunity to do something that could make the world a better place. She used every fiber of her being within her moment in time to lift up everyone around her and never asked for anything in return. That is a leader. My hope for my children and their children and future generations is that all men and women could feel this way about their mothers.

Mom, I know you'll be comfortable up on that mountain. You deserve to be there and I don't think being lumped in with those great historical figures will faze you one bit. I'm sitting in the United States Senate today because of what you gave me and taught me.

I wish more of our leaders would take my mother's calm and reflective approach to life and to solving problems. I've often said that I would like to see our national leaders sit quietly in their offices every now and then and just stare out the window for a few hours and actually think about what they're doing and ask themselves the tough questions about the future.

Eisenhower received criticism because he played a lot of golf. His critics said he should have been in the office more. Likewise, Reagan was criticized for his short workday. Rather than being drawbacks, I believe the down time, the time away from constant meetings, babbling people, news conferences, and the daily demand of official schedules gave them the opportunity to get their arms around the big issues. By finding time for the quiet moments of reflection, they were able to listen to their inner selves, rely on their deepest instincts, and recall the personal experiences that shaped them and conditioned their lives. That ability to stop and reflect is what made them leaders in the first place: They knew who they were, what they believed, and where they wanted to go. My dear friend and former business partner Mike McCarthy says, "Leaders are a special lot, different from managers. We can hire managers, but it is the followers that must choose their leaders."

In the army there is a term for using a compass to set your course toward an objective. It's called "shooting an azimuth." The origin of the word is Arabic; it means "the ways." In other words, out of all the possible paths toward a goal, the azimuth is the straightest, truest line.

The greatness of a leader in battle, or in the day-to-day combat of political life or running a company or an organization, is the ability to shoot an azimuth that is true, even under hostile fire. A good leader can communicate that goal and bring the people along in common purpose to accomplish it. This doesn't mean that you don't adjust to circumstances. The platoon leader might have to go around a hill or skirt an enemy's defensive perimeter, deviating from a certain course, but always returning to it. A political leader must be just as resilient. Leaders instinctively know how to set that azimuth and bring people along. As long as the people have a clear picture of the mission and how to accomplish it, they will not hold back their support.

This kind of effective and inspiring leadership always has and always will alloy the ideal with the practical. The result is neither purely one nor the other, but it is always moving toward a common goal. For America that goal has never been anything other than freedom and a better life for all people. How we adjust to the currents and riptides of history will determine the ultimate success of the historic venture known as America.

In that sense, America's next chapter is but another variation on the theme first set forth on a long-ago July day when the Continental Congress met in Philadelphia. The truths and inalienable rights that the Founders put forward on that day are now, as they were then, our nation's one true north. It is only to the extent that we citizens are vigilant in its defense, and our leaders both wise and bold in their pursuit, that America can remain "the pride of each patriot's devotion" and a beacon of hope in a better world. That is America's next chapter.

ACKNOWLEDGMENTS

Woven into the fabric of my life have been the threads of so many people who have helped me along the way. My family, friends, colleagues, teachers, and bosses have all prepared me and provided me with the wonderful opportunities I've had in life. This book is a product of their belief in me. Whenever I was in need, they have been there for me with their support.

My wife Lilibet, daughter Allyn, and son Ziller deserve the most credit. This book would not have been possible without them. Lilibet's uncommon wisdom and grace have given me perspectives on life I would never have known without her. And Allyn and Ziller—well, who matters more than your children?

Peter Kaminsky, my faithful collaborator, deserves special thanks for his devotion to this project, his powerful abilities, and his unique instincts. We made an effective team—and even had some fun with a serious subject. My agent, Lisa Queen; my publisher, Ecco, in particular Dan Halpern and Millicent

Bennett—all deserve great credit and my gratitude for believing in me and our purpose.

My senate staff provided invaluable input on their own personal time. The indispensable Lou Ann Linehan, my chief-of-staff, who came with me to Washington and as my campaign manager twelve years ago had a lot to do with getting me here, played an invaluable role with her contributions and her faith in our common goals. Mike Buttry, my communications director, was critically important with his contributions and collaboration. Rexon Ryu, my foreign policy counselor, provided a reality check on my memories and helped sharpen every point. The same goes for my Banking Committee counsel, Joe Cwiklinski; and my former Foreign Policy counsel, Andrew Parasiliti. My special assistants Katie Ringenberg and Adrienne Sullivan were always there to help, even before I asked.

I could not undertake any project without the soul and heart of my brothers, Tom and Mike. They have been sustaining forces in my life, along with the memory and influence of my mother, whom I discuss in the last chapter; my father, who died on Christmas Day when I was sixteen; and my youngest brother, Jim, killed in a car accident at age sixteen. My friend and former business partner, Mike McCarthy, an accomplished writer, student of literature and life, and close confidant, has always given me wise counsel on all matters. Finally, we are each inspired in life by certain individuals, heroic deeds, and acts of courage and humanity. My friend John Becker, a veteran of World War II, voracious reader, collector of great books, and humanitarian of large proportions, has provided me with that inspiration and, by his example, with a role model—I'm sure while never knowing it.

No one ever accomplishes anything in life without the support of others. We've all required a little help from time to time—and received it. I've always believed that was God's plan—we need each other. I hope this book is worthy of those who have done so much for me in my life—those listed above and many more.

INDEX

Abbas, Mahmoud, 73
Abdullah II, king of Jordan, 40, 73
Abilene, Kansas, 274
Aboud (West Bank village), 70–71
Afghanistan, 7, 82, 95, 161, 166, 182
  clearly defined U.S. goals in, 50–51
  cost of U.S. presence in, 247–48
  Iranian aid to U.S. in, 86–87, 96–97
  unfinished business in, 39, 51, 162
Africa:
  Chinese influence in, 108
  economic development lagging in,
    137–38
  endemic disease in, 122, 135
  end of colonialism in, 28, 31
  energy resources in, 228
  failed states in, 68
  famine in, 135
  genocide in, 135
  population growth in, 137–38
  poverty in, 122, 135
  U.S. influence in, 108
African Americans, civil rights of, 125
agriculture, mechanization of, 226

Ahmadinejad, Mahmoud, 77
Ainsworth, Nebraska, 1–2, 178,
  179–80, 217
Alamo, 5
al-Qaeda, 29
  Israeli-Palestinian conflict and, 72
  post-9/11 plots of, 143–44
  Saddam and, 50
alternative energy:
  China's need for, 111–12, 229
  as economic opportunity, 228–30
altruism, 183–84
American Enterprise Institute, 46
American Idol, 14
American Legion, 3, 177, 178
American Society of Civil Engineers, 12
American Spirit Honor Medal, 151
Angola, 108
anti-Americanism:
  Israeli-Palestinian conflict and, 72
  in Middle East, 69, 78
  as outcome of colonialism, 146
anti-Semitism, 128
appeasement, diplomacy mistaken as, 86

Arab-Israeli conflict, 66, 67–82
  Clinton administration initiatives in,
    73–76, 79
  Iranian nuclear aims and, 83–84
  peacemaking as high-risk endeavor
    in, 73
  U.S. leadership role in, 72
  see also Israeli-Palestinian conflict
Arafat, Yasser, in Camp David negotia-
    tions, 74–76, 79
Armey, Dick, 208
Armitage, Richard, 48
Army, U.S., 161, 162
Army National Guard, 161
Asia:
  economic development lagging in,
    137–38
  endemic disease in, 122
  population growth in, 137–38
  poverty in, 122
  see also Southeast Asia
Assad, Bashar al-, 40
Assad, Hafez al-, 74–75
Athens, democracy in, 176, 194
Atta, Mohammed, 138
Australia, 123
autobahns, 217
avian flu, 144
"axis of evil," 50, 88
azimuth, 281

Baikal, Lake, 129–30
Baker, Howard, 194
Baker, James, 75, 76
Baker-Hamilton report, 61, 162
balance of power, Cold War and, 23
Balfour Declaration, 68
Balkans, 68
Ban Ki-moon, 62
Barak, Ehud, 73, 75–76

Barzan, Iraq, 43
Barzani, Masoud, 41
Base Realignment and Closure Com-
    mission (BRAC), 167
Becker, John, 264
Begin, Menachem, 76
Beijing, 104–5, 106
Berlin wall, 23, 30
Bible, 72
Biden, Joe, 54, 55, 210
  Iraq surge opposed by, 64
  2002 Middle East trip of, 40–44
Biden-Lugar-Hagel Iraq War resolu-
    tion, 55
Billington, James, 98
Bill of Rights, 205
bin Laden, Osama, 130, 138
bipartisan ticket, 210
Blackwater Worldwide, 167–68
Bliss, Fort, 67–68, 151–52
Blix, Hans, 46, 49
Blum, Steven, 163
border security:
  in postwar Iraq, 63, 64
  in U.S., 142
Bosnia and Herzegovina, 32
Bowen, Stuart, 169
Bowles, Erskine, 223
Bradley, Omar, 132
Brazil, 30
Breaux, John, 210
Bremer, Paul, 167
Brown v. Board of Education, 275
Brzezinski, Zbigniew, 60, 125–26
Burke, Edmund, 176
Bush, George H. W., 76
Bush, George W.:
  "axis of evil" mantra of, 50, 88
  diplomatic and coalition approach
    to Iraq promised by, 55–56, 58

Hagel's Iran proposals sent to,
  95–96
Hagel's Iraq mediator proposal
  ignored by, 62
Israeli-Palestinian conflict and,
  76–77
limited foreign policy experience
  of, 50
military surge authorized by, 64
supplemental budget requests of,
  248
war powers of, 53
Bush administration:
  Baker-Hamilton report ignored by,
    61
  Chalabi and, 46–49
  democracy-building agenda of, 59, 77
  European missile system plan of,
    126
  fear of further terrorist attacks
    exploited by, 50, 51
  go-it-alone penchant of, 34,
    49–50, 57
  hubris of, 50, 51, 52
  incompetence of, 52
  intelligence failures of, 38, 50, 93
  Iraqi WMD claims of, 44–45, 48
  Iraq War resolution sought by,
    54–57
  Middle East policy of, 32, 51
  neoconservative ideology of, 50, 77,
    93
  permanent U.S. military Middle
    East presence envisioned by, 50
  untrue and misleading statements
    by, 58
  war sloganeering by, 38, 49, 58

Cambodia, 37, 110
campaigns, political, 198–99

Campbell, Kenneth, 264
Camp David negotiations, 74
Canada, 133
  U.S. exports to, 134
Canton (Guangzhou), China, 105
capital, debt and, 11
Card, Andy, 53–54
Castro, Fidel, 200–202
Catechism of a Revolutionary
  (Nechayev), 138
cellular telephony, 103–4, 107, 227
Center for Strategic and International
  Studies, 96
Central Command, U.S. (USCENT-
  COM), 40, 168
Central Intelligence Agency (CIA), 86
  Chalabi and, 46, 47
Chafee, John, 106, 210, 277
Chalabi, Ahmad:
  Bush administration and, 46–49
  Clinton administration and, 46
  Congress and, 46–48
  Iran ties of, 48
Chamberlain, Neville, 120
Chavez, Hugo, 134
Chechens, 126
Cheney, Dick, war sloganeering by, 38
Chengdu, China, 106
child labor, 107
China, People's Republic of, 6, 82
  Africa and, 108
  economic growth in, 102–3, 106–7
  energy demands of, 106–7, 108,
    111–12, 228–29
  environmental issues in, 112, 229
  expanding world role of, 29
  foreign policy of, 108
  in global economy, 102, 110
  human rights issues in, 101, 102,
    107, 109, 114, 125

China, People's Republic of (*cont.*)
    intellectual property rights in, 101
    isolation of, as ill-considered, 102,
        115
    job flight and, 110
    Latin America and, 108
    middle class in, 102
    military strength of, 113
    North Korea and, 83, 113–14
    oil imports of, 108
    poverty in, 102
    quality of goods made in, 110–11
    Taiwan and, 114
    tax policy in, 238
    2008 Olympics in, 108
    U.S. balance of trade with, 101
    U.S. economy and, 110–13, 114–15
    U.S. engagement with, 102
    U.S. national debt holdings of,
        112–13
China-Africa Cooperation Forum, 108
Churchill, Winston, 120, 142
citizenship:
    educational system and, 186
    idea of service and, 177, 181–82,
        184–89
    military service and, 177, 181
    political system and, 175–76
    rights vs. responsibilities of, 6,
        176–77, 186
Civilian Conservation Corps, 187
civilizations, complacency and, 21
civil liberties, national security vs., 142,
    165
Civil Rights Act (1957), 275
Civil Rights Act (1964), 125, 265, 275
Civil War, U.S., 141, 176
Clausewitz, Carl von, 149
Clay, Henry, 194
climate change, 6, 23

multinational efforts needed to deal
    with, 144–45
    U.S. policy on, 32
Clinton, Bill, 58
Clinton administration:
    budget surpluses of, 249
    Chalabi and, 46
    Middle East peace initiatives of,
        73–76, 79
Cold War, 8, 23–24, 25, 30, 92, 121,
    123–24, 131, 179
Collins, Hagel and Smith, 104
colonialism:
    as based on military might, 30–31
    end of, 28–29, 31
    heritage of, in Muslim world,
        146–47
Columbus, Nebraska, 25–26, 178
Commager, Henry Steele, 157
Commission on the National Guard
    and Reserves, 163
Communism, 8, 25, 108
    fall of, 222, 267
complacency, 21
Comprehensive Test Ban Treaty, 92
Congress, U.S., 239
    Chalabi and, 46–48
    checks and balances and, 209
    constitutional war powers of, 65–66
    Defense Department budget and,
        166–67
    earmarking by, 166
    fiscal discipline lacking in, 247–49
    Iraq War resolution of, 54–57
    in Iraq War run-up, 4, 5, 38, 53–58,
        65–66
    LBJ and, 265
    Nebraska delegation in, 159–60
    oversight responsibility of, 58, 65
    partisanship in, 207

Republican majority in, 241–42
Shinseki's testimony to, 58–59
Vietnam War failures of, 158
see also House of Representatives, U.S.; political system, U.S.; Senate, U.S.
Congressional Budget Office, 244
Congressional Executive Commission on China, 107
Congressional Record, 215
consensus, 193, 194, 207, 210, 278
Constitution, U.S., 150, 198, 205
  checks and balances in, 209
  congressional war powers in, 65–66
  original intent in, 65–66
  political system in, 175
  presidential war powers in, 53–54
Continental Congress, 281–82
court system, U.S., checks and balances and, 209
crabs, politicians as, 191–92
Crusades, 147
Cuba, 200–202
Cuban Missile Crisis, 26–27, 131, 265–66
currency manipulation, 234
"Curveball," 48
Cyprus, terrorism in, 139

Daschle, Tom, 54–55
D-Day, 275
de-Baathification program, 48
debt:
  capital and, 11
  public, *see* national debt, U.S.
Declaration of Independence, 194, 272
Defense Department, U.S.:
  accountability lacking in, 163, 166, 167
  Chalabi and, 47–48

postwar planning of, 56
private contractors and, 167–69
supplemental budgets of, 247–48
2007 budget of, 163
2008 budget of, 166
waste and fraud in, 163, 166–67
deficit spending, 11
  see also national debt, U.S.
de Gaulle, Charles, 28
democracy:
  definition of, 176
  impossibility of external imposition of, 51–52, 57, 59
  realistic promotion of, 117–18
  in Russia, 124–25
  in U.S. history, 125
Democracy in America (Tocqueville), 177
Democratic Party, 206–7
  narrowing ideology of, 208
demos, 176
Demosthenes, 194
Depression, Great, 187, 233, 264, 266, 268
developing world, 137, 225–26
Dewey, Thomas E., 180
DeWine, Mike, 210
Dien Bien Phu, 28
diplomacy:
  ideology vs., 77, 86
  ignored in Iraq War, 60–61
  mistaken as appeasement, 86
  war as failure of, 149
Dirksen, Everett, 194
disarmament:
  failures of, 92
  U.S. commitments to, 92
disease:
  multinational efforts needed in combating, 22, 120, 122–23, 135, 144
  poverty and, 122–23

Dodd, Christopher, 215–16, 219–20
Dole, Robert, 13, 194
draft, military, 170, 181, 186–87
Dr. Strangelove, 26
Dunn, Joseph Patrick, 217, 218, 250–51
Dunn, Katie, 251
Durant, Will, 85–86
Durrell, Lawrence, 139

East Jerusalem, 75
  as capital of Palestinian state, 80
economy, global, 6, 11, 135
  capital flow in, 221
  China in, 102, 110
  energy sector of, 72, 84, 86, 106–7, 108, 111–12, 227–29
  infrastructure of, 221
  manufacturing sector in, 226
  total output of, 221
  see also free market economies; global marketplace
economy, U.S., 6
  challenges to, 12–13, 110, 220
  China and, 110–13, 114–15
  Cold War and, 23, 222
  educational system and, 221, 222, 225
  foreign capital in, 12, 112–13, 236, 246
  GDP of, 232
  innovation and, 225–26
  job flight and, 110
  manufacturing sector in, 225–26
  openness of, 22, 221
  outsourcing and, 6, 22, 182, 231–32
  productive capacity of, 6, 20, 111, 221
  protectionist policies and, 109–10, 226, 232–33
  skilled labor force in, 111, 225–27, 229
  technology and, 111–12, 221, 222–24, 225
  see also financial markets; free market economies
educational system, U.S.:
  citizenship and, 186
  economy and, 221, 222, 225
  humanities in, 119
  mathematics programs in, 6, 119, 223–24
  openness of, 22
  reform of, 6, 11, 119
  science and engineering programs in, 6, 119, 223–24
Egypt, 73, 78, 82
  Iraq War opposed by, 39
Eisenhower, Dwight D., 13, 27–29, 202, 280
  farewell address of, 163–65, 275–76
  interstate system and, 217
  leadership qualities of, 274–76
  on Middle East, 52
  on military industrial complex, 163–65, 167
  in 1952 election, 179–80
  nuclear nonproliferation policy of, 91, 131
Eisley, Loren, 129–30
ElBaradei, Mohamed, 45–46, 49
elections:
  of 1952, 179–80
  of 2000, 75
  of 2008, 211
energy resources:
  Africa and, 228
  alternative, 111–12, 228–30
  carbon-based, 228
  Iran and, 84, 86

Latin America and, 228
Middle East and, 72, 228
need for innovation in, 227–29
entitlement programs, 6, 11, 12, 207,
    219, 239, 241–58
    see also Medicaid; Medicare; Social
    Security
environmental issues, 10
    in China, 112, 229
    as economic opportunities, 229–30
    in Southeast Asia, 229
    see also climate change
equity markets, 11–12, 236
Erbil, 42
European Union (EU), 60, 77, 91
    expanding world role of, 30, 121–22
    Israeli-Palestinian conflict and, 126
    U.S. and, 121–22
extremism, *see* religious extremism

Faisal, Prince Turki al-, 40
Fatah, 79
Federal-Aid Highway Act (1956), 217
federal budget, 246
    Social Security and, 249
    supplemental spending and, 247–49
Federal Health Care Board Act (2007)
    257–58
Federalist Papers, 19
Federal Thrift Savings Plan, 254
Feinstein, Dianne, 210
Feith, Douglas J., 47
financial markets, 11–12, 236
Financial Times, 60
Foreign Affairs, 102
foreign policy, U.S.:
    domestic consensus needed for,
        118–19
    ideology vs. diplomacy in, 77, 86,
        109

inconsistency of Middle East policy
    in, 77, 79, 81–82
Iran dialogue lacking in, 32–33, 39,
    60–61, 84–85, 86, 87, 93–99
Iraq War as failure of, 4, 10, 35, 52
JFK on purpose of, 24
multilateral engagement needed in,
    34, 60–61, 119
one China policy of, 114
Russia and, 123, 125–27
UN and, 120–21
"Fortress America," 33, 142
fossil fuels, 228
Founding Fathers, 65–66, 209–10,
    241, 282
Four Freedoms, 268–69
France, 44, 238
    Indochina and, 28–29
Franklin, Benjamin, 277
Franks, Tommy, 40
free market economies, 8, 110, 226–27
    investment and, 247
    outsourcing and, 231–32
    protectionism and, 232
free trade, 34, 221, 233–35
Friedman, Thomas, 69
Fulbright, J. William, 158

Gallup polls, 194, 206
Gates, Bill, 227
Gaza, 67, 69, 79
"Gaza First" plan, 81
Gelb, Leslie, 65
General Agreement on Tariffs and
    Trade, 233
genocide, 135
Gephart, Richard, 54
Germany, 118, 144, 217, 238
Germany, Nazi, 120
Gettysburg Address, 194, 272, 275

global marketplace, 110–11
  assembly of products in, 111
  competition in, 110, 220, 221–22, 234
  currency manipulation and, 234
  health and safety issues in, 234
  intellectual property rights in, 234
  quality issues in, 110–11
  unfair trade practices in, 234
  see also economy, global
global warming, *see* climate change
Golan Heights, 67, 75
Gonzales, Alberto, presidential war
  powers and, 53
Gonzalez, Elian, 200–202
Gonzalez, Juan Miguel, 201
Gorbachev, Mikhail, 128, 262
Government Accountability Office,
  168–69
Graham, Bob, 210
Grand Island, Nebraska, 217
Grassley, Chuck, 210
Great Britain, 31, 44, 238
  intelligence operations of, 143
  terrorist attacks in, 140
  U.S. viewed unfavorably in, 33–34
Great Depression, 187, 233, 264, 266,
  268
Great Society, 15
Greenspan, Alan, 243–44
gross domestic product (GDP), 232
Gruening, Ernest, 158
Guangzhou (Canton), China, 105
Gul, Abdullah, 40
Gulf War (1991), 41, 45, 46

Hadley, Steven, 62
Hagel, Allyn, 183
Hagel, Bertha, 1
Hagel, Betty, 3–4, 41–42, 177–78, 180
  leadership qualities of, 278–80

Hagel, Charles (father), 3–4, 179–81,
  217, 218
  American Legion uniform of, 3–4
  death of, 251, 279
  idea of service and, 177–78
  importance of voting to, 178–79
Hagel, Chuck:
  Assad's meeting with, 74–75
  attack on patriotism of, 58, 157
  cell phone business of, 103–4, 107,
    227
  China visits of, 104–7
  on Elian Gonzalez case, 200–202
  Hariri's meeting with, 45
  health care proposals of, 257–58
  international mediator for Iraq
    proposed by, 61–63
  Iran policy proposals of, 94–96
  Iraq surge opposed by, 64
  Middle East interest of, 67–68, 73
  in mock UN debate, 195–96
  Mt. Rushmore additions of, 274–80
  National Infrastructure Bank Act of,
    216, 220
  1999 Vietnam visit of, 8–9
  nuclear nonproliferation bill of,
    92–93
  party loyalty and, 209
  Russian visit of, 127–30
  in Senate Foreign Relations Com-
    mittee, 39–40
  Social Security reform proposals of,
    252–55
  2002 Middle East trip of, 40–44
  in Vietnam War, 2–3, 27, 149,
    153–56
  Washington Post op-ed piece by, 63
Hagel, Herman, 1, 218
Hagel, Jim, 279
Hagel, Leo, 179–81

Hagel, Lilibet, 183
Hagel, Tom, 3, 8, 27, 153–56, 180–81
Hagel, Ziller, 183
Hagel family, Social Security and,
    250–51, 268
Halabja, Iraq, 43
Hamas, 72, 77, 78, 79–80, 87
Hannah, John, 47
Hariri, Rafik, 45
Hart-Rudman Report, 222
Hastert, Dennis, 54
Hatfield, Mark, 158
health care:
    costs of, 6, 237, 255–57
    as economic opportunity, 230
    Hagel's proposals for, 257–58
Herrod, Mildred, 188
Hessian mercenaries, 168
Hezbollah, 72, 78, 87
Hitler, Adolf, 142
HIV/AIDS, 122, 144
Hoar, Joseph, 60
Ho Chi Minh, 9, 28
Ho Chi Minh City (Saigon), 8–9
Hong Kong, 105, 110
Hosseinian, M. H. Nejad, 97
House of Representatives, U.S.:
    Armed Services Committee of, 162
    in Iraq War run-up, 4
Hubei province, China, 106
humanities education, 119
human rights issues:
    in China, 101, 102, 107, 109, 114,
        124
    in Iran, 125
    in Russia, 124, 125–26
hunger, multinational effort needed in
    combating, 120, 135–36
Hussein, Saddam, 39–40, 51, 57, 157
    al-Qaeda and, 50

containment of, 44, 49
Kurds and, 42–43
WMDs and, 44–45, 48, 55

Ignatius, David, 78
Ike: An American Hero (Korda), 52
immigration policy, 6, 11, 32, 34,
    224–25
immunity, of military contractors, 167
India, 6, 82
    expanding world role of, 29
    nuclear weapons possessed by,
        91–92, 130
    Pakistan and, 68, 130
Industrial Revolution, 103
Indyk, Martin, 75
infrastructure, U.S., maintenance and
    modernization of, 6, 11, 12, 216,
    219–20, 229
initial public offerings (IPOs), 12, 236
Institute of Medicine, 223
integration, 275
intellectual property rights, 101, 234
intelligence gathering, as key to com-
    bating terrorism, 143–44
International Atomic Energy Agency
    (IAEA), 45, 92
International Monetary Fund (IMF),
    8, 60
Internet, 9, 10, 227
    political process and, 211–12
interstate highway system, 217–18
IPOs, *see* initial public offerings
Iran, 54, 69, 77, 82, 83–99
    in "axis of evil," 88
    ayatollahs 'power in, 88, 98
    Chalabi's ties with, 48
    democracy in, 88–89
    destabilizing behavior of, 87, 94–95
    economic incentives for, 94

Iran (*cont.*)
  factionalism in, 89–90
  hostage crisis in, 87
  human rights issues in, 125
  integration into global economy as
    goal for, 95, 98
  Iraq War lessons and, 93
  lack of U.S. dialogue with, 32–33,
    39, 60–61, 84–85, 86, 87, 93–99
  Lebanon and, 84, 87
  long history of, 85
  nuclear weapons sought by, 83–84,
    87, 90, 92, 94
  parliament (Majles) of, 89
  pro-American attitudes in, 88, 97–98
  regime change in, 94–95
  regional diplomatic strategy re-
    quired for, 95
  Russia and, 96
  shah overthrown in, 87, 94
  and Shiite-Sunni split, 84, 97
  as terrorism sponsor, 85, 87, 94, 97
  U.S. efforts at isolation of, 85, 87,
    93, 94
  and U.S. occupation of Iraq, 84, 88,
    97
  U.S. war on Taliban aided by,
    86–87, 96–97
Iraq, 7, 68, 69, 77, 87, 95
  Kurds in, 40–44
  legitimate U.S. interests in, 62–63, 64
  no-fly zones in, 41, 44
  oil reserves in, 38, 42
  Shia in, 44
  trade embargoes against, 44, 49
  WMDs in, 44–45, 48, 55
Iraq, postwar:
  border security in, 63, 64
  Chalabi and, 48
  civil war in, 63, 64

  counterterrorism efforts in, 63, 64
  de-Baathification program in, 48
  Defense Department planning for, 56
  impossibility of imposing democ-
    racy through force in, 57, 59
  international mediator proposed for,
    61–63
  Iran and, 84, 88, 97
  long-term goals in, 60
  military contractors in, 167–69
  phased troop withdrawal from,
    63–64
  reconstruction failures in, 57, 62
  Security Forces training in, 63, 64
  U.S. military as occupation force in,
    63, 163
Iraqi Liberation Act (1998), 46
Iraq National Congress (INC), 47–48
Iraq Study Group, 61, 162
Iraq War, 5, 166, 182
  cost of, 219, 247–48
  counterterrorist efforts subverted
    by, 51
  as destabilizing influence in Middle
    East, 64, 140
  exit strategy lacking in, 59
  finger-pointing for failures in, 49, 57
  flawed premises and strategy for, 4,
    93, 160, 161
  as foreign policy disaster, 4, 10, 35,
    52, 109
  international diplomacy ignored in,
    60–61
  lessons of, 64–65, 66, 93
  Middle East policy goals obscured
    by, 79
  regime change goal of, 39, 46, 51
  Shock and Awe campaign in, 45
  terrorist recruiting aided by, 79,
    139–40

Iraq War, run-up to, 4–5, 37–59
  Arab support lacking in, 40
  Congress in, 4, 5, 38, 53–58,
    65–66
  go-it-alone approach in, 10, 32, 39,
    49–50
  Hagel's statements in, 39–40, 157
  intelligence failures in, 38, 50, 93
  media complicity in, 4, 38
  Powell in, 29
  Vietnam lessons ignored in, 37–38
  war sloganeering in, 38, 49, 58
Islam:
  jihadist perversion of, 138
  submission as literal meaning of,
    147
  West and, 146–48
Israel, 40, 87
  go-it-alone penchant of, 79
  Jordanian treaty with, 74
  Lebanon attacked by, 78–79, 80
  neoconservatives and, 50
  right to exist of, 68, 70
  security walls built in, 71
  Syria and, 74
  terrorist attacks in, 71, 72, 78, 97,
    140
  U.S. relationship with, 81–82
Israeli-Palestinian conflict, 39, 40,
    69–72
  al-Qaeda and, 72
  anti-Americanism increased by, 72
  Camp David negotiations in, 74
  as destabilizing influence in Middle
    East, 72
  Quartet and, 126, 127
  "road map" to peace in, 77
  Russia and, 126, 127
  two-state solution to, 70, 74, 126
  see also Arab-Israeli conflict

Japan, 83, 110, 112, 113, 118, 123, 238
  economic resurgence of, 103
Jefferson, Thomas, 176, 194, 272
jihad, jihadists, 10, 126, 130, 140, 141,
    147
  Islam perverted by, 138
Johnson, Lyndon, 27, 187
  leadership qualities of, 264–65
  loss of public trust in, 15
  Vietnam War and, 15, 265
Joint Chiefs of Staff, 162
Jordan, 47, 73, 78, 82
  Iraq War opposed by, 39
  Israeli treaty with, 74
  refugee camps in, 69
Joyce, William, 67, 151–53, 154
Juarez, Benito, 148

Katrina, Hurricane, 182–83
Kennedy, John F., 24, 27, 131, 195,
    202, 247
  leadership qualities of, 265–66
Kennedy, Robert F., 27
Kennedy administration, Vietnam War
    and, 27
Kerrey, Bob, 210
Khalilzad, Zalmay, 62
Khamenei, Ayatollah Ali, 89
Khatami, Ayatollah Mohammad, 85, 89
Khomeini, Ayatollah Ruhollah, 89
Kim Jong Il, 83
Kirkuk, 42
Kissinger, Henry, 118
Kohl, Helmut, 262
Korda, Michael, 52
Korea:
  division of, 68
  see also North Korea; South Korea
Korean War, 28, 179
Krasnoyarsk, Russia, 127–28

Kurdistan, 40–44
  civil war in, 41
  refugee camp in, 42–43
Kurdistan Democratic Party, 41
Kurdistan National Assembly, 43
Kurds:
  chemical weapons used on, 43
  in Iraq, 40–44
  peshmerga guerrillas of, 41, 43
  Saddam and, 42–43

Laos, 37
Latin America, 110, 134
  Chinese vs. U.S. influence in, 108
  energy resources in, 228
  poverty in, 134
leadership, 6–7, 239, 258
  current dearth of, 262–63
  public trust and, 269
  qualities of, 263–82
  reelection vs., 7, 14, 193, 198–200, 242
"Leaving Iraq, Honorably" (Hagel), 63
Lebanon, 69, 78, 82
  as failing state, 77
  Iran and, 84, 87
  Israeli attack on, 78–79, 80
  refugee camps in, 69
Lebed, Alexander, 128–29
Lee, Robert E., 186
Lemann, Nicholas, 267
Lenin, V. I., 138–39
Levin, Carl, 64
Libby, I. Lewis "Scooter," 47
liberty, as core Western value, 147
Library of Congress, 187–88
Lieberman, Joe, 210
life span, average, 252–53
Lincoln, Abraham, vii, 14, 141, 176, 194, 204, 272

Lincoln, Nebraska, 41
Li Peng, 106
Little Rock, Arkansas, 275
Livy, 229
lobbies, 197–98
Los Angeles Times, 168
Lott, Trent, 54
Louisiana Purchase, 272
loyalty, political, *see* partisanship
Lugar, Richard, 54, 55, 210

MacArthur, Douglas, 149
McCain, John, 210
McCarthy, Mike, 280
McGovern, George, 158
McKinley, William, 273
McLaughlin, John, 86
Macmillan, Harold, 28
McNamara, Robert, 27
McNeill, William, 123
Madison, James, 194
Majles, 89
malaria, 122
Malaysia, 110
malpractice insurance, 237
Mansfield, Mike, 194
Mao Zedong, 107, 139
March of Folly, The (Tuchman), 52
Marine Corps, U.S., 162
Marshall, George C., 13, 274
Marshall Plan, 118
mathematics education, 6, 119, 223–24
media:
  in Iraq War run-up, 4
  public discourse and, 196–97
  and U.S. political system, 193–94, 203, 212
Medicaid, 207, 244, 255
Medicare, 207, 244–45, 255, 265
Mekong Delta, 154

mercenaries, 168
Mexico:
 U.S. exports to, 134
 U.S. relationship with, 133–34
Middle East, 6, 37
 anti-Americanism in, 69, 78
 attempts to impose democracy in, 51
 destabilizing influences in, 64, 72
 economic development lagging in, 137–38
 Eisenhower on, 52
 global economic integration needed for, 81
 Hagel and Biden's 2002 trip to, 40–44
 Hagel's interest in, 67–68, 73
 history of religious violence in, 69
 inconsistent U.S. policy toward, 77, 79
 legitimate U.S. interests in, 62–63, 64
 NATO and, 121
 population growth in, 137–38
 pro-American governments in, 69
 U.S. policy in, 32, 51, 54, 81–82
military, U.S., 159–71
 as all-volunteer force, 169–71, 181
 antiterrorist role of, 143
 Cold War and, 23
 draft and, 170, 181, 186–87
 extended tours of duty in, 160, 161
 idea of service and, 2–3, 4, 156, 171, 177, 181
 as occupation force in Iraq, 63, 163
 phased Iraq withdrawal and, 63–64
 recruitment efforts of, 161–62, 171
 reenlistment rates in, 161, 171
 reequiping costs of, 162–63
 troop strength of, 170
 unreasonable burdens on, 160–63, 170–71

military contractors, 167–69
 immunity of, 167
 as mercenaries, 168
military industrial complex, 163–65, 166–67, 275
 national security policy set by, 165
Minneapolis, bridge collapse in, 216
Mitchell, George, 45
Mitterrand, François, 262
mock United Nations debates, 195–96
Moldova, 128
Morocco, 78
Morse, Wayne, 158
Moynihan, Daniel Patrick, 13, 194, 210
 leadership qualities of, 277–78
Mubarak, Hosni, 73
Musharraf, Pervez, 130–31
Muslim world:
 colonial heritage of, 146–47
 totalitarian and corrupt governments in, 135, 147
 U.S. viewed unfavorably in, 33
 West blamed for problems of, 147

NAFTA (North American Free Trade Agreement), 133–34
National Academy of Engineering, 223
National Academy of Sciences, 223
National Archives, 188
national debt, U.S., 6
 foreign holdings of, 12, 112–13, 236, 246
 growth of, 242–43, 244, 246, 248
National Infrastructure Bank Act (2007), 216, 220
national security, 165–66
 border control and, 142
 civil liberties vs., 142, 165
 military industrial complex and, 165
 private contractors and, 167–69

national service, 181–82
National Youth Administration, 187
NATO (North Atlantic Treaty Organization), 8, 60
  Arab-Israeli conflict and, 81
  expanding role of, 121–23
  humanitarian and economic roles of, 122
  Israeli-Palestinian conflict and, 72
  U.S. and, 121–22
Nazi Germany, 120
Nebraska, 177
  congressional delegation of, 159–60
Nechayev, Sergei, 138
Nelson, Ben, 210
neoconservatives:
  Bush administration policy set by, 50
  and finger-pointing for Iraq War failures, 49
Newbold, Greg, 59
New Deal, 187, 268
New Orleans, 182–83
Newsweek, 26
New Yorker, 267
New York Times, 200
Nigeria, 108
Nixon, Richard, 27, 102, 169
Norris, George, 194
North American Free Trade Agreement (NAFTA), 133–34
North Carolina, University of, 223
North Korea:
  China and, 113–14
  nuclear weapons possessed by, 83, 91–92, 113–14
nuclear club, 90, 91
nuclear weapons:
  disarmament failures and, 92
  Iran's expected possession of, 83–84, 87, 90

new international regime needed for, 90–93, 131–32
  proliferation of, 22, 90–91, 95
  Russian arsenal of, 124
  Soviet arsenal of, 123–24
  terrorists and, 90, 139
  U.S. arsenal of, 91

Obama, Barack, 92–93
oil resources, 38, 42, 108, 125, 146, 228
Organization for Economic Cooperation and Development (OECD), 238
Oslo Process, 74
outsourcing, 6, 22, 182
  free market economies and, 231–32

Pace, Peter, 162
Pakistan, 82
  as haven for jihadists, 130
  India and, 68, 130
  nuclear weapons possessed by, 91–92, 130–31
Palestinians:
  economic aid needed for, 80–81
  radicalization of, 72, 147
  right to independent state of, 70, 80
  see also Israeli-Palestinian conflict
pandemics, *see* disease
parties, political, 205–11
  loyalty and, 208–9
  narrowing ideologies of, 208
partisanship, 13, 193–94, 196–97, 208, 210
  patriotism vs., 158
  public interest vs., 208–9
Party of Six talks, 113, 126, 127
Patriotic Union of Kurdistan, 41
patriotism, 58, 157–58, 177
  politics vs., 158

Patton, George S., III, 154
Paulson, Henry, 238
Peace Corps, 188
Pearl Harbor, Japanese attack on, 5, 141
People's Bank of China, 112
Peres, Shimon, 73
Pericles, 194
Perle, Richard, 47
peshmerga, 41, 43
petroleum resources, 38, 42, 108, 125, 146, 148, 228
Pew Research Studies, 108
Philippines, 110
Pickens, Slim, 26
Pine Ridge Reservation, 218
Plagues and Peoples (McNeill), 123
Poland, 147
political system, U.S., 6
  campaigning in, 198–99
  checks and balances in, 209, 271
  citizenship and, 175–76
  common good and, 13, 197–98, 278
  consensus in, 193, 194, 207, 210, 278
  Constitution and, 175
  debate in, 194–97
  independent administration in, 210–11
  independent voters and, 206–8, 211
  inertia and gridlock in, 192–93, 203–4
  Internet and, 211–12
  loyalty vs. public interest in, 208–9
  media and, 193–94, 203, 212
  openness of, 20, 22
  parties in, 205–11
  partisanship in, 13, 193–94, 196–97, 208, 210
  primaries in, 211–12

  public trust in, 14–15, 64, 194, 242
  special interest lobbies and, 197–98
politicians:
  as crabs or prairie dogs, 191–92, 199
  leadership vs. reelection interests of, 7, 14, 193, 198–200, 242
  as representatives of public interest, 197–98
  self-preservation as goal of, 192, 199
Pol Pot, 139
poverty, 9–10
  disease and, 122–23
  extremism and, 9, 29
  multinational efforts needed in combating, 22, 120
Powell, Adam Clayton, Jr., 275
Powell, Colin, 48, 57, 60, 63, 75
  "you break it, you own it" philosophy of, 29
power grid, 219
prairie dogs, politicians as, 191, 192, 199
preemptive strikes, 50–51
presidency, U.S., 207
  checks and balances and, 209
  fiscal discipline and, 247–49
  leadership and, 239
primaries, political, reform of, 211–12
protectionism, 109–10, 226, 232–33
public discourse, media and, 196–97
public interest, political loyalty vs., 208–9
public trust, 14–15, 64, 194, 242, 269
pundits, 196–97
Putin, Vladimir, 124

Qatar, 40
quality, of goods, 110–11

Quartet, 126
Q'uran, 72

Reagan, Ronald, 34, 202, 262, 280
    leadership qualities of, 266–67
Red Guards, 107
Reed, Jack, 127, 129
reelection, leadership vs., 7, 14, 193,
    198–200, 242
refugee camps, 42–43, 69
regime change, 39, 46, 51
religious extremism, 5, 9, 10, 22, 38,
    130, 140, 141, 148
    disaffection and poverty at root of,
        29, 138, 146–47
    multinational efforts needed in
        combating, 126
    strengthened by U.S. go-it-alone
        penchant, 32
    see also terrorists, terrorism
religious tolerance, 148
Republican Party, 206–7
    founding of, 14, 204
    Hagel attacked for disloyalty to, 58
    as majority party in Congress,
        241–42
    narrowing ideology of, 208
responsibility, 188–89
rhetoric, 194–97
Rice, Condoleezza, 60, 62, 63
Rockefeller, John D., 228
Roman Empire, 21, 168
Roosevelt, Eleanor, 187
Roosevelt, Franklin D., 141, 176
    Four Freedoms of, 268–69
    leadership qualities of, 267–69
    on Social Security, 249–50
Roosevelt, Theodore, 176, 200, 268
    leadership qualities of, 272–74
Ross, Dennis, 76

Rostow, Walt, 27
rule of law, 175
Rumsfeld, Donald, 56, 59
Rushmore, Mount, 7, 271–74
    Hagel's personal additions to,
        274–80
Rushville, Nebraska, 218
Rusk, Dean, 27
Russell, Richard, 15, 265
Russia, 6, 77, 83, 113
    anti-Semitism in, 128
    corruption and inefficiency in,
        128–29
    democracy in, 124–25
    economic growth of, 124
    European missile plan opposed by,
        126
    Hagel's visit to, 127–30
    human rights issues in, 124,
        125–26
    Iran and, 96
    Israeli-Palestinian conflict and, 126,
        127
    media in, 124, 126
    natural resources of, 125
    oil and gas reserves of, 125
    in Party of Six, 113, 126, 127
    U.S. relationship with, 123,
        125–27

Sadat, Anwar, 76
Saddam Hussein, see Hussein, Saddam
Sadr, Muqtada al-, 48
Saigon (Ho Chi Minh City), 8–9
St. Bonaventure High School, 25, 188,
    195
Sanders, Bernie, 210
SARS, 122
Saudi Arabia, 40, 44, 73, 78
    Iraq War opposed by, 39

savings, individual, 12, 225, 242, 250
Saving Social Security Act (2005),
    252
Schmidt, Helmut, 147, 261–63
science education, 6, 119, 223–24
Selective Service, 181
Senate, U.S.:
    Foreign Relations Committee of,
        39–40, 55, 60, 62
    Intelligence Committee of, 62
    in Iraq War run-up, 4
September 11, 2001 terrorist at-
        tacks, 7, 29, 38, 50, 88, 137,
        138, 141
    emotional fallout from, 51, 58
    pro-American response to, 88
service, idea of, 2, 6, 158, 265
    altruism and, 183–84
    citizenship and, 177, 181–82,
        184–89
    military and, 2–3, 4, 156, 171, 177,
        181
Sharon, Ariel, 40, 73
    "Gaza First" plan of, 81
Sheridan, Tom, 25–26, 27, 195–96
Shia:
    in Iraq, 44
    Sunnis vs., 97
Shinseki, Eric, 58–59
Shock and Awe campaign, 45
Siberia, 129
Sichuan province, China, 106
Singapore, 110
Singh, Manmohan, 132
Six-Day War, 67–68
Slaughter, Anne-Marie, 65
Snowe, Olympia, 64, 210
Social Security, 207, 243, 245–46
    average life span and, 252–53
    Bush's proposals for, 245

FDR on, 249–50
Hagel family experiences with,
    250–52, 268
Hagel's proposed reform of,
    252–55
retiree/worker ratios in, 252–53
as safety net, 249–52
soldiers, 149–58
    bond between, 151, 153
    mutual dependence of, 152–53
    politicians 'responsibility to, 150
Sorensen, Ted, 27
South America, see Latin America
Southeast Asia:
    environmental issues in, 229
    expanding world role of, 30
South Korea, 83, 110, 113, 122
Soviet Union, 23–24, 25, 30, 92,
    123–24
    collapse of, 124, 222, 267
    nuclear weapons of, 123–24
Spain, 34
    terrorist attacks in, 140
Stalin, Joseph, 139
State Department, U.S.:
    Chalabi and, 46–47
    Future of Iraq Project of, 48
Stevenson, Adlai, 179
Strategic Air Command, 124
submission, as literal meaning of Islam,
    147
subprime mortgage crisis, 11–12
Sudan, 108
Summers, John T., III, 154–55
Sunnis, Shia vs., 97
supplemental spending, 247–49
Supreme Court, U.S., 75, 275
Syria, 40, 82
    Israel and, 74
    U.S. relations with, 39, 60–61

Taiwan, 114

Taiwan Relations Act, 114

Talabani, Jalal, 41

Tale of Two Quagmires, A (Campbell), 264

Taliban, Iranian aid in U.S. war on, 85, 86–87, 96–97

Tanner, John, 257

tariffs, 32, 233

taxes, 246–47

  capital gains, 237–39

  in China, 238

  corporate, 237–38

  investment and, 247

  payroll, 249

Tehran, U.S. consulate in, 97–98

terrorists, terrorism, 137–48

  anti-Israel attacks of, 71, 72, 78

  in Cyprus, 139

  disaffection and poverty at root of, 29, 138, 139, 146–47

  fear of further attacks by, 50

  in Great Britain, 140

  intelligence gathering and, 143–44

  Iran as sponsor of, 85, 87, 94, 97

  Iraq War as aid to recruiting by, 79, 139–40

  multinational efforts as key to combating, 22, 29, 119, 120, 126, 143–44, 145–46

  nuclear proliferation and, 90, 139

  as ongoing phenomenon, 140

  preemptive strikes against, 50–51

  religious, *see* jihad, jihadists; religious extremism

  in Spain, 140

  "war" as misleading paradigm for, 140

  see also September 11, 2001 terrorist attacks; *specific organizations*

Thailand, 110

Thatcher, Margaret, 262

Three Gorges Dam, 106

Tianjin, China, 105

Time, 26

Tocqueville, Alexis de, 2, 177

tolerance, religious, 148

Tolstoy, Leo, 267

Tonkin Gulf resolution, 27

totalitarianism, 8

Toynbee, Arnold, 21

trade, 11, 23, 34, 44, 49, 94, 101, 133–34, 221, 233–35

Treasury Department, U.S., 11

Treasury securities, Chinese holdings of, 112

Truman, Harry S., 13, 180, 202

tuberculosis, 122

Tuchman, Barbara, 52

Turkey, 34, 40, 44

  Iraq War opposed by, 39

two-party system, 205–7

ululating, 43

United Arab Emirates, 78

United Nations (UN), 8, 31, 57, 60, 97, 106, 277

  Arab Human Development Reports of, 69

  in end to Arab-Israeli conflict, 81

  General Assembly of, 120

  and Israeli-Palestinian conflict, 72, 77, 126

  North Korea and, 83

  Security Council of, 55, 61, 77, 94

  U.S. and, 120–21

United States:

  go-it-alone penchant of, 10, 32–33, 49–50, 79

isolationism in, 232
leadership role of, 10–11, 20–21, 30
legitimate Middle East interests of, 62–63
as member of world community, 5, 20, 23, 30
moral authority and trustworthiness of, 23, 78, 109
as sole superpower, 5, 7–8, 24–25, 84
as symbol of West, 146
unfavorable world opinion of, 7, 33–34, 78, 108, 109
United States–India Civil Nuclear Cooperation agreement, 131–32
United States–India Peaceful Atomic Energy Cooperation Act (2006), 131–32
USCENTCOM (U.S. Central Command), 40, 168

Valenti, Jack, 265
veterans, 3–4, 177, 178, 179, 270
and obligation to speak out, 150
Veterans Administration, 150
Veterans of Foreign Wars (VFW), 177, 178
Viet Cong, 154–56
Vietnam, 37, 110
economic recovery of, 9
Hagel's 1999 visit to, 8–9
Vietnam War, 33, 67
casualties in, 37
Congress's failures in, 158
Hagel in, 2–3, 15, 27, 149, 153–56
LBJ and, 15
lessons of, 37–38, 64–65, 66, 119, 158
Voinovich, George, 210

voters:
independent, 206–8, 211
responsibility of, 178–79
Voting Rights Act, 15, 125

war:
as easier to get into than out of, 29, 38, 84, 270
as failure of diplomacy, 149
as last alternative, 38
unknowable consequences of, 157
Vietnam lessons on, 37–38
War and Peace (Tolstoy), 267
war on terror, as misleading concept, 140
Washington, DC, 277
Washington, George, 176
farewell address of, 271–72, 275
Washington Post, 63, 65
weapons of mass destruction (WMDs), 10, 19
proliferation of, 81, 91, 120
Saddam and, 44–45, 48, 55
see also nuclear weapons
Webb, Jim, 210
Webster, Daniel, 194
West:
Islam and, 146–48
liberty as core value of, 147
U.S. as symbol of, 146
West Bank, 67, 70–71, 79
Wolfowitz, Paul, 47, 56, 59
women, rights of, 125
Works Progress Administration, 187
World Bank, 8, 60, 94
World Factbook (CIA), 166
World Trade Organization (WTO), 94, 233, 234
World War I, 232
World War II, 268, 275

World War II (*cont.*)
  economic causes of, 232
  U.S. role in aftermath of, 8, 13, 31,
    118, 233
  veterans of, 3–4, 179

Yeltsin, Boris, 128

Yichang, China, 106
YouTube, 211

Zarif, Javad, 97
Zawahiri, Ayman al-, 138
Zinni, Anthony, 60
Zogby International, 78